JUNIA ARISE

APOSTOLIC WOMEN
ON THE FRONTLINES

Axel Sippach

TABLE OF CONTENTS

INTRODUCTION

By Axel Sippach

"*I was the elephant in the room with a skirt on!!*" Beth Moore

"#MeToo goes to church: Southern Baptists Face a Reckoning over Treatment of Women" is the title of a June 8, 2018 NBC News online article by Alex Johnson with a subtitle that reads - *"Many women have experienced horrific abuses within the power structures of our Christian world,"* Beth Moore, an evangelical teacher, wrote in a letter [https://www.nbcnews.com/storyline/sexual-misconduct/metoo-goes-church-southern-baptists-face-reckoning-over-treatment-women-n880216]. This was referencing an open letter to *"Dear Brothers in Christ"* that she posted on her blog on May 3, 2018 [https://blog.lproof.org/2018/05/a-letter-to-my-brothers.html] where she told friend Ed Stetzer to make sure and interview her when she was on her deathbed "about what it's been like as a female leader in the conservative Evangelical world." When he asked her why they couldn't do it before then, she answered, "Because you know good and well what will happen - I'll get fried like a chicken." She also speaks of feeling "dismissed and ridiculed" at events by fellow evangelical leaders who were also speaking, making her feel like she was "the elephant in the room with a skirt on."

Beth Moore has been a well-known Bible teacher in Southern Baptist and other conservative evangelical circles for over 20 years, although recently, she is being received more and more by Charismatics. Her "open letter" has not only intensified the national discourse on this subject, but is helping fuel a woman's movement in the evangelical world that is creating a major shake-up. #MeToo has now "gone to church."

The train has left the station and is not coming back. Many are saying that "2018"—the year this anthology, *Junia Arise: Apostolic Women on the Frontlines,* is being published, has definitely become, "The Year of the Woman." I believe God is focusing attention on the empowering of women in this time in a greater way than ever before, both in the secular world and in the Christian world. God is up to something. This is not a time to resist what the Lord is doing, but to come into agreement and alignment with Heaven. We must have the prophetic Tribe of Issachar "understanding of the times" as written in 1 Chronicles 12:32 in order to "know what Israel ought to do." God has need of "Apostolic Women on the Frontlines" in ministry, media and marketplace—in fact, on all 7 Mountains of Cultural Influence to pioneer and lead change that will result in the discipling and transformation of generations and nations.

What is a Frontline?

A "frontline" according to Merriam-Webster is; *1) a military line formed by the most advanced tactical combat units; also, an area of potential or actual conflict or struggle. 2) the most advanced, responsible, or visible position in a field or activity.* So this can refer to the "frontlines" of the conflict in war, but also the "frontlines" of, say, research to find a cure for cancer, or to educate the poor, or the frontlines of advocacy of a particular cause regarding injustice, or the frontlines of innovation in the corporate world. There are many different applications. But it has to do with pioneering and breaking through when there is great resistance; solving challenging problems and achieving powerful victories.

Jesus said in Matthew 16:18 that he was building his church right at the very "gates of hell" which could not prevail against what he was building. The implication here is that the Church should be on the offensive, with satan's domain clearly on the defense. The frontline of a Kingdom advance is also where the greatest conflict zone is, and where the warfare is the most intense – right at the closest proximity to the gates of hell. These gates of hell are ruling cities, territories, nations and the 7 mountains of cultural influence—the kingdoms or systems of this world. We are called to rule and reign with Christ at these gates and establish God's Kingdom rule. And not only are men called to these frontlines, but God has always called women there as well—and there is a fresh clarion call from Heaven sounding at this time that is awakening a new generation army of women to strategically take their places on the frontlines again.

What Does Apostolic Mean?

Apostolic is an ecclesiastical term coming from the Greek word for "apostle" which is "apostello", meaning a "sent one" in its simplest definition. Jesus chose this term for a new "office" he was implementing for the church that had not existed in the Old Covenant. He specifically chose this Greek word when he commissioned his 12 disciples as "apostles" in Mark 3:13 and "sent" them out to preach the Kingdom, and to have authority over demons and heal the sick. This secular term was taken from the Greeks and Romans who would send out an "apostle" like an admiral of a fleet of ships or a general of an army who would be "sent out" to conquer a territory for the empire, and then with a team that came with them, to take time to "disciple" the new territory and its people to the culture of the Greeks or Romans. Jesus said we were to pray for God's Kingdom to be on Earth as Heaven, and that as the Father had sent him, so he was sending us, now to disciple nations for him in what is called the Great Commission.

After Christ's resurrection, Paul was not chosen to replace Judas, but Matthias was. So Paul was not part of the original 12. He was part of what we call the Ephesians 4:11, post-ascension grace-gift apostles. The New Testament mentions other apostles also, beside the 12 and Paul: Silas, Barnabas, Timothy, Andronicus and Junia, Titus, Epaphroditus and James. So the ministry of the "apostle" continues on even today. And while everyone in the church is not an apostle, there is a sense in which every believer is called and "sent," and therefore "apostolic"—an "ambassador of the Lord Jesus Christ"—called and sent to participate in God's cosmic plan of the ages to bring Heaven to Earth, as the original mandate of the first Adam is now through the cross, death, burial, resurrection, and ascension restored through the last Adam, Jesus Christ. So the term "apostolic" in the title of our anthology, is loosely describing this "sent one" dimension of every son and daughter of God.

The Old and New Testaments, plus 2,000 years of church history, are full of examples of how God called, chose, prepared, anointed, and *sent* women to the frontlines in their generation in order to advance his plans and purpose for the nations. And most of those times and cultures were primarily very male-dominated, in which those women lived and worked, making it very challenging to fulfill their calling. And although the modern-day women's liberation movement is now over 50 years old, having pioneered many changes in primarily western countries, there is still a long way to go regarding equality for women. In fact, many non-western nations in regions like the Middle East, Africa, and Asia have not made much progress at all. It was just this year, 2018, that women were given the legal right to drive in Saudi Arabia. In many Muslim nations, they must still wear the hijab and be fully covered outdoors and have very limited legal rights. Things are changing in these developing nations, but slowly.

In America and other western countries, much progress has been made as far as women's equality, but much work is yet to be done. Women still have to be almost twice as good as a man in order to climb the corporate ladder and be promoted. In some parts of the Christian world, women also still have been very restricted in terms of preaching, teaching, leading, and pastoring, primarily because of a faulty interpretation of Scriptures written by the Apostle Paul regarding women in the Church. But there is an incredible amount of research and theological scholarship that has been accomplished over the past few decades that is bringing great clarity to these texts as the light of truth begins to shine on them from a fresh and very convincing theological perspective. I don't have space here to address those theological controversies and the mountain of research that has been compiled, but I have written about one incredible discovery that is becoming a tremendous "game-changer" in my chapter on *"Junia the Apostle"*—the "outstanding" female apostle after whom this anthology is named.

Who is Junia?

Junia, along with her husband Andronicus are greeted by the Apostle Paul in Romans 16:7 and are both said to be "outstanding" among the apostles. Out of 28 individuals greeted in Romans 16 by Paul, ten are women—and one of these women is an outstanding "apostle"—Junia. For the first 1,200 years of the Church, almost all documents from church fathers and others have the name of this apostle as "Junia"—a female name. 700 years ago, some Bible translators and commentators started to change her name to the male version by adding an "s"—"Junias." It was a conspiracy that lasted 700 years, but the tremendous scholarly research of the past two decades has caused light to shine into the prison of this misogynistic darkness, liberating this female apostle back to her rightful place in church history to shine as the incredible and "outstanding" Junia. She truly is a "game-changer" and the hermeneutical lens through which we must view Paul's misunderstood writings on women. Paul had many women on his apostolic team—and he honors a female apostle in his letter to the Romans. You can read more in-depth about this in my chapter.

Why This Anthology?

I believe this anthology is timely. As we embarked on this writing project, as lead author, I said to the writers that have contributed a chapter each, that I felt *"Junia Arise"* was to be informational, revelatory, inspirational, and motivational—an anthology of women who would be chosen from Scripture or church history and whose stories would empower women today to break through every resistance barrier and challenge, and take their place on the "frontlines" of the conflict as history-makers and world-changers—as "Apostolic Women on the Frontlines." May the *Junia* in you, whose full potential may have been hidden, **arise** as you read through this anthology. May each chapter powerfully speak to you, causing the spirit of faith to come alive, awakening the apostolic dimension of a "sent one" inside of you. You have come to the Kingdom for such a time as this!

CHAPTER 1

JUNIA, THE APOSTLE: SHE'S A GAME-CHANGER

By Axel Sippach

"Greet Andronicus and Junia, my fellow Jews who have been in prison with me. They are outstanding among the apostles, and they were in Christ before I was." **(Romans 16:7)**

She was an "apostolic woman on the frontlines" of the Gospel of Jesus Christ in the first century as it quickly spread from Jerusalem all the way to Rome. Her name is Junia. She was an apostle. And Paul the Apostle calls her "outstanding" among the apostles in Romans 16:7. But a centuries-old dark conspiracy changed her name to Junias—a man's name. She was meant to be hidden forever, buried under the deceptive lies of a cover-up forged by numerous religious misogynists that would seek to eradicate her memory from the pages of Holy Scripture and early church history.

But recent "truth-seekers" among highly-respected academics, scholars, and theologians over the past 20 or more years have "resurrected" her from the ashes of this deception to shine the light of truth on the reputation of this incredible woman of God—Junia the Apostle. Junia was lost, but now she is found—and she is a huge **game-changer**.

Paul's Apostolic Ministry Team of Women

In Romans 16, the Apostle Paul spends much of this last chapter of his letter to the growing church at Rome, greeting and commending those who have worked hard in laboring with him in the Gospel. It is very interesting that the list begins first with a woman named Phoebe who was a deacon of the church in Cenchrea and had a recognized ministry role there, most likely leading the local church.

Highly regarded theologian Dr. N.T. Wright writes this about Phoebe: *"He entrusted that letter to a "deacon" called Phoebe whose work was taking her to Rome. The letter-bearer would normally be the one to read it out to the recipients and explain its contents. The first expositor of Paul's greatest letter was an ordained travelling businesswoman."* What an amazing woman she must have been. She was an "apostolic woman on the frontlines." Paul also commented that she was a patron or benefactor who had financially supported him and many others.

As Paul continues his warm greetings to those who were part of his apostolic ministry team, he mentions as second in the list another "apostolic woman on the frontlines"—the very capable Priscilla. She and her husband, Aquila, ministered together as a married couple, but in most places in Scripture, she is mentioned first. She and her husband risked their lives for Paul. Out of 28 people mentioned in this chapter, ten were women. That is pretty impressive to be written in the context of the fairly male-dominated society of Rome.

By the way, did you ever notice that Paul had a "spiritual mother?" Check it out in verse 13 where he says that Rufus' mother was a mother to him too. Some people have labeled Paul a "chauvinistic woman hater" who is viewed by some as wanting to keep women quiet. It certainly doesn't look like it from Romans 16. He is not ignoring women, but passionately applauding them, mentioning three times how "hard some of them worked in the Lord." Without this apostolic ministry team that included so many women, Paul would have been very handicapped in doing as much as he did for the Gospel of Jesus Christ.

Andronicus and Junia—A Power Couple

We could spend much more time highlighting the other tremendous women in this chapter, but let us focus on the one after whom this anthology is named—Junia. In Romans 16:7 "Andronicus and Junia" are greeted together. Andronicus could have been Junia's brother or close relative, but most scholars believe he was her husband. I hold that view as well. They were Paul's kinsmen, which can imply they were either relatives or fellow Jews.

This was a *power couple* who were also great risk-takers for the Gospel, with the authorities feeling threatened by their ministry and association with Paul, and getting thrown into prison with him as a result of it. Paul says that they were believers in Christ before he was, and he calls them "outstanding" or "noteworthy" among the apostles. Not only were they "apostles", but they were outstanding. They stood out among the other apostles. They were **impressive**.

For more than the first one thousand years of the Church, it was for the most part, a given that Junia in Romans 16:7 was a female apostle. Junia was a common female name found in many secular Greco-Roman writings of that day. Junias, the male version, is not found in any writings. Here's what The Anchor Bible Dictionary says: *"Without exception, the Church Fathers in late antiquity identified Andronicus' partner in Rom 16:7 as a woman."* [1]

The early church fathers, some of whom were not even necessarily pro-women, believed Paul was referring to a woman apostle. Here is a quote from 4th century church father Chrysostom: *"And indeed to be apostles at all is a great thing. But to be even amongst those of note, just consider what a great encomium this is! But they were of note owing to their works, to their achievements. Oh! how great is the devotion of this woman, that she should be even counted worthy of the appellation of apostle!"* [2]

Temple University scholar Dr. Leonard Swidler writes: *"To the best of my knowledge, no commentator on the text until Aegidus of Rome (1245-1316) took the name to be masculine."* [3]

The Deception to Bury Junia

So we see that for the first 1200 years of the church, the prevailing opinion was that "Junia" was a **female apostle**. Then the dark conspiracy of this religious misogyny begins with this Catholic archbishop "Aegidus (Giles) of Rome" and continues on with other medieval commentators and translators including Martin Luther, changing Junia to Junias, which begins a 700 year old cover-up. Its purpose is to reflect the institutional prejudice against women to function in any kind of leadership capacity. They could not have a woman apostle "shining brightly" in Scripture. They had to "bury" her. We who have discovered the truth about Junia have been accused of being "revisionists." But these medieval theologians are the revisionists, revising history to fit their misogynistic agenda.

It's interesting to note, that the Eastern Orthodox Church that split from the Roman Catholic Church in 1054AD, always revered both Andronicus and Junia (female) as apostles who converted many pagans to Christ, consequently shutting down their pagan temples and planting numerous churches in their place. They venerated them to sainthood status 1400 years ago in Constantinople (Istanbul). There is so much documentation that Junia as a female apostle, was the prevailing view of the first 1200 years of the church.

It's hard to understand why we are still having any kind of argument regarding this today. The only reason is that satan is fighting hard to give up this ground that he gained over 700 years ago. But he has lost. And it is just a matter of time now that because of the intense scholarship that has been invested in this over the past 20 years, that "Junia—the female apostle" becomes again the prevailing theological position of most of the Church.

Here's what Dr. N.T. Wright says in his article among one of many very respected scholars, persuasively arguing for the ordination of women to the ministry: *"All Christian ministry begins with the announcement that Jesus has been raised from the dead. And Jesus entrusted that task, first of all, not to Peter, James, or John, but to Mary Magdalene. Part of the point of the new creation launched at Easter was the transformation of roles and vocations: from Jews-only to worldwide, from monoglot to multilingual (think of Pentecost), and from male-only leadership to male and female together. Within a few decades, Paul was sending greetings to friends including an "apostle" called Junia (Romans xvi, 7)."* [4]

Two very in-depth scholarly books on Junia that I highly recommend are *"The Lost Apostle: Searching for the Truth About Junia"* by Rene Pederson

(2006), and *"Junia the First Woman Apostle"* by Eldon Jay Epp (2005). Both can be found on Amazon. They will give you a wealth of information on the subject that I am not able to cover in this short chapter.

Mysterious Junia is Rising from Obscurity

The *mysterious* Junia is arising out of the obscurity of the past 700 years into her rightful place through the "light of truth," and she is about to "shine." Junia is the big "game-changer!" She becomes a major hermeneutical lens through which other Scriptures regarding women must be seen and understood.

If this Junia is an apostle, and if she is a woman, then that means she was a preacher, teacher, church planter, leader, etc. She is a game-changer. And wow—she is "outstanding!" She is an "apostolic woman on the frontlines" and she is about to give voice to a new generation of outstanding women who also are arising out of obscurity and are about to shine with the glory of God upon them to powerfully advance God's Kingdom.

The Greek word for outstanding is "episemos," and it can mean *stamped; having a mark; coined; illustrious; to brand; seal; a mark of being yoked; well known; remarkable; eminent; conspicuous; notable; and even notorious.* [5] She is the *notorious* Junia. And she is becoming conspicuous again. She was an apostle—an anointed sent one on a mission for the King of Kings.

She did everything an apostle does—she preached, taught, was a wise visionary leader, evangelized the lost, planted churches, discipled new converts, raised up leaders, healed the sick, cast out demons, confronted satanic principalities, and pioneered and broke through into new territories with the Gospel, risking her life. But she was not *just* an apostle; she was an **outstanding** one. She was amazing. She was impressive. She was on the frontlines. She was a history-maker and a world-changer.

She stood out among the other male apostles of that generation. There was something so very special about Junia, that the Apostle Paul shows her such huge respect, giving her this badge of honor in Romans 16:7 so she will never be forgotten, even two thousand years later, in the 21st century. Junia is *the* "game-changer" for women in the Church. And the Apostle Paul's commendation of this tremendous woman is proclaiming in a fresh and loud voice today an incredible revelation here for us never to forget: we cannot do it without the women of God—**apostolic women on the frontlines!**

Arise and Shine, for your Light has Come

So JUNIA ARISE and shine, for your light has come, and the glory of the Lord has risen upon you!! It's time to come out of obscurity. You may have felt like you have been buried and hidden with no one to advocate for you. You may have felt persecuted and stifled by religious misogynists that would not look past your gender to see your potential. But there is a shift taking place in this season and in this generation. The Kingdom has need of you. God has heard the cry of multitudes of women across the Earth and major changes are taking place, both in the Church and outside the Church.

Are you ready to hear the call and be *sent* by the Spirit of God? Are you ready to take your place on the frontlines? Are you ready to go from ordinary to extraordinary—from average to outstanding? Your best days are just ahead. Believe it. Your dream is not dead; it was just buried under years of *stuff*. You may have felt like you were in a prison of limitations. But just like Junia got out of prison, so shall you break free from limitations to run with wild abandonment toward all God is calling you to. Junia lived in the time of a very male-dominated culture. But yet she stood out as remarkable; "outstanding" in her calling.

I believe that many women of God are about to stand out and shine in what God has called them to. And the Church will take notice. And the world will take notice. And Jesus will be glorified in and through them. Junia—it's time to Arise! Shake yourself from the past. They may have mislabeled you just like Junia, with the intent that you will be long forgotten. But God has not forgotten you. You are a daughter of the Most High God. Abba is you Father. You are royalty. So get ready for His spotlight of favor to shine on you brightly. You may have felt concealed, but your true identity is about to be revealed. A company of Junia's are about to arise. Declare by faith— I'm one of them!

Declarations for Junia Apostolic Women on the Frontlines:

1. This is my time to come out of obscurity, I will be who God says I am
2. They have mislabeled me, but I am awakening to my true identity in Christ
3. I will not stay in the shadows, but will arise and shine, for my light has come
4. I will not be timid and fearful, but courageous and bold, full of faith
5. I am breaking out of every prison of limitations and will be free indeed
6. God is giving me a voice to proclaim Good News to my generation
7. I will go from ordinary to extraordinary—from average to outstanding

References:

[1] https://www.fulcrum-anglican.org.uk/articles/women-bishops-its-about-the-bible-not-fake-ideas-of-progress/

[2] Freedman, David Noel, ed., *The Anchor Bible Dictionary*, (New York: Doubleday) 1997, 1992

[3] Chrysostom, Homily on the Epistle of St. Paul the Apostle to the Romans XXXI

[4] Leonard Swidler, Biblical Affirmations of Women, (Westminster Press), 1979, p.299

[5] http://biblehub.com/greek/1978.htm

CHAPTER 2

THE DEBORAH EFFECT: CHARACTER TRAITS OF ISRAEL'S MOTHER, JUDGE, PROPHETESS, AND GENERAL

By Axel Sippach

"Warriors were scarce, they were scarce in Israel, until you arose, Deborah, until you arose as a motherly protector in Israel."
(Judges 5:7 NET Bible)

An "effect" according to various dictionaries, is a change that is a result or consequence of an action or other cause. It can refer to the power that brings about desired results—an influence or force that is able to make something happen and achieve a successful outcome.

This chapter, *"The Deborah Effect"* taken from the pages of Old Testament history in Judges chapters 4 and 5, is about one apostolic woman on the frontlines that was called, anointed, and sent by God at a critical time in Israel's history to deliver her people out of the oppressive, cruel bondage of an occupying enemy nation through a single supernatural and victorious decisive battle. I encourage you now to take about five minutes to go through those two chapters before you continue reading.

So, the *Deborah Effect* is about the private internal qualities of the character and personality of this incredible woman, including her mind, emotions, and spirit that create the external public persona of authenticity that flows from those internal qualities, causing people to be attracted to her for her leadership, wisdom, judgment, and prophetic insight. All of this ultimately inspires the people of Israel's willingness to not only follow her, but to execute and carry out her life or death decisions regarding going to battle with the enemy, the result of which sees the hand of God bring deliverance and great victory to the nation.

Obadiah 21 in the NIV Bible states, *"Deliverers will go up on Mount Zion to govern the mountains of Esau. And the kingdom will be the LORD's."*

Psalm 68:11-12a in the Amplified Bible states, *"The Lord gives the command [to take Canaan]; The women who proclaim the good news are a great host (army); The kings of the [enemies'] armies flee, they flee…"*

God is raising up and sending forth in this generation an apostolic company of women deliverers—Deborah deliverers to defeat His enemies and liberate multitudes. They are arising with the *mantle of Deborah* and they will carry and release *The Deborah Effect* upon nations!

…Until I Deborah Arose a Mother in Israel

In Judges 5:7 it says in many translations that, "Village life in Israel ceased, ceased until I Deborah arose, arose a mother in Israel." Some of the wording in the original text is difficult to translate, and so other translations have the perspective translating the first part that "rulers, or leaders, or warriors, or valiant men" ceased, were not there to protect them, and that people would no longer fight for themselves because of the lack of leadership, and basically just allowed the oppressive occupying enemy to do what they wanted to do to them. They became complacent and lethargic with no courage or passion to fight, **until**…Deborah arose a mother in Israel.

This is powerful! Times were so bad—so dark—so seemingly hopeless. The people lacked inspiration, and a passionate and courageous leadership that could motivate them beyond their gripping and crippling fears to take action. There was no fight in them…until Deborah arises as mother in the nation. And this mother is about to birth new strength, new courage, new passion, new vision, new faith in her people. She is about to birth a move of God that will take them to victory and ultimate deliverance from their enemy.

14

Deborah, the mother in Zion, a matriarch, a world-changer, a history-maker, a game-changer, a global player, an epic hero, a champion of the nation who is ready to take on the seemingly impossible, because God is with her. She is *an apostolic woman about to take her place on the frontlines* to save a nation. She's a warrior—She's a general.

The Mantle of Deborah

There are some things that will not change until someone arises and takes their place of leadership to birth fresh hope and faith, and passionately inspires courage that will motivate action that will lead to victory. And many times the best equipped and anointed to answer the call and go will be a woman with the capacity to birth something extraordinary.

Deborah's are about to arise with an apostolic authority and prophetic anointing to challenge dead religious patterns, oppressive systems, and destructive mindsets of limitations. Deborah deliverers—it's time to arise! Our generation needs heroes. They need authentic Deborah's who have the capacity to birth movements that inspire change. It's time to receive the *mantle of Deborah*. A mantle is a Scriptural metaphor or symbol for a calling, a ministry, an anointing and even an office given to individuals by God. There is a *mantle of Deborah* and it contains apostolic authority and prophetic anointing and insight for the assignment at hand. God is about to wrap a company of women in the mantle to change nations. What Deborah will now birth in Israel—the very qualities that are on the inside of her that will lead a nation to victory.

So What's in a Name?

So, what's in a name? We know that Biblical names can be very prophetic. What's in Deborah's name? Her name actually means a "bee," perhaps being seen as a queen bee may be what is meant. Perhaps, as in the words of Muhammed Ali, she can "float like a butterfly and sting like a bee."

The etymology of her Hebrew name shows that it comes from "dabar", meaning "commanded; counseled; declare; proclaimed; preached; speak; utter; to properly arrange; cause; revealed from the Lord." Deborah's name is very prophetic – she is a "prophetess."

Prophets in the Old Testament were considered *friends of God* who had access by invitation to the Heavenly Divine Council of Yahweh. In Judges 5:31 ESV says, *"So may all your enemies perish, O LORD! But your friends be like the sun as he rises in his might." And the land had rest for forty years."* Deborah considered herself a friend of God. She had an intimate relationship with Yahweh Elohim, the God of Israel. And he was also her friend. I believe as a prophet, she had invited access to the Heavenly Divine Council and was privy to the deliberations there in order to prophesy his decrees. And when the *"dabar"* the word of the Lord came forth, she had to prophesy it to Yahweh's nation.

Her name is Deborah, she was also a living *dabar* —a living word, a living epistle written by the Spirit for her people to read. This is **The Deborah Effect**—the influencer, the change agent, the leader who would lead Israel to triumph. God had been preparing her as a judge, and she judged the people righteously with fairness and justice under the palm tree, which was her court. God had been preparing her as a prophetess and friend of God. All of that preparation was for her now to step up to the plate as a brave warrior and strategic general to lead the army of Israel into battle, trusting God for the victory. Heaven moved on her behalf, and Israel was powerfully delivered.

10 Characteristics that Helped Create the Deborah Effect

1. **CAUSE:** When young David in the Bible was sizing up the situation with a giant named Goliath that was challenging the armies of Israel, he said, "Is there not a cause?" The word "cause" here in Hebrew is "dabar"— the same word Deborah's name derives from. He was saying, isn't there anyone here who has the *word of the Lord* regarding what to do? Goliath became David's cause right there. He must have heard the word of the Lord of how to take down this giant, and that God had chosen him to become the champion in Israel to do it.

Deborah had a cause. She had the word of the Lord, knowing she was called for such a time as this. And she had the strategy of Heaven regarding how to move forward. Deborah was an apostolic woman on the frontlines, right at the very gates of hell of the enemy. She knew her cause. She knew her *why*.

What is your cause? What is your *why*? Why do you get out of bed every morning? Once you know your why, your what to do, and how to do it, everything comes much easier.

2. **IT**: Do you have **it**? Do you have that **secret sauce**? Is it showing? Deborah had it. She didn't even have to go to the people; they came to her under the palm tree. She was a woman of wisdom, counsel, justice, fairness, humility, authenticity, access and they daily came to her. She had *it*. You know when someone has *it* and you know when they don't. **It** was attractive—magnetic—it had drawing power. She had *it*. Deborah was full of grace, full of "charis", the Greek word for grace meaning, "the divine influence upon the heart and its reflection in life." Out of your belly shall "flow"…What is "flowing" out of your innermost being? Deborah knew her *why* and she had **it**. When she called for her general, Barak, he came without question. Barak knew she had **it**.

3. **FRIEND OF GOD**: Deborah had that close, intimate friendship with Yahweh, Israel's God. She was a woman of prayer, a worshiper of the Most High. She was privy to the Heavenly Divine Council. She heard God's voice. She was a prophetess with that keen prophetic insight from Heavenly places that gave her the winning advantage. She knew what Israel must do, and she had the right timing. I believe her intimate friendship with Yahweh caused her face to shine like the Sun, like Moses when he came down from the mountain. The Deborah Effect could not have been possible without her incredible relationship with Yahweh.

4. **LEADERSHIP**: Judges 4:1 in most translations says Deborah is the wife of Lappidoth. But it can also be understood as "woman of Lappidoth." Scholars have different opinions. Lappidoth means "fiery" or "flames" or "torches." So it's unclear whether Deborah coming home late at night after a hard day at work, started singing to Lappidoth, "Baby won't you light my fire", since names are prophetic and that is what it means. Or, the other possibility is that if Deborah is the "woman" of Lappidoth and not wife, the

"fiery" description could refer to her personality. Now that's something to think about. Either way, Deborah is also a take-charge *sista*. But she was also an accessible servant leader to the people.

God did not choose Deborah to be the exception to the rule regarding male-only leadership. He chose her because she was exceptional She had amazing leadership skills. People easily followed her. They trusted her. She was authentic—the real deal. She had insight. She was fair and just. And men like Barak quickly came when she called. Deborah was a tremendous leader.

5. **PRESENCE**: She carried the presence. There was something about Deborah that even her general, Barak, would not go to war without her. It's like when Israel would take the ark with them into battle. There was a great grace about her that exuded hope, faith, strength, and victory. She was confident. And God's grace and presence adorned her.

6. **SOCIAL JUSTICE WARRIOR**: Deborah was stirred because of the oppression of the enemy against Israel. It created a compassion in her for her people, and a passion to see them free. She wanted to see the "light of God's justice" dispel the darkness over Israel. What stirs you with passion? Deborah was not only a prophetess, but also a judge. She judged with equity.

7. **DISRUPTOR**: She disrupted the status quo. She was willing to go against the grain of "what was" to see the possibility of "what could be." She was a visionary. She could see the future—a future of living in freedom and prosperity. She was willing to be a risk-taker and lead a battle that would disrupt the enemy's plans.

8. **COURAGEOUS**: Deborah was fearless! She went into battle with Barak against 900 "iron chariots"—these are the tanks of that day, the latest in war machinery technology. But she was not afraid. She had the "dabar", the word of the Word. Deborah was courageous. Four letters in "couRAGEous" are "rage." To be courageous means at times you have to "rage" against something; against injustice, oppression, sex trafficking, racism, the prison industrial complex, unjust wars, child labor, etc. Rage can

be a holy righteous anger that passionately rises up inside of you where you find your courage to act decisively, and that leads to victory.

Sometimes that *rage* must also be against what you know is holding you back in your life; what the enemy is using to hold you back. Do you have sufficient rage against those things to find "courage" to defeat them? Such as a holy rage against rejection, fear, negative effects of abuse or toxic relationships, feelings of worthlessness, insecurity, poverty, shame, guilt, past failure, betrayal, etc. Are you tired enough yet of being sick and tired? Of always getting knocked down and overlooked? Enough is enough!! Find the courage to defeat those dream thieves and destiny killers. Be intentional. You are more than a conqueror through Christ who loves you so much.

9. **STRATEGIST**: She knew exactly what to do when going into battle. She had the word of the Lord with impeccable detail and timing. God will give you the strategies. He says in Jeremiah 29:11-13 that He is thinking thoughts toward you to prosper you and give you a future and hope. God has awesome plans for you. He has the blueprint. Why not let Him give you a "designer life?" The scroll of Heaven with your name and destiny on it are ready for you to discover and explore by the help of the Holy Spirit. Are you ready to embark on the most exciting journey of your life, accomplishing great exploits along the way as you advance God's Kingdom on Earth? It's your time. God is calling you. He has brought you to the Kingdom for such a time as this!

10. **POET**: Judges Chapter 5 is The Song of Deborah—it is her life as a poem. Deborah is a general, a warrior, a judge, but she's also a poet. What incredible creativity is within Deborah. She is strong, bold, and courageous ready to fight every enemy. But she also has the creativity of a poet. Ephesians 2:10 declares that we are God's workmanship—his masterpiece, which comes from the Greek word "poima" which can mean "poem." Your life is God's masterpiece. You are His "epic" poem that is being written as you pursue your journey of destiny.

There is a *mantle of Deborah* coming on those who are reading this chapter. Some of you are sensing the weight of it now as these words are becoming "dabar" in your spirit, stirring and moving you toward destiny and purpose as clarity and strategy are coming to you regarding your next assignment. You are getting ready to birth something powerful as you "arise" to take your place as a "mother in Israel."

Deborah definitely broke a glass ceiling for women then and still today. She is a game-changer, a prototype of an apostolic and prophetic company of Deborah's to come that will take their place on the frontlines. The "Mountain of Religion" could not contain her prophetic gift and calling within the four walls of its limitations. No—her calling includes judging, governing, and warring. Her call was to the "Mountain of Government." It was to create a better future for a nation in bondage.

The people of Israel had cried to the Lord for help in their backslidden state, and God answered by raising up a deliverer named Deborah. And He will do it again in every generation where one is needed. Are you one of them?

Pray this prayer of faith after me:

Father, in Jesus' name, I ask you to help me victoriously break through every limitation in my life that is holding me back from walking in the fullness of my calling and destiny. Let me be full of grace, find my cause and arise as a "mother in Zion" that is pregnant with the prophetic "word of the Lord" for this generation. May the mantle of Deborah come upon me now! Help me pursue an intimate relationship with You as a "friend of God"—one who can clearly hear Your voice and boldly declare it. Let me rise up with courage as a warrior that brings deliverance to others. Let me arise as one that has the authority of a general, and yet maintains the humility of servant-leader. I ask You to change me and rearrange me until I am transformed into one who can authentically and powerfully release "The Deborah Effect" that will influence many for Your Kingdom. Help me to take my place as an "apostolic woman on the frontlines." Amen and amen! Let it be so, and it is so!

Mantle of Deborah Declarations:

1. I will take up my "cause" as an "apostolic woman on the frontlines" ready for action
2. I declare that the "mantle of Deborah" comes upon me now with power and authority
3. I declare that "The Deborah Effect" shall be seen and felt through me as an influencer
4. I will arise as a "mother in Zion" to bring deliverance and freedom to this generation
5. I will be a bold and courageous leader and never shrink back because I am a woman
6. I am a "friend of God," highly favored with access to His Heavenly Divine Council
7. I am an agent of change, called to an epic journey to make "his-story" for my King

CHAPTER 3

GIRL—GET UP!
THE STORY OF TABITHA AKA DORCAS
INFLUENCER ON THE MT. OF BUSINESS

By Axel Sippach

"It's not over till God says, It's over!"

There is an amazing story in the Bible of an incredible woman named Tabitha. It's found in Acts 9:36-42. She is named as a disciple—a follower of Christ, and a witness for him. This is noteworthy and stands out because even though Jesus had a number of women disciples, it is the only place in the New Testament where the female form of the word "disciple" is used— "mathetria."

She is commended for good works and charity. She wove clothing and gave robes and garments to many people. Tabitha was an entrepreneur—a businesswoman. And the town of Joppa loved her for it, especially the widows. Her name in Greek is "Dorcas," which means *gazelle*. Names in the Bible are very prophetic, including this "apostolic woman on the frontlines."

She is an influential *7 Mountain* marketplace minister. We could say Tabitha was a fashion designer and clothing manufacturer. She was a woman of means, able to help the poor, a model in her community, and most likely a widow herself. Tabitha was a transformational leader, an influencer for the Kingdom of God on the Mt. of Business in Joppa, a seaport town.

The church in Joppa, which is believed to have been established earlier by

Phillip, was a center of fervent evangelism. It is very possible that this church met in the home of Tabitha. She may even have been one of its leaders, like the deaconess called Phoebe in Cenchrea, mentioned in Romans 16:1,2 who is a benefactor and credentialed member of the Apostle Paul's ministry team.

Let us speculate for a moment, and read between the lines of what is written regarding Tabitha's story, and consider that this entrepreneur and humanitarian concerned with the disenfranchised, was not only giving people *fish*, but also teaching them *how* to fish. It is likely that she was not only involved in weaving herself, but providing opportunities for many poor widows to become self-employed, working at sewing and selling clothing. This was one of the reasons she was so beloved in Joppa.

Prophetic Implications of her Name in Greek—Dorcas

Even though Tabitha is a Jew with an Aramaic name, it is possible that she also was well known in Greek circles in Joppa, and thereby called Dorcas, the Greek equivalent. As mentioned earlier, names in the Bible are very prophetic, and the name "Dorcas" means "gazelle." I believe her name can give us some powerful prophetic insights regarding the characteristics that caused this woman of God to become the kind of leader who could make such an impact in her community.

Let's look at some of these traits. Gazelles are swift. They can run 50-60 miles per hour, sometimes even reaching 80 mph, zigzagging to confuse their predators. They are survivors that can adapt to harsh climates where there is little water, living without it for long periods of time. They are very beautiful, nimble, exceptionally alert to sounds and movement, and they are graceful. They have a keen sense of smell, which helps them find food. That keen sense of smell, hearing, and sight balances their vulnerabilities.

They not only run fast, but are able to do what is called *stotting* or *pronking* to display strength. This is called the "behavior of fascination," a bluff tactic where they captivate and confuse their predator by leaping up and down to keep any threat under control and to maintain the upper hand. Their enemy becomes hypnotized in a sense by this fascinating movement of the gazelle, allowing them to control the potentially deadly situation, while mapping out a quick escape.

Gazelles know how to move and how to survive in the worst of situations, whether dealing with extremely harsh environments or potentially dangerous predators. Tabitha (Dorcas) was a gazelle. She knew how to move and survive in life in the midst of challenges, whether in navigating harsh deserts or climbing mountains. And she knew how to prosper in spite of those challenges because of what God had put inside of her.

Tabitha was an "apostolic woman on the frontlines—a disciple of Jesus Christ—a "sent one" on assignment for the King. She was an entrepreneur; a marketplace minister who loved her city, and was moved with compassion to help the most marginalized, not only with handouts, but equipping them to become self-employed. How beautiful and anointed on the "mountains of cultural influence" in Joppa were the feet of this amazing woman—an ambassador of Christ who was proclaiming the Good News of the Kingdom through word and deed. She was a model for her generation. And she is still a model for us today, two thousand years later.

Sometimes Your Story Begins after Something in Your Life has Died

Tabitha's powerful story in the Bible actually begins with a tragedy; her sickness and sudden death. There are times where your real story may actually begin when something has first died in your life. Disciples from the Joppa community of believers hear that the Apostle Peter is just a few miles away and bring him to where Tabitha is lying in an upstairs room.

There is so much grief in the room from the widows who deeply loved her, that Peter had to take control of the atmosphere and ask them to leave. He knelt down and began to pray, turning to the dead woman and saying, "Tabitha, get up!" In today's vernacular, he might have said, "GIRL—GET UP!" And she opened her eyes, and he helped her to her feet, and presented her to the believers and widows alive.

What an amazing miracle, and what an amazing story. Many people came to believe in Jesus all over Joppa as word of the miracle spread. The church grew and the Kingdom expanded.

Where are you today in regards to your story, your dream and purpose? God has placed tremendous gifts and abilities both in the natural and spiritual inside of you. There are leadership and destiny in you, ready to come forth to bless a community, a city, or a nation. Theologians believe Tabitha herself was a widow, meaning she would have had to overcome many things when her husband died. That was most likely a very challenging time in her life, where she had to trust in the gifts and talents God had put inside her. But out of processing the pain of loss, she discovered her greater purpose that would bless many.

Some of you may feel, as you are reading this, that your dream or prophetic promise has died because of circumstances beyond your control. But I want to say to you that there is a "gazelle" inside of you that can overcome the harshest environments and escape from the most dangerous predators. Your dream—your vision is not dead. Resurrection is coming. Heaven has called you, and the Kingdom has need of you. New life is coming. You're an apostolic woman getting ready to take your place on the frontlines. Death cannot hold you down.

So there is only one thing to do: GIRL—GET UP! It's time to get up and live again.

The Amplified Bible in Isaiah 60:1-3 reads like this:

Arise [from the depression and prostration in which circumstances have kept you— rise to a new life]! Shine (be radiant with the glory of the Lord), for your light has come, and the glory of the Lord has risen upon you!
² For behold, darkness shall cover the earth, and dense darkness [all] peoples, but the Lord shall arise upon you [O Jerusalem], and His glory shall be seen on you.
³ And nations shall come to your light, and kings to the brightness of your rising.

It's time to Arise and Shine. It's time to Get Up!! Your light has come. Darkness must flee! It's the "dawning of a new day" for your life. GIRL— GET UP!

Principles from the Life this Apostolic Woman on the Frontlines:

1. Tabitha knew her identity – a gazelle that would survive and prosper
2. Tabitha modeled what it was to be a true disciple of Jesus Christ
3. Tabitha understood her gift to prosper in business was the key to her mission
4. Tabitha was passionate and selfless about helping and empowering others
5. Tabitha was very comfortable in multi-cultural settings with both Jews and Greeks
6. Tabitha was a servant leader whose example transformed many lives
7. Tabitha understood how to do ministry in the church and the marketplace

Pray this prayer of faith after me:

Father, in the matchless name of Jesus, I want to thank you for every gift and talent you invested in me as part of my destiny and purpose on Earth. I thank you that no weapon formed against me and the dream you have given me will prosper. Thank you that your tender mercies are new every morning, and that your grace is sufficient for me. Lord, I make a conscious decision to get up and to arise and shine every day. I receive new life and strength from you for the journey ahead. I will be intentional about moving forward into my future. Help me to create and pursue with passion a life of servant leadership that will impact others as Tabitha's did. Lord, I ask you to equip and prosper me that I may have all the resources needed to bless and empower others. Amen and amen. Let it be so—and it is so!

CHAPTER 4

THE STORY OF MARY SMITH: REBEL WITH A CAUSE!

By Axel Sippach

"...being sent out by the Holy Spirit, they went down to..." **Acts 13:4**

This is the story of Mary Smith. She was a disciple of the Lord Jesus Christ, and she was a fisher of men. She was an "apostolic woman on the frontlines." She was a sent one—sent out by the Holy Spirit.

I have used Mary as an example a number of times in my preaching over the years, and felt her story needed to be immortalized in a chapter in this anthology. If she had ministered three decades later, her name would be all over social media, but as it is, few have heard her testimony. I will try to recall it here to the best of my memory.

Mary was a retired African-American postal worker from New Jersey in her mid to late 60's. I met her on my first apostolic ministry trip to Africa in 1985. The location was Nairobi, Kenya. I had been ministering in Ethiopia, Djibouti, Sudan, and now was in Kenya, on my way to Egypt and Israel. Someone had told me about this amazing retiree from Jersey that God had sent to Kenya, and I wanted to meet her. It was an incredible encounter, and such a joy to hear her powerful story.

Mary Smith had no Bible School degree. She was not an ordained minister. She had no title she went by. But she had something special from God. She had such a heart of compassion for people, and loved to evangelize. She loved praying for people to be healed and delivered. And she had a special faith and anointing to see people baptized with the Holy Spirit. Mary was a faithful member of her Pentecostal church for many years. But they, unfortunately, could not see the call of God in her life.

On a Mission with a Mandate

When she retired, her dream was to go as a missionary to Kenya and spend her remaining years investing her life in that nation. Her pastor and the elders of her church could not see the vision God had put in her heart. She asked them to bless and send her, but they refused, and basically encouraged her to just enjoy her retirement until Jesus took her home.

But Mary would not be dissuaded. And she was not going to spend her retirement in a rocking chair. She heard the voice of the Lord and His call to Kenya, and made preparations to go. If her church would not send her, the Holy Ghost would send her. She wanted to do her part in fulfilling the Great Commission, and she was on a mission with a mandate from Heaven.

So, this retired postal worker from Jersey made arrangements to have her monthly small retirement and social security checks wired to an account in Kenya, and she got on a plane headed for Nairobi. After she arrived, she secured a small apartment in a suburb of Nairobi called Buru Buru, and bought a used little Japanese car to get around in. Now she was ready to go to work. She knew God was with her.

She was a Move of God Getting Ready to Happen

Mary discovered that during weekdays, people working in downtown Nairobi would have their lunch in the beautiful Uhuru Park. She decided to begin preaching and ministering the Good News there during lunch hour. People were drawn to her and touched by her message, and something was ignited by the Holy Spirit. Souls began to get saved. Healings started happening as she prayed for many people. Others got filled with the Spirit. Amazing things began to happen. Mary Smith was a move of God getting ready to happen.

People began to find out where Mary lived. And most days of the week, when Mary awoke at sunrise and pulled back her curtains, she would see a line of 50 to 100 or more people, both rich and poor, lined up outside her apartment, patiently waiting for her to open her door for ministry. Her reputation was beginning to spread.

One retired postal worker, full of the Holy Ghost and sent by the Holy Ghost was about to touch the lives of multitudes in Kenya and beyond.

Within a short period of time, Mary was regularly preaching in the public schools with many students receiving salvation and others being filled with the Spirit. Evangelists who were having big crusade meetings in Kenya began to call for her to minister in the crusades. When it came time to pray for people to be baptized with the Holy Spirit, they gave her the microphone to pray. Soon she was also speaking in many churches and a variety of events.

Mary Smith was a move of God, and wherever the river in her flowed, it brought life, healing, deliverance, and restoration. Miracles, signs, and wonders followed her ministry. Multitudes were being touched. Lives were being changed.

Her Latter Years were Greater than Her Former Years

When I first visited Mary at her humble little Nairobi apartment in Buru Buru, she brought out many huge and heavy accounting-type ledgers for me to look at. As I opened the ledgers, I saw the names of thousands who filled the pages with their names, dates, and what God had done for them through the ministry of Mary Smith. Those names represented the poorest of the poor, along with wealthy business and high-level government leaders. They were blessed to give testimony in these ledgers that showed the success and fruit of Mary's ministry. It was an incredible feeling holding those ledgers as a young man on his first apostolic journey to the nations. What an inspiration this woman of God was.

In that season of my life in the mid to late 1980's, I was in Nairobi once or twice a year ministering. A few years later, I remember walking down a street in Nairobi past a magazine stand and seeing a well-known secular women's magazine with Mary's photo on the front cover featuring an article telling her story. I was so excited to see that.

Mary Smith blessed a nation in her retirement years. The glory of her latter years was so much greater than her former. The Lord used her to plunder hell and populate Heaven with many souls that are credited to her Heavenly account.

Mary was a woman of courage. She was bold. She was intentional. She was radical. She was obedient to the One who had called her. She was an ambassador for Jesus Christ. She would not be talked out of her destiny — out of her dream. She was willing to go it alone if necessary, in order to do what God had called her to do. She was an anointed evangelist.

Mary Smith had a move of God in her spirit that touched a nation. She was a rebel *with* a cause. She was *sent* out by the Holy Ghost.

I hope this powerful story will inspire and motivate you to dream big and believe God can use you to even touch and bless a nation. They may have thought she was too old or not qualified enough. This was over 30 years ago, so perhaps it was because she was a woman. Whatever the reason, Mary would not take "no" for an answer. She intimately knew the One who was sending her, and that He had also equipped and anointed her for the assignment. His grace was sufficient for her. All it took was her obedience to say yes.

That's all God is looking for from you; your YES! Listen for his voice. He will give you the desires of your heart as you delight yourself in Him. Those desires are motivational forces that will propel you forward toward your destiny. His sons and daughters are led by His Spirit. You can be led by His Spirit every day. Don't let anyone talk you out of your dream. It's connected to your destiny. You are a *sent one*. Just say yes, and watch how God will prepare the way and open the doors. You are a move of God getting ready to happen.

Apostolic Principles

1. Mary walked with Jesus and was intimate with him through prayer and knew his voice

2. Mary had to obey God rather than man and make an uncomfortable decision
3. Mary was intentional, bold, and courageous. She knew God had sent her
4. Mary did her research and was strategic in making proper preparations for ministry
5. Mary was moved with love and compassion for those she was sent to
6. Mary trusted in the Holy Spirit and the gifts given to her to carry out the assignment
7. Mary's humility kept her in a place to continually access the grace she needed

Pray this prayer of faith for yourself now:

Father, I ask you in Jesus' name to help me to clearly hear your voice regarding my future, and to give me the courage to obey what you will speak to me, and the strength to overcome every challenge that is hindering me. Help me to be intentional every day to pursue your purpose for my life. I resist discouragement, fear, and the opinions of those who cannot see the treasure you have deposited in me. Help me to grow daily in my relationship with you and to develop every gift and talent you have put in my life. I acknowledge you have called me to your Kingdom for such a time as this, getting ready to be sent on my next assignment. I ask for your grace to empower and equip me to walk in the fullness of my calling as a sent one—as an apostolic woman on the frontlines. Amen and amen. Let it be so—and it is so!

CHAPTER 5

THE INCREDIBLE DAUGHTERS OF ZELOPHEHAD: GOD SAID, "THEY RIGHT ABOUT IT, MOSES!"

By Axel Sippach

"So Moses brought their case before the Lord..." **(Numbers 27:5a NIV)**

These daughters of Zelophehad were apostolic women on the frontlines—incredible game-changers and reformers in the time of Moses. Take a moment to read their amazing story in the Bible in Numbers 27:1-11.

Their father had died without a son. And under the existing law, without a male heir, they had no legal right to the family inheritance. Only sons could inherit the family land. These women were marginalized. They experienced gender discrimination. But they were bold, courageous, and assertive. They decided to fight for their inheritance.

They challenged their challenges. They confronted Moses and demanded their inheritance. God stepped in, and a new law had to be created for them.

They were game-changers. They challenged the rules. They were reformers.

We know that names in the Bible can be prophetic, so let's have a quick look at what their names mean to perhaps gather insight regarding their personality traits, looks or challenges.

Here is what their names mean:

1. Mahlah: fat; weak; sick; born during a time of infirmity or suffering from wounds;
2. Noah: male form means rest, but female form means movement; motion; shake; rattle; shaky girl; lady wanderer
3. Hoglah: dancing; hopping; partridge with a broken wing
4. Milcah: queen; counsel
5. Tirzah: pleasing; favorable; delight; beauty; pleased with; accepted

Only two out of the five were "prom queens" so to speak, Milcah and Tirzah. The other three had some difficult personal challenges in their lives, including possible health issues or a physical handicap. However, they all stood together as one voice to challenge the system.

These daughters raised before Moses the case of a woman's right and obligation to inherit property in the absence of a male heir in the family. Women were considered property and could be sold or traded, but these five daughters were absolutely fearless. They were bold. They were change agents who disrupted "the system." They wanted the family name carried out through their inheritance.

This was a first for Moses to have to deal with. Change came. New laws were established. These women did not keep silent. They invaded the place where men dominated. They were determined. Continuity of the family name depends on inheritance of the land. And they found the loophole in the law—an omission in the law. And they trusted in Yahweh's justice— that he is a just God. They were wise. They argued their case masterfully as skilled attorneys.

THEY CONTENDED FOR THEIR INHERITANCE. NO DEFEAT— NO RETREAT.

Moses concluded that the women then must marry within the tribal clan. The DNA of the tribe of the father must be preserved. So the tribal land would stay in the tribal allotment of the Promised Land. These warrior daughters of Zelophehad defied the patriarchal system of their day and earned a special place in Biblical history. They were pioneering women preparing the way for others. They challenged the system. They were lionesses.

And what did God say about them? Let me paraphrase Numbers 27:7, "They're right about it Moses—they're right!"

God contradicts centuries of prejudice and wrongheaded tradition. He makes it clear that in His Kingdom women have value. They are not an afterthought. They got their inheritance. Somebody reading this should shout about now—"I'm going after my inheritance!"

Pray this prayer of faith after me:

Father, in Jesus' name, I ask you to give me the boldness and courage of these daughters of Zelophehad to stand up for justice and what I believe should be my rights and the rights of others. Let me not settle for second best or even miss out on my inheritance because of a "system" that favors men. Abba—I am your daughter and I believe I am highly favored by you. Let an anointing for breakthrough come upon me and give me the wisdom to speak with irresistible clarity and persuasion. I will take back everything the enemy has stolen from me and recover all. And I will be a voice of reformation to prepare the way for other women to do the same. Thank you Lord, that when I am weak, your strength is made perfect in my weakness, and your grace is sufficient for me. I will walk in victory because you are with me. I also declare, Lord, that I am an apostolic woman on the frontlines of issues in this generation that require reformation. I declare that I am sent to be a voice for change. Amen and amen! Let it be so, and it is so!

Declarations:

1. I will not allow any limitations to keep my voice from being heard
2. I will boldly speak as a woman, even if some still think it is not proper
3. I will go after everything I believe God has promised me and not doubt
4. I will trust in God's love, mercy, grace and justice
5. I will stand in the gap as a reformer for issues near to God's heart
6. I will fearlessly walk in the courage of the daughters of Zelophehad
7. I will receive all the inheritance Abba Father has for me as his daughter

CHAPTER 6

KINGDOM FINANCIERS: WOMEN WHO FUELED & FUNDED THE FRONTLINES OF JESUS' MINISTRY

By Dr. Yolanda Powell

"Soon afterward Jesus began a tour of the nearby towns and villages, preaching and announcing the Good News about the Kingdom of God. He took his twelve disciples with him, 2 along with some women who had been cured of evil spirits and diseases. Among them were Mary Magdalene, from whom he had cast out seven demons; 3 Joanna, the wife of Chuza, Herod's business manager; Susanna; and many others who were contributing from their own resources to support Jesus and his disciples." **(Luke 8:1-3 NLT)**

The Kingdom Campaign and Gospel Tour

In all of the New Testament writings about women, this is one passage I hold dear to my heart. It centers on the important work of the Lord Jesus Christ and his dedication to "tour" the surrounding towns and villages of his day, openly ministering to enormous populations of followers and spreading the **good news** of the Kingdom. This wide-spread ministry campaign was not political, social, or temporal. It was personal, spiritual, and eternal. The Kingdom was a rare and valuable commodity that many desperately needed in order to be healed, delivered, and set free in their spirit, soul, and body. So Jesus spent days and nights generously campaigning and distributing this *supernatural empowerment* to whosoever desired it, and his generosity was both effective and contagious. He rebuked death, spoke life, assaulted darkness, brought light, and turned the bittersweet. A true "Miracle Worker" was in the midst of the masses. Therefore, his ministry gained popularity among hurting people desperate for a better life; a life filled with joy, freedom, and abundance.

Jesus, the Mega-Popular Rock Star

Almost overnight, this lowly carpenter and motivational teacher becomes a "rabbinical rock star" and a popular "household name." Jesus was hitting towns and cities en masse with the sound effects of liberation from demons and extraordinary healing from disease. Good news was being written upon real lives in full demonstration and tons of testimonies were everywhere regardless of race, gender, or age. The Kingdom of Heaven was at hand! It was a fresh move of Heaven on Earth that defied religion and removed the exclusion. Wow! That's just how Jesus rolls!

The Twelve & the Cost of Full-Time Ministry

And yet, he didn't do it alone! With him on this life-changing tour and ministry campaign are a twelve-man team he has personally trained outside of that same religious box. They are commoners and ordinary fishermen—unlearned in the Law of Moses and untrained in scholastic Judaism. They have no religious credentials or university understanding. But they are dedicated to the Messiah and committed to him as Master. Without a doubt, these disciples of Christ turned fishers of men are primed to be the next *Movers and Shakers* on the planet and they have left ALL to follow Him on this incredible journey of ministry, power, and might.

Yet, outside of the fanfare of the crowds and the non-stop action of miracles is the reality that following Jesus, the Quintessential Rock Star costs! These men have left their fishing boats, medical practice, tax business, farming fields, and other varied occupations on temporary hold, as well as the earnings that come with them. Think about the call and test of this for a moment. How will they eat, pay bills, buy groceries and take care of their families while on tour? Who will work their boats, run their enterprises, and overview their matters while ministry is going forth?

They have gone into full-time ministry with this popular and powerful "Ministry Magnet" who is upsetting systems and shaking the status quo. As awesome as this is, they still have to trust the process. Each of them has left families and businesses, and forsaken all to proclaim the Gospel of the Kingdom. Therefore, Almighty God must bring provision and avail resources to sustain the enormous work they are doing, especially in the absence of their normal income. This is a faith walk, but it must be financed. Undoubtedly, ministry requires money, and mission tours, like this, must be sponsored and underwritten by those with heart-strings and expense accounts that are tenderly tied to the Messenger and his Mandate.

Women in Ministry on Tour with the Messiah

So, this is where Luke's tiny verse gets extraordinarily good. Inside this touring company with the miracle-working Messiah and his traveling band of sacrificing disciples, are a group of women who are placed on the campaign trail by both *inspiration* and *invitation*. These women have experienced Jesus' ministry first-hand and can testify to his bonafide anointing and authentic power. Wherever he goes and whatever he does, they are committed to "aid and assist" because their lives have been drastically changed by Christ the Lord who "breaks yokes and destroys burdens." These women were **inspired** and devoted to serving the One who set them free.

Among them were Mary Magdalene, from whom he had cast out seven demons; Joanna, the wife of Chuza, Herod's business manager; Susanna; and many others.

According to Bob Deffinbaugh, a writer for Bible.org, "Luke identifies the three women by name so as to indicate how different each was. But regardless of the diversity among the women who followed Jesus, they all seemed to have this in common: Jesus had miraculously delivered (healed) them of conditions for which there was no human solution. Some, like Mary Magdalene, were delivered of demon possession. Others were healed of sicknesses and disease. Others, may have been healed of injuries and disfigurations. But all were beyond human help. All of those who went with Jesus to be of help to Him were those who had experienced His help in their lives."[1] Truly, Jesus had touched these women deeply and inspired their hearts for a lifetime.

Mary Magdalene is well known in Gospels and is characterized as one who was under severe demonic oppression when she encountered the Ministry of Jesus. He actually cast seven demons out of her. Up until that point, her life was severely troubled and full of vexation of spirit. "Some paint Mary as a prostitute or *loose* woman, but the New Testament clearly distinguishes the demonized from sinners and prostitutes. How this demonic activity manifested itself, we don't know. Perhaps in some kind of mental illness or self-destructive behavior."[2] Even to the bitter end, Mary is serving Jesus at the tomb and crying out her assignment to show benevolence to him by dressing his body for burial. The other women named are, "Joanna the wife of Chuza, the manager of Herod Agrippa's household, Susanna, 'and many others.' Susanna, too, is mentioned with no husband, so she may have been a widow. Joanna's husband had a very prominent position in the Galilean king's court. That she had the freedom to travel with Jesus while her husband was still living and active is remarkable."[3]

Women in the Line-Up & Fueled for Christ

Additionally, this text also reveals that these women were **invited** to be a part of the touring team and ministry campaign that Christ was leading. *"He [Jesus] took his twelve disciples with him, along with some women who had been cured of evil spirits and diseases."* From the viewpoint of Jesus, these women were vital to His ministry; so he included them in the official line-up and enjoyed their company as he traveled near and far. "But the way Jesus treats women, ministers to their needs, and allows them to travel as a regular part of his team is unparalleled in ancient history. Though the New Testament doesn't tell us, doubtless the scandalous presence of women traveling in Jesus' group was a theme of his critics."[4]

Nevertheless, they were given a repeated invitation to share their stories and personally interact with many who were quietly suspecting or openly questioning the validity and authenticity of the Son of God. They had been undeniably delivered from evil spirits and dramatically cured of major diseases. As a result, the "good news" brought to the public square would not just be in teaching and preaching, but in power and demonstration, as these women gave bold testimony to the Living Christ. Joyfully, these women shared the stage with the twelve disciples and were even given space to "minister at the microphone" with their Rock Star Savior. I can envision them facilitating small groups around their personal testimonies and intimately sharing, with both seekers and doubters, what the Lord had done for them. And even now, I can hear the voices of these women openly introducing Christ before massive crowds as "The Deliverer" and "The Healer" of their lives.

The Extraordinary Leadership of Christ

In his article, *"Serving the Savior,"* Steven J. Cole writes, "It is interesting that nowhere in the gospels is a woman recorded as being an enemy of Jesus; all His enemies were men. The prevailing Jewish attitude toward women was less than exemplary. The rabbis refused to teach women and restricted them to the outer court in the temple, along with the Gentiles. They did not regard the testimony of women in a court of law. But Jesus showed personal concern and respect for women. He healed them, forgave them, taught them, and accepted their ministry on His behalf. When you view it in light of the cultural context, Jesus' treatment of women was nothing short of radical."[5] Oh, yes! A radical revolutionary leader indeed!

Without flinching, Jesus was radically poised to break with religion and tradition concerning women in ministry. He knew that these ladies would be game changers who would serve as social proof and living examples of the power of His Apostolic and Prophetic ministry among the people. Everyone knew that women were not to be taken seriously or regarded publicly. This was a cultural no-no. Yet, Jesus simply doesn't care. He breaks the mold of gender bias and defies the social insanity of misogyny. Women have value and are rich in what they carry and possess. "O MAN," as contributing writer Nicole Davis pens, "Hear the Heart of A Woman."[6] Jesus, the God-Man can both hear and speak!

The Funding Sources of Female Financiers

"...who were contributing to their support out of their private means [as was the custom for a rabbi's disciples]." Luke 8:3b AMP

Interestingly, the same women who fueled the Ministry of Jesus with their powerful testimonies and caring presence also put their money where their mouth was! They were both women of financial means and hard working sacrifice that poured out praise and profit over their Lord and his disciples. Like many women today, they flooded the forefront of ministry and were always a workforce of *willing workers* who bring their blood, sweat, and tears to the calling of Christ. They are not afraid to share their substance with the one who delivered them both the elements of the spiritual oppression and infirmity, and they found creative ways to showcase their thanksgiving with their treasures. They took care of the back office and made sure that monies were in place, meals, services, and ministry to the masses were both fielded and funded with Kingdom order and extravagance.

Once again, Author Bob Daffinbaugh confirms these Scriptural assessments, "The women who had been healed by Jesus and who now accompanied Him, were those who also supported the whole group out of their own means. Luke wants us to know that these women were not mere "clingers-on," they were active contributors to the proclamation of the gospel of the kingdom. Humanly speaking, this campaign could not have been waged without their support. The party had to eat, and the food was provided by these women. I cannot say for certain that no men contributed to the support of our Lord's mission, but we do know that many women played a crucial role in this matter."[7]

Without equivocation, these women were *Kingdom Financiers* who rejoiced in giving their riches and resources to ensure that the Ministry Tour and Campaign of Christ were covered with appropriate amounts of food, water, sandals, tunics, lodging, transportation, and other varied expenses. So as women today, we should square our shoulders and lift our heads high, because we have a place at the table, on the stage, and in the accounting sheet of Jesus' Ministry. He highly regards us for our love and sacrifice and He proves both in Holy Writ and in our personal lives. So, come forth, wealthy woman. Jesus' works on Earth still require your treasured touch.

References (listed in the order used in the chapter)

1   *"Ministry, Money & Women" by Bob Deffinbaugh bible.org - https://bible.org/seriespage/24-ministry-money-and-women-luke-81-3*

2   *"Jesus' Traveling Band - Luke 8:1-3" by Dr. Ralph F. Wilson Jesus Walk Bible Study Series http://www.jesuswalk.com/lessons/8_1-3.htm*

3   *Ibid*

4   *Ibid*

5   *bible.org "Lesson 33: Serving the Savior" by Steven J. https://bible.org/seriespage/lesson-33-serving-savior-luke-81-3*

6   *"O Man - Hear the Heart of a Woman" Poem by Nicole Davis, 2018*

7   *"Ministry, Money & Women" by Bob Deffinbaugh bible.org - https://bible.org/seriespage/24-ministry-money-and-women-luke-81-3*

CHAPTER 7

PRISCILLA AND AQUILA:
ONE IN SPIRIT AND APOSTOLIC AUTHORITY

By Nicole Davis

Success in marriage does not come merely through finding the right mate, but through being the right mate. - Barnett R. Brickner[1]

Who Priscilla is—her apostolic identity—was not determined after she married Aquila. Her virtue, character, passion, and calling were established before she was formed in the womb. Yet, her ability to fully become the woman God created her to be, was actualized because she was fitly joined with the *right* mate: her husband and supporter, Aquila. Those two were the perfect complement to one another. Scripture does not show us competition, but compatibility. There were no signs of superiority, just synergy. Since marriage made them one flesh, and Jesus made them one in the spirit, apostolic authority and anointing rested upon them both *equally*. Wisdom says, the right mates will come alongside one another to offer each other full support to achieve God's best expression for them both: individually and collectively. When these conditions are met, the result will be powerfully successful marriages, with two fulfilled people who glorify God.

The Bible provides two dynamic examples of what a man and woman's partnership should look like as husband and wife. In the Old Testament, we

---

[1] http://proverbicals.com/marriage-proverbs/

see God's example through Adam and Eve. In Genesis 1:27-28, God provided the blueprint for all marriages to follow. Before the Fall, His plan was for man and woman to be fruitful, multiply, subdue, and have dominion *as one*. This picture of unity and equality was so important to God that He gave it to us again in the New Testament, through Aquila and Priscilla. Their example gives us still another model of how man and woman should co-exist at home, in business, and in ministry. Priscilla and Aquila's story can be found in Acts 18. They are also mentioned in Romans 16, 1 Corinthians 16, and 2 Timothy 4.

While today, hearing that a husband and wife are leaders in ministry together is not Earth-shattering, in the 1st Century Church, it was practically unheard of in Greek/Roman culture. Unless she had great wealth, a woman was otherwise thought of as property and relegated to a life of child rearing, hard-labor, and caring for her family.[2] Wives were completely subject to their husbands and not educated. It was only men who studied God's Law who were considered learned.[3] Notwithstanding these facts, it appears Aquila *chose* unashamedly to honor Priscilla as a woman. He also honored her gifts, abilities, knowledge, and apostolic position in the Kingdom. Priscilla is an example of an *apostolic* woman, an *apostolic* wife, an *apostolic* entrepreneur, and an *apostolic* minister of the Gospel. In this chapter, we're going to look at the life story of Priscilla the woman, her marriage, and her ministry.

The Apostolic Woman

Priscilla was a leader, pioneer, warrior, hard-worker, and standard bearer. She was a Jewish woman with an apostolic mantle. These three variables made her dangerous to the status quo. Before the rise of Christianity, men

---

[2] Keller, M. N. (2010). *Priscilla and Aquila: Paul's coworkers in Christ Jesus.* Collegeville, MN: Liturgical Press.

[3] Taylor, M. A. (2012). *Handbook of Women: Biblical interpreters* (pp.244-247). Grand Rapids, MI: Baker Academic.

were viewed as superior in areas of marriage, society, and government.[4] However, this viewpoint began to change with the emergence of the Church. We can see it through much of the early teachings by the Apostle Paul, who encouraged men and women to submit to one another (Ephesians 5:21-25, Galatians 3:26-29). This was an extremely difficult challenge to rise above for those whose culture and training taught them to treat women as inferior people. Priscilla enters at a time when the new Church needed to see what it looked like for a wife to work alongside her husband, as equals, through tumultuous situations. Acts 18, Scripture hints at the difficulties they endured through forced exile and wide-spread persecution of Christ followers.

Priscilla was a tent-maker by vocation and an apostle by purpose. She was a woman who worked hard with her hands, yet had a soft heart for the lost—no matter the physical, financial, or emotional cost. She served with her husband on the frontlines to bring the Good News of the Gospel, and she did so knowing it could cost her her life (Romans 16:3).

Her Apostolic Marriage

Even though Priscilla served faithfully in ministry, her oneness with her husband appeared to be her priority. Her ability to understand and accept her role as a wife made it possible for her to willfully submit to her husband, and Aquila submitted likewise to her. It's no wonder Scripture is intentionally equally showcasing their influence and power, making it virtually impossible for us to rank them. Marriage truly made them one in every way. It can be implied that all ministry opportunities were considered, discussed, and agreed upon because they always showed up together. It's not by coincidence that God gives this example to us in the canon of Scripture. Their union was often acknowledged and promoted by Paul. Some scholars believe that when Paul wrote about love in 1 Corinthians 13, he was referencing the relationship between Priscilla and

---

[4] Women in Church History (n.d.). In *Wikipedia*. Retrieved 12/15/2017 from https://en.wikipedia.org/wiki/Women_in_Church_history

her husband.[5] Their bond, centuries ago, demonstrated what godly love should look like between a man and a woman; and, it continues to serve as a significant representation for marriages today.

Her Apostolic Ministry

While theologians and ministers debate her worth, her leadership, her calling, her contribution, and the order in which her name should appear in Scripture with her husband's name, Priscilla will be forever remembered for doing the "works" of ministry. She was a *solutionist* at heart. She was teaching, preaching, evangelizing, and working alongside the Apostle Paul to see people redeemed, healed, and delivered. Along with Aquila, they served as church house leaders. Many recognized and respected their authority (1 Corinthians 16:19) and excelled under their tutelage.

Priscilla was also equipped and anointed to discern error, as we see in their encounter with Apollos in Acts 18. Apollos being a well-learned and influential person (Acts 18, 1 Corinthians 3), willfully submitted himself to the teachings of both Priscilla and Aquila. It demonstrates that even religious leaders believed they operated at an advanced level of intelligence and spiritual power. One of the most important aspects of Priscilla's ministry was the respectability she received from her male contemporaries: her husband who lived, worked, served, and ministered with her; Paul who lived, worked, and ministered with her; Apollos who learned from her; and, Luke, who wrote about her in the Book of Acts. Through every Bible interpretation, Priscilla's apostolic position and her influence in the Church remains undeniable. Priscilla, with the support of Aquila, exercised the spiritual freedom God had given her. Marriage truly enhanced her shine in ministry—God's Masterplan.

---

[5] Keller, M. N. (2010). *Priscilla and Aquila: Paul's coworkers in Christ Jesus.* Collegeville, MN: Liturgical Press.

Our Challenge

With relentless determination, satan works overtime to reinforce tension and competition between men and women to keep us distracted with a matter we are powerless to change: God has irrefutably chosen us both to be joint-heirs with Him (Romans 18:17). Like Jesus, we too must stand against Satan and decide that God's will for our lives is greater than our own personal ambitions. We start by responsibly and consistently assessing and correcting all dysfunction within ourselves and in our marriages, in light of God's Word.

Choosing the right mate *and* being the right mate are two of the most important choices you will ever make. As wives, like Priscilla, we too must become secure in our identity *in* Christ, yet, be submitted to complete partnership with our spouses. Your apostolic calling should encompass every aspect of life.

Handled properly, it's a function of Christ's Body to advance the Kingdom of God and to positively influence culture. Husbands and wives demonstrate their level of value for one another based on the degree of acceptance and acknowledgment of each other's spiritual role in the Kingdom. Agreement here is vitally important.

Finally, responding to who you are apostolically should entice you to, not exempt you from, fully submitting to doing marriage God's way. Based on our Biblical examples, we have a mandate to be the modern-day Priscilla and Aquila. After all, your marriage is your first ministry.

Apostolic Traits of Priscilla

A. Priscilla confidently and unapologetically did the "works" of ministry as a Bible teacher, preacher, evangelist, church planter, and minister.

B. Priscilla operated as a leader with the full encouragement and support of her husband.

C. The apostolic anointing flowed equally through Priscilla and Aquila because they were married.

D. Priscilla joined her entrepreneurial and pioneering abilities with those of her husband so that they could work in ministry together.

Prophetic Prayer

I decree that God will showcase godly marriages to exemplify the power of God through the love men and women have for one another. Like Aquila and Priscilla, I call forth a greater level of unity, stronger commitment to marriage, and purpose-filled conversations that will illuminate God's vision and assignment for every marriage and household. I bind competition, misunderstanding, and rivalry, and I release mutual acceptance, mutual honor, and mutual respect. Let 1 Corinthians chapter 13 be our guiding Scripture to promote faith, hope and love, in Jesus' name, Amen.

CHAPTER 8

PROPHETESS DEBORAH:
WOMEN INSPIRING WOMEN

By Deborah Sheppard

"God is within her, she will not fall." **(Psalm 46:5)**

And Deborah, a prophetess, the wife of Lapidoth, she judged Israel at that time. And she dwelt under the palm tree of Deborah between Ramah and Bethel in mount Ephraim: and the children of Israel came up to her for judgement (Judges 2:4-5). Prophetess Deborah was the fourth judge in the chaotic and disorderly time of the Judges. God raised her up as a deliverer to rescue the children of Israel as they once again attempted and failed to take possession of their promised land after the death of Joshua. It was a challenging time that the Bible described as "Every man was doing what was right in his own eyes."

The only female judge mentioned in the Bible, Deborah, whose name is an anagram for "she spoke" but actually means "honey bee" according to myjewishlearning.com, came onto the scene as the cycle of idolatry, bondage, and deliverance was repeating itself once more. And according to Scripture, God had sold them into the wicked hand of Jabin, king of Canaan who had "900 chariots fitted with iron and had cruelly oppressed the Israelites for 20 years." It was in answer to these cries for mercy that God raised Deborah up as a prophetic leader, spiritual mother, and military strategist to deliver His people once again and to rule over them. The first part of The Song of Deborah, an ancient poem most notably written around the XXI century BC by her describes life under cruel Canaanite oppression.

"In the days of Shamgar, son of Anath,
In the days of Jael,
The highways were deserted,
And the travelers walked along the byways.
Village life ceased, it ceased in Israel,
Until I, Deborah, arose,
Arose a mother in Israel.
They chose new gods:
There was war in the gates:
Not a shield or spear was seen among
Forty thousand in Israel."

From under the palm tree where she sat judging the children of Israel, to the battlefield where under her leadership King Jabin's great general Sisera was soundly defeated, Deborah indeed proved herself as Mother of Israel. It was this motherly love, coupled with her great faith in God that caused Deborah to call upon Barak, a skilled warrior and military general who would help deliver the children of Israel from Sisera's great army and company of chariots.

And the Bible says, according to Judges 4:4-9, "And she sent and called Barak the son of Abinoam out of Kedeshnaphtali, and said unto him, Hath not the Lord God of Israel commanded, saying, Go and draw toward mount Tabor, and take with thee ten thousand men of the children of Naphtali and of the children of Zebulun? And I will draw unto thee to the river Kishon Sisera, the captain of Jabin's army, with his chariots and his multitude; and I will deliver him into thine hand? And Barak said unto her, if thou wilt go with me, then I will go: but if thou wilt not go with me, then I will not go. And she said, I will surely go with thee: notwithstanding the journey that thou takest shall not be for thine honour; for the Lord shall sell Sisera into the hand of a woman."

And it was then that Deborah arose, and went with Barak and his 10,000 men to Kedesh, where the Lord "routed Sisera, the commander of the army of Canaan and all his chariots," and gave the victory into their hands. The Lord sent a fierce torrent of rain and a severe mudslide and flash floods to discomfit them. Sisera's army of 900 war chariots was bogged down in the resulting mire as they attempted to scale the mountain where Barak's army was stationed. As the ancient Kishon overflowed its banks, both horses and chariots were swept away, and the warriors were killed. Sisera, the great general of the Canaanite armies, was later slain when a tent peg was driven through his skull while he slept by the woman Jael, another Biblical heroine.

Chosen and gifted by God to undertake this task of liberating His people, Deborah was not only a prophetic leader, poet, and judge, but a woman who possessed a great military spirit. She had an inner strength and faith in God that would not fail, and it was because of this faith that, "the Lord came down for me against the mighty." The latter part of the Song of Deborah celebrates this victory and the great things God did in this spectacular time of Jewish history and remembers those who were instrumental and called by God to participate in it! Readers may want to experience this joy and blessing of this poem for themselves by reading Judges Chapter 5.

Deborah was backed by the authority of Heaven, a prophetess of the Old Testament with a New Testament apostolic mantle upon her life. The definition of an apostle in the New Testament is "the sent one." Deborah was definitely sent by God; anointed and appointed as Israel's' spiritual governing authority in her role as its fourth judge. Just as the apostles of the New Testament changed the lives and the cities to which they were called, so also did Deborah change the lives and cities where the Israelites dwelled in the 11th century BC. The position she held over God's people was truly apostolic.

Apostolic Traits that Apply to Deborah:

1. Apostles are called by God alone.
2. Apostles are chosen by God to lead His people from bondage to freedom.
3. Apostles are spiritual fathers or mothers who love and are truly concerned with the spiritual condition of their children.

4. Apostles are anointed to gather God's people and impart the unity of faith.

5. Apostles prophesy, encourage, and speak the truth into the lives of God's people.

6. Apostles teach, instruct, and release Kingdom strategy into their realms of influence.

7. Apostles are backed by the government authority of Heaven.

Deborah, who called herself the mother of Israel, birthed a nation unto God from ruins to greatness. From judging under the palm tree in Israel, to leading Barak and the 10,000 soldiers to victory, Deborah reformed the nation of Israel through her apostolic identity and caused the children of Israel to turn their hearts towards God once again.

Prayer:

It is my prayer for you, dear reader, as you take hold and embrace this chapter, that God will illuminate your thoughts and bring you to a place of peace, purpose, and prosperity in the revelation of Christ. I believe that the words written here will help you discover your true identity in Christ as new doors of opportunity are opened to you, and that, like Deborah, you will become an atmosphere shifter, able and equipped to speak forth the mind and counsel of the One who has sent you to exercise dominion authority in the Earth realm. May God continue to bless you, dear reader, and sing songs of victory over you!

CHAPTER 9

MODERN DAY ESTHER'S COME FORTH: APOSTOLIC GOVERNMENTAL LIONESSES EMERGE

By Michelle Brown-McKoy

"Women must become revolutionary. This cannot be evolution but revolution." - Shirley Chisholm, First African-American Congresswoman & Female Presidential Candidate

LEAVING BEHIND A LASTING LEGACY!

We're seeing more emergent apostolic female leaders on the rise who know who they are, are aware of the power that they possess, and are unapologetically walking into their purpose. This grand awakening is not only ushering them into the world as change agents but also propelling them to ignite a similar passion into future forerunners. As we take a look at the life of Queen Esther, we are captivated by her outward beauty, inward power, and commitment to honoring God's will for her life.

In fact, we see her reverence for God in action in one of her defining moments as a leader. When Esther approached the king when she was forbidden to do so, it displayed her act of heroism that left a lasting impression on the hearts of women. The fact that she was willing to do what other women were afraid of doing by sacrificing it all separated her from the rest. She had the courage to confront man-made laws that restricted women and the underprivileged from having a voice to speak up against injustice and unrighteousness.

When we look at apostolic women in government, such as Congresswoman and Presidential candidate, Shirley Chisholm; Florida State Representative, Apostle Kimberly Daniels, and countless others, we see that they had to walk in the spirit of boldness and courage to maintain their positions of influence. Upholding godly law and principles were part of their political agenda which positioned them to have their light shine before men in such a way that they were able to see their good deeds and moral excellence (Matthew 5:16, AMP). They knew that in order to be effective change agents they had to be willing to break barriers and come against demonic systems of government within legislation. These women have been instrumental in paving the way for other believers to rise in prominence and power. They helped to create a legacy for those that will follow their lead in standing up against the social ills of society. I believe God is releasing *Esthers* throughout the nations of the world to continue to break ground, expose corruption, and champion change by promoting the Kingdom of God! ESTHERS ARISE…ARISE…ARISE! YOUR TIME HAS COME!

NEVER ALLOW FEAR TO WIN

Fear is a paralyzing emotion that scares us from wanting to lunge forward into God's promises for our life. By succumbing to this harmful emotion, we're easily held captive and can live with thoughts of defeat where it's hard to trust God. I am so glad that Esther decided to look fear in the face and let it know that it wasn't going to stop her from pursuing her destiny. When she said, "…if I perish, I perish" (Esther 4:16, KJV), it was a time that she rejected the spirit of fear and allowed the spirit of boldness to have its perfect work. I'm sure the devil wanted her to buckle under pressure and begin to fret and worry, having not known what the outcome would be. However, Esther decided to trust God and step out in faith. As Joyce Meyer points out, "Fear wants you to run, to withdraw and to hide. God wants you to finish what you began." Fear was set by the kingdom of darkness to undermine the key Kingdom component, which is faith. When we live in fear, we cripple the power of faith from manifesting and being able to move in our lives. As the Bible says, "For God has not given us a spirit of fear and timidity, but of power, love, and self-discipline" (II Timothy 1:7, NLT), which helps to remind us that we have to constantly speak to the spirit of fear and let it know that it can't influence or direct our paths. There is power that lies inside of us all and as we tap into this supernatural strength, we'll begin to have the courage to do things that we never thought were possible. Thus, allowing fear to lose its grip off our mind, heart, will and emotions—which then causes those same spirits that had us in bondage that threatened the Christ in us to become our target to destroy.

YOUR MISERY IS YOUR MINISTRY

When we evaluate the lives of women that have moved into great positions of influence, we oftentimes discover that they had major odds stacked against them. Esther was an orphan that was taken from the only family she knew and had to prepare for a king that could potentially choose her as a wife. Some of us may have grown up in a single-parent home, an abusive or poverty-stricken household, etc. Yet, despite the cards we were dealt, we somehow pushed ourselves to tap into the inner power that helped unlock our destiny.

It amazes me how God is able to take our tragedy and turn it into triumph. Our life lessons help to prepare us for our Kingdom mandate and assignment. The world may make us feel as if our struggles and issues have disqualified us to be used by God to help others. However, it's quite the contrary! We should never allow anyone's perception of us or our life journey negatively impact or direct our paths.

Just know that the world will always try to judge you through a gray-colored lens, but it's up to you to keep your eyes fixed on Jesus. As Judy Jacobs says, "Don't adjust your life and ministry to the limitations of the world's culture around you. God has called you to believe Him and stand out to make a difference in this world by embracing your calling." So, although Esther lost a lot at a young age and existed in an era where women didn't have many rights, God allowed her to step into her apostolic call to impact many people. As she was a rejected orphan that was used to deliver a rejected people, you can also be used to set multitudes of people free. God essentially turned her misery into her ministry and can do the same for you!

HIDDEN FOR GOD'S ASSIGNMENT

There are times when God will conceal our true identity and have us remain hidden until the appointed time because it allows Him to work out various things behind the scenes. God doesn't reveal anything before it's time because he is a God of kairos timing. Looking at the Merriam-Webster definition of kairos, we see that it means a time when conditions are right for the accomplishment of a crucial action, the opportune and decisive moment. As the Hebrew root of Esther is 'hester' which means hidden, we see it in every aspect of the life and assignment of Esther because as the word states,"…to everything there is a season, and a time to every purpose under the heaven" (Ecclesiastics 3:1, KJV).

Esther was a Jew and her husband did not even know her place of origin until she decided to reveal her identity to save her people. When God hides His people, there's no telling when He will reveal that which is hidden. We see that with Esther, as her heritage and lineage was unknown, but she quickly progressed to a place of prominence. As Michelle McClain-Walters says, "one day she was an orphaned Jewish refugee. One year later she was crowned queen of Persia." So, her assignment shows that there was an unnatural progression that proved to be supernaturally orchestrated by God. She was hidden so no one could challenge or question all that was taking place in her life. The average person would've seen it as impossible that someone was an orphan one minute, then the next moment a queen. But, when it comes to Kingdom assignment and progression, God uses "…the foolish things of the world to confound the wise…" (I Corinthians 1:27, KJV).

I DECLARE & DECREE IN THE NAME OF JESUS THAT THESE AFFIRMATIONS SHALL BE YOUR PORTION!

1. No weapon formed against the health, family, finances, ministry, and destiny of God's women servants shall prosper. **Isaiah 54:17**
2. All women in the Body of Christ will have and exude the spirit of patience, boldness, and confidence. **Ephesians 3:12**
3. This is the season where women of God will no longer be timid to fulfill

their God-given mandates to change the world. **Proverbs 28:1**

4. Women of God will arise out of fear and obscurity to proclaim the Good News and release the Word of the Lord in due season. **II Timothy 1:7, Mark 16:15, Proverbs 15:23**

5. There's a fire anointing falling from Heaven on God's women servants to break them out of the box of being lackadaisical and complacent with status quo. **Isaiah 66:15**

TRAITS THAT ESTHER HAD AND I DECREE SHALL TRANSFER UNTO YOU!

1. <u>Strength</u> – Esther was able to withstand adversity from early on in her life and trust God to deliver her, AND SO SHALL YOU! **Esther 2:7**

2. <u>Synchronized with the Holy Spirit</u> – She was a woman who communicated with God and was able to clearly hear His instructions for her assignment, AND SO SHALL YOU! **Esther 4:17**

3. <u>Prayer Warrior</u> – Esther was a woman that understood the power of prayer and how to connect it with a strategy of fasting so Heaven could respond to her petitions, AND SO SHALL YOU! **Esther 4:16**

4. <u>Fearless</u> – She was a fearless woman who stared fear in its face and did the unthinkable of facing the king when people were forbidden to do so, AND SO SHALL YOU! **Esther 4:14**

5. <u>Favor with the King</u> – Esther was a woman that had great favor with the king and was able to get her godly aligned desires and Kingdom mandate fulfilled, despite it being contrary to the law, AND SO SHALL YOU! **Esther 5:2**

References:

1. Jacobs, J. (2013). *You Are Anointed For This!* Lake Mary, FL: Charisma House, 46.

2. Meyer, J. (2006). *The Confident Woman.* New York, NY: Hatchette Book Group, 204.

3. McClain-Walter, M. (2014). *The Esther Anointing.* Lake Mary, FL: Charisma House, 21.

CHAPTER 10

COLLIDING WITH DESTINY: THE RISE OF WOMEN APOSTLES IN GOD'S ARMY

By Thapelo Kgabage

"…but the godly are as bold as lions." **Proverbs 28:1 NIV**

The book of John 1:6 states, "There was a man sent from God whose name was John." Furthermore, church history records that there was a Christian Dutch watchmaker woman that was sent from God whose name was Cornelia Arnolda Johanna "Corrie" ten Boom. Corrie's story of World War II; her arrests and detentions together with her family; the death of her family members; her mysterious release, and her life after the war is encouraging in its nature. Her character and service to the Lord and the world reflects true qualities of an apostle, commissioned in her generation to serve God and God's people. History records that Corrie was born on 15 April 1892 and lived during World War II. Corrie, named after her mother, the youngest child of Mr. Casper ten Boom, was born to a working-class family in Haarlem, Netherlands, near Amsterdam. Mr. Casper was a jeweler and watchmaker. He was so fascinated by the craft of watchmaking that he often became so engrossed in his own work that he would even forget to charge his customers for his services.

Corrie's life can be likened to that of Jesus Christ, born unto Joseph the Carpenter; she, being born to a jeweler, was also trained to be a watchmaker, inheriting and learning from her father. In 1922, it is recorded that Corrie became the first woman licensed as a watchmaker in Holland, and over the next decade, in addition to working in her father's shop, she established a youth club for teenage girls, which provided religious instruction as well as classes in the performing arts, sewing, and handicrafts. She can be described as one of the greatest apostolic scribes and a pioneer raised by the Lord in her generation to communicate the message through arts and handicrafts, and raising as well as impacting the next generation. Corrie came from a family with strong Christian roots and beliefs, as they were strict Calvinists in the Dutch Reformed Church, following the teachings of John Calvin. She and her family's faith inspired them to serve society, offering shelter, food, and money to those in need.

According to history, in May 1940, the Nazis invaded the Netherlands. Among their restrictions was banning the youth club. In May 1942, a well-dressed woman came to the ten Booms' with a suitcase in hand and told them that she was a Jew, her husband had been arrested several months before, her son had gone into hiding, and Occupation authorities had recently visited her, so she was afraid to go back. She had heard that the ten Booms had helped their Jewish neighbors, the Weils, and asked if they might help her too. Casper ten Boom, Corrie's father, readily agreed that she could stay with them, despite the police headquarters being only half a block away. As devoted Old Testament readers, they believed that the Jews were the chosen people of God, and he told the woman, "In this household, God's people are always welcome." The family then became very active in the Dutch underground hiding refugees; they honored the Jewish Sabbath. The family never sought to convert any of the Jews who stayed with them.

Thus, the ten Booms began "The Hiding Place." Corrie and Betsie (Corrie's sister) opened their home to refugees, both Jews and others who were members of the resistance movement being sought by the Gestapo and its Dutch counterpart. They had plenty of room but, due to war, there was food scarcity.

During the time, every non-Jewish Dutch person was receiving a food ration card to receive weekly food coupons; she miraculously one day received more than she expected from the father of a disabled woman that was a civil servant and was in charge of the local ration cards office. They gave them to Corrie, as she was known for her charitable work; she received 100, of which she later gave to every Jew she met.

It later happened that the refuge work done at the Beje by ten Boom and her sister became known by the Dutch Resistance. The Resistance sent an architect to the ten Boom home to build a secret room adjacent to ten Boom's room for the Jews in hiding, as well as an alert buzzer to warn the refugees to get into the room as quickly as possible.

On the 28 February 1944, Jan Vogel (Dutch informant) told the Nazis about the ten Booms' work, which led to the entire ten Boom family's arrest. Casper (Corrie's father), died 10 days later after the release of some of Corrie's family members. Corrie and Betsie were imprisoned at the Ravensbruck Concentration Camp, which was the women's labor camp in Germany. They would hold worship services in prison after the hard days at work, using a Bible that they had managed to sneak in. While at Ravensbruck, Betsie's health continued to deteriorate and she died on the 16 December 1944 at the age of 59. Fifteen days later, Corrie was released; it was said that this happened due to a clerical error. Afterward, Corrie returned home during the winter of hunger, and she again opened her doors still to the mentally disabled that were in hiding for fear of execution.

After World War II, ten Boom returned to the Netherlands to set up a rehabilitation center in Bloemendaal. The refugee houses consisted of concentration-camp survivors and sheltered the jobless Dutch who previously collaborated with Germans during the Occupation exclusively until 1950, when it accepted anyone in need of care. She returned to Germany in 1946, where she met and forgave two Germans who had been employed at Ravensbruck, one of whom was particularly cruel to Betsie. Corrie went on to travel the world as a public speaker, appearing in more than 60 countries as an Evangelist, of which she even wrote many books during that timeIn 1978, Corrie suffered two strokes, the first rendering her unable to speak, and the second resulting in her paralysis. She went to be with the Lord on her 91st birthday on the 15 April 1983, after a third stroke.

Characteristics or apostolic traits of an apostle on Corrie ten Boom and her family

Corrie ten Boom was one of the godliest, soul-rich individuals in Christian history. Corrie and her entire ten Boom family that were Dutch Christians demonstrated the following apostolic traits accordingly:

1. **Apostles are willing to suffer regardless of challenges and rejections (Acts 9:16)** - Corrie and the family suffered for their good course of hiding the Jews and were arrested and treated badly.

2. **Gentleness and humility is the mark of an apostle (1 Thessalonians 2:19)** - Corrie and her family were the actual caring people with meek heart, they did hide many Jews and non-Jews including the Jew woman whose husband had been arrested several months before, her son had gone into hiding, and Occupation authorities had recently visited her, so she was afraid to go back, Casper ten Boom, Corrie's father, readily agreed that she could stay with them, despite the police headquarters being only half a block away.

3. **Apostolic leaders have great Love, are zealous for God, God's mission, and for God's people** - The ten Booms loved the people of God. God's people were always welcome in their homes.

4. **Apostolic leaders are Selfless individuals and have Undivided Loyalty to Christ in their services (Philippians 1:21)** - Casper (Corrie's father) was imprisoned and died 10 days after the release of some of Corrie's family members for serving God's people. Corrie and Betsie (Corrie's sister) were imprisoned at the Ravensbruck Concentration Camp, that's where Betsie's health continued to deteriorate and she died as well.

5. **Apostolic Leaders don't run away but respond to challenges regardless of how risky it can (see 2 Corinthians 4:8-12 and Acts 16:6-10).** - The ten Booms began "The Hiding Place" for hiding the refugees and having them stay with them despite the police headquarters being only half a block away from their home.

6. **Apostolic people are focused on equipping the next generation and they are pioneers** - In addition to Corrie's work in her father's shop, she

established a youth club for teenage girls, which provided religious instruction as well as classes in the performing arts, sewing, and handicrafts.

7. **Apostolic leaders run toward new adventures and embrace risk thus includes going to new places, facing new challenges, and trying new things at most times** - After Corrie's release and after World War II, ten Boom returned to the Netherlands to set up a rehabilitation center in Bloemendaal.

Apostolic Prayers:

- May the Lord raise many mighty women of great stature that shall manifest Christ across nations of the world.
- May the Lord raise women of greater influence that shall turn the hearts of many lost souls unto God.
- May the Lord raise fearless women that are bold enough to stand in marketplaces and declare and manifest Christ, thus the watchmen of the cities in this generation.
- May the Lord raise women of influence, women that will positively influence their surrounding areas, their families, their workplaces, their friends, and the world as a whole.
- May the Lord raise women leaders who shall lead big corporations, local and international assemblies, countries, and various nations of the world.
- May the Lord raise mighty women with the transforming word of God in their mouths that brings healing to the entire world.
- May the Lord raise mighty women of greater visions and pioneers in this generation.

Daily Apostolic Declarations/Affirmations:

1. I am a world changer.
2. I was raised for greater impact and exploits.
3. I am called to bring Christ to the nations of the world.
4. I have the mind of Christ in me.
5. I manifest God's glory wherever I go.

6. I am a vision carrier.
7. I am commissioned from above to fulfill God's mandate and raise many sons of Glory.

References:

https://en.wikipedia.org/wiki/Corrie_ten_Boom

CHAPTER 11

ARISE, MODERN-DAY DEBORAH: BECOMING A POWERFUL WOMAN OF INFLUENCE IN THE 21ST CENTURY

By Cherie Banks

The villages were unoccupied and rulers
ceased in Israel until YOU arose — YOU,
Deborah, arose — a Mother in Israel (emphasis added).
Judges 5:7 (AMPC)

Arise, Woman of God, arise like Deborah, who led the Israelites to victory over the Canaanites, saving a nation and creating a legacy for generations. The Old Testament introduces Deborah as a prophet, a judge of Israel, and the wife of Lappidoth (Judges 4:4). She was a powerfully influential matron, courageous mouthpiece, and bold warrior living in the fullness of her calling under God's authority. Deborah rendered judgments beneath a palm tree between Ramah in Benjamin, and Bethel in the land of Ephraim (Judges 4:5). Ramah is known as a place of barrenness, weeping, and great mourning, and Bethel as the House of God (Wikipedia, *see Ramah and Bethel*). In between these two significantly meaningful places, Deborah's life was purposed to serve as a chief intercessor, military strategist, and deliverer of the oppressed. She is a Biblical icon of a Kingdom woman trailblazer liberating God's people with supernatural power. Her keen ability to understand wisdom, attain knowledge, discern hearts, receive revelation, and execute godly timing, represents the divine power of Deborah's anointing. These spiritual gifts manifested in Deborah, increasing her spheres of influence that were vital to the call upon her life.

Deborah's story begins in the Book of Judges when the people of Israel had been oppressed by Jabin, Canaanite King of Hazor, for twenty years (Judges 4:2-3). Stirred by the dreadful condition of Israel, Deborah incites a rebellious attack against Canaan (Hirsch, Emil G., et. al., *see also Judges 4-5*). She summons Israel's military commander, Barak, telling him of God's command to muster ten thousand troops of Naphtali and Zebulun (Id., *see also Wikipedia, Barak*). Deborah delivers military strategies for Barak to concentrate his warriors upon Mount Tabor, the mountain at the northern angle of the great plain of Esdraelon (Id.). She then prophesies that the Lord of Israel will draw Sisera, Commander of the Canaanite Army, to the River Kishon (Id.). Barak refuses to go into battle unless Deborah accompanies him (Id.). She consents, but declares that the glory of the victory will belong to a woman (Id.). Her prophetic words foretell God's will and specific intent to use a "woman" to bring victory for His glory. While Deborah is the central female figure in this Biblical narrative, her prophetic words seemingly transition into a Scriptural reference of yet another woman who is critical to carrying out God's mission. Once the news of rebellion reaches Sisera, he collects nine hundred chariots of iron and a host of people (Id.).

Deborah said to Barak, "Go! This is the day the Lord has given Sisera into your hands. Has not the Lord gone ahead of you?" (Judges 4:14) Barak then went down Mount Tabor with ten thousand men following him (Hirsch, Emil G., et. al., *see also Judges 4-5*). Barak begins the battle with his warriors against Sisera, pursuing the Canaanite army as far as Harosheth of the Gentiles (Id.). Suddenly, God engages in the battle and causes a flood storm on the River Kishon (Frymer-Kensky, Tikva, *see also Judges 5:21*). This disabled the Canaanite chariots and enabled Israel to win (Id.). All the Canaanites were destroyed except Sisera, who escaped on foot and came to the tent of a woman named Jael (Hirsch, Emil G, et. al., *see also Judges 4-5*). He lies down to rest and asks her for a drink (Id). Jael gives Sisera milk and while he is asleep, she hammers a tent-pin through his temple, killing him (Id.). Jael is the woman who seals Sisera's fate, fulfilling Deborah's prophesy. This victory had a revolutionary impact for women because, traditionally, they were trapped in an antiquated age, plagued by cultural prejudices and societal injustices of gender inequality. The victory originating from Deborah's anointing and Jael's courageous act had the miraculous strength and power to break through these barriers. They overcame obstacles that faced women's ills throughout thousands of years. With God, all things are possible (Matthew 19:26). There is no other heroine like Deborah in the Hebrew Bible, but other women had some of her many roles (Frymer-Kensky, Tikva).

Despite prevailing female discrimination, Deborah's gender and femininity were compelling characteristics in bringing forth the liberation of God's people as "a Mother in Israel" (Judges 5:7). Remarkably, this victory celebrated her natural instinct to nurture a generation with a mother's heart. Under Deborah's maternal-servant leadership, she exhibited God's love, grace, and mercy unto His children in a time of grave despair and desolation. This earned her great influence in an archaic male-dominated society. As a wife, Deborah's honor for her husband surely would have demonstrated the utmost dignity, reverenced submission, and unfailing love; authenticating her loyalty and integrity in cultural community circles. Today, Deborah's anointing rests upon modern-day women, waiting for YOU to arise! Your living history is being written in this very moment. God is calling you to establish and expand your spheres of influence for His glory. Your destiny under Deborah's anointing is leading you to become a mighty matriarch; marking a new historic era in the millennium epoch of iconic female heroism.

Since Deborah's appointed time, God has been calling women in wondrous ways over the centuries to fulfill His purpose on Earth. The 21st Century marks YOUR appointed time! The modern world suffers from deadly nuclear threats of worldwide warfare and devastating natural disasters of epic magnitudes causing chaos, confusion, and catastrophic fatalities. These are times of great adversity, but not without promised purpose. The Kingdom of God is in great need of YOU to arise in these turbulent times. The Lord has granted you access to spheres of influence to affect cultural change aligned with His Word. There are desires that God has secretly placed inside of you embodying divine creativity, intellect, and solutions to transform the world. You are being summoned by the throne of God to receive Deborah's anointing with spiritual gifts added on to you to complete your mission. Your womanhood is a critical component for the clarion call and to bring forth victory. These are Kingdom keys that were essential for Deborah to circumvent a corrupt culture and preserve a nation. In this hour, the Lord is directing you to your divine destiny.

As you live in the fullness of the Holy Spirit, you are given God's power and authority to free people from bondage and usher them into peace. The Bible states that after the battle was won, there was peace in the land for 40 years (Judges 5:31). This peace preserved Deborah's legacy, which is bestowed unto you right now. Deborah's anointing is one of legacy because it requires you to leave a remnant on Earth that carries peace forward to the next generation. Becoming a modern-day Deborah requires sowing seeds to advance the Kingdom and harvest peace on the planet. As a descendant of Deborah's legacy, you have the gifts and grace to minister deliverance for liberty and freedom in the new millennia. Woman of God, take up the sword of the Spirit for world compassion and reformation. You are spiritually armed to confront the powers of darkness and attain victory with the power of God. For our struggle is not against flesh and blood, but against the rulers, against the authorities, against the powers of this dark world and against the spiritual forces of evil in the Heavenly realms (Ephesians 6:12).

Arise, Woman of God, arise! Deborah's life narrative pours out an oil of anointing that brings women into the full manifestation of their purpose. Woman of God, this oil is upon the crown of your head. By the power of the Holy Spirit, I anoint your head with this oil and release Deborah's anointing upon you in Jesus' name! Its fragrance is a sweet, sweet aroma, quick to stir up your spiritual gifts and increase your spheres of influence in becoming a modern-day Deborah. I call forth and activate the apostolic leadership and prophetic mandate of the "Matriarch" to fall upon your ministry mantle. Woman of God, be confident that the Lord will finish the good work that He has started in you (Philippians 1:6). Seek God for His strategic downloads for impacting the world, healing a hurting humanity, bringing peace to nations, and leaving a legacy for generations. Awaken yourself to the destiny calling and Deborah anointing on your life. Like Deborah, you are called to pioneer a powerful movement of unprecedented maternal-servant leadership in this lifetime for which you were born to live for God's glory. In the Holy Spirit and under Deborah's anointing with God's authority, I boldly, courageously, and unashamedly prophesy that the glory of the victory belongs to a woman—YOU!

References (listed in the order used in the chapter)

1. Bible Gateway (2018, February). Judges 5:7, Amplified Bible, Classic Edition (AMPC). Retrieved from https://www.biblegateway.com/passage/?search=Judges%205:6-8&version=AMPC
2. Biblica, The International Bible Society (2018, February). Judges 4-5, New International Version. Retrieved from https://www.biblica.com/bible/?osis=NIV:Judg.4-Judg.5
3. Wikipedia (2017, October). Ramah. Retrieved from https://en.wikipedia.org/wiki/Ramah_in_Benjamin
4. Wikipedia (2017, October). Bethel. Retrieved from https://en.wikipedia.org/wiki/Bethel
5. Wikipedia (2018, February). Barak. Retrieved from https://en.wikipedia.org/wiki/Barak
6. Hirsch, Emil G., Levi, Gerson B., Schechter, Solomon, Kohler, Kaufmann (2011). "Deborah," Jewish Encyclopedia. Retrieved from http://jewishencyclopedia.com/articles/5027-deborah
7. Frymer-Kensky, Tikva (2009, March). "Deborah: Bible." Jewish Women: A Comprehensive Historical Encyclopedia. Jewish Women's Archive. Retrieved from https://jwa.org/encyclopedia/article/deborah-bible
8. Bible Gateway (2018, February). Matthew 19:26, New International Version (NIV). Retrieved from https://www.biblegateway.com/passage/?search=Matthew+19%3A26
9. Bible Gateway (2018, February). Ephesians 6:12, New International Version (NIV). Retrieved from https://www.biblegateway.com/passage/?search=Ephesians+6:12

10. Bible Gateway (2018, February). Philippians 1:6, New International Version (NIV). Retrieved from https://www.biblegateway.com/passage/?search=philippians+1%3A6&version=NIV

CHAPTER 12

JEHOSHEBA: DARE TO BE DIFFERENT

By Anita McCoy

But Jehosheba, the daughter of King Jehoram and sister of Ahaziah, took Joash son of Ahaziah and stole him away from among the royal princes, who were about to be murdered. She put him and his nurse in a bedroom to hide him from Athaliah; so he was not killed.
2 Kings 11:2 NIV

Positioned for Preservation

Jehosheba's name literally means – *"Yahweh Is An Oath; or The Lord's Oath."* An oath is a solemn appeal to a deity; to keep a promise. In Genesis 22:16 God said to Abraham concerning the promise to bless him and make him the father of many nations, that when He could swear by none greater, God swore by Himself to keep His promise. So convinced was Abraham of the promise that in the face of adverse events opposing the promise, Abraham *knew* that God was faithful! To read of the bravery performed by Jehosheba, it's evident that *she knew* of some future event to come and positioned herself accordingly. Why else would a princess marry a high priest? I'll come back to this later! A further look into the meaning of her name reveals that the *"sheba"* of "Jehosheba" translates to the meaning of *"Seven."* This seemingly small detail holds great significance when you understand what I call *"the power of Seven."* You see, according to the Bible, the number *seven* is *God's Divine or Perfect Number!* The number seven reveals to us that which represents perfection and is complete in the Mind of God. The seemingly tiny detail of Jehosheba's name containing *seven* is actually extremely

69

significant as we look at what Scripture reveals concerning her extraordinary fortitude, courage, and heroic actions that caused her name to be added to the chronicles of Biblical history.

2 Kings 11:2 – But Jehosheba, the daughter of King Jehoram and sister of Ahaziah, took Joash son of Ahaziah and stole him away from among the royal princes, who were about to be murdered. She put him and his nurse in a bedroom to hide him from Athaliah; so he was not killed.

Evil Interceptions Overturned by Divine Interruption

Princess Jehosheba was the daughter of Jehoram, son of King Jehoshaphat, who ruled in the Southern Kingdom of Judah—a kingdom that had sought to fortify itself against the Northern Kingdom of Israel, and of which it was spoken by God's holy prophets, Christ the Messiah would come. Wars and conflict were not uncommon in the reign of the kings and history reveals that much of the conflict in this time period resulted from making *unholy alliances*.

For example, to ease the conflict and establish a treaty between the two kingdoms Jehosheba's grandfather, Jehoshaphat arranged the marriage of his son Jehoram to Athaliah, daughter of King Ahab and Queen Jezebel, who ruled the Northern Kingdom. All the righteous acts of King Jehoshaphat in returning the Southern Kingdom of Judah to the ways of God were reverted in his death when his son Jehoram took the throne. King Jehoram was so impressed by the evil deeds and the Baal worship of Athaliah and his in-laws that he had all of his brothers killed to eliminate any challenge to him sitting on the throne! What? Who kills their own flesh and blood? It didn't stop there. After seven years of Jehoram's volatile rule, he dies a horrible death and his sons are carried into exile with only the youngest son, Ahaziah, surviving to take the throne and preserve the lineage of David. King Ahaziah's reign was cut short but not without a further downward spiral of the Southern Kingdom that was now mainly under the influence of Ahaziah's mother, Athaliah, the daughter of Jezebel. If you thought Jezebel was bad, what about Athaliah! It seemed everyone was under the control of Athaliah who, after her son died, secured the throne for herself by killing all her grandchildren who would have had legal right to the throne.

No one attempted to stop Athaliah's massacre except her daughter, Jehosheba, who put her own life in jeopardy to save the life of her infant nephew, Joash, the only remaining son of her brother, Ahaziah. This was truly remarkable because in Jehosheba's heroic act, she not only saved a natural dynasty; she secured a spiritual legacy, interrupting a hell-inspired plan to abort the line of Judah from which Jesus the Messiah would come!

Performing Under Pressure - Doing Your Best When it Matters Most

Imagine the pain Jehosheba must have felt to learn that all the men in her family tree were being destroyed. For many, such rapid loss and devastation would leave us emotionally traumatized and totally incapacitated. What empowered Jehosheba to perform so boldly and not succumb to the devastating blows of her pain and despair? First, I believe she *"refined in the fire of affliction,"* as described in Isaiah 48:10. Secondly, Princess Jehosheba married the High Priest Jehoiada, whose name means, *"Knowledge of the Lord,"* and no doubt was comforted, trained and inspired by the God and faith of her husband. I believe Jehosheba observed all the unholy alliances and the enemy's threat to her ancestry and decided this union with her husband would offer a *holy alliance* that would strategically position her to preserve her royal seed, as now she would have the *perfect* place—a secret place to hide young Joash! Because temple worship was deemed defunct under the wicked influence of Athaliah, she would never think to look for the missing child there. Jehoiada took an active role with Jehosheba to preserve and train Joash while keeping him hidden for six years. As High Priest, Jehoiada used his spiritual authority to govern the affairs of safety and spiritual development of the young prince, while Princess Jehosheba would ensure Joash's training to rule as king over a kingdom!

The Influence of Jehosheba for Today's Godly Woman

What We Can Learn from Jehosheba:

1. Jehosheba became a *foster* mother. The word *"foster"* means to encourage, promote, or develop. In view of other words associated with

foster, Jehosheba inspires us to be *promoters, developers,* and *nurturers.*

2. Jehosheba *risked self-preservation* to preserve a nation and ultimately helped prepare the way for the salvation of the world! Perhaps you, too, have been faced with making a life-changing decision that will impact others. We live in a time where it seems easier to just maintain "status quo," but remember, *"the only thing necessary for evil to triumph is for good people to do nothing."* You've been designed by God to *make a difference.* I like to say it like this: *"When you do that little something extra, your ordinary becomes extraordinary!"*

3. Jehosheba teaches us the value of *aligning with the eternal purposes and promises of God to fulfill destiny.* As a princess, she was of a natural royal bloodline but sacrificially laid that aside to be aligned with the promise of a spiritual inheritance exceeding the natural. History doesn't speak of her giving birth to offspring from her natural womb, but what she birthed spiritually was a remarkable courage and strength preserved the *seed of a nation.*

4. Jehosheba possessed a *finishing anointing* to secure the rightful destiny of Joash and to *transfer or reproduce* in him a passion for the things of God. For six years, she and her husband raised Joash in temple worship, teaching him to honor the covenants of God and His ways. Joash became king at seven years old and reigned for forty years. In 2 Kings 12:2 the Scripture says, *"Joash did what was right in the eyes of the Lord..."* He carried the love of the temple of God that was taught and caught from his spiritual parents, Jehosheba and Jehoiada. Has God called you to be a spiritual mentor in someone's life? I guarantee that the anointing God has placed inside of you carries the *Finisher's touch* that will equip you to teach, guide, direct, encourage, counsel, and strengthen another who is destined to reign victoriously in life!

Scripture References:

2 Kings 11:2; 2 Chronicles 22:11 (NIV)

Other References:

Book: All the Women of the Bible –author: Herbert Lockyer

www.meaning-of-names.com/israeli-names

http://www.abarim-publications.com/

www.merriam-webster.com/dictionary

CHAPTER 13

THE P.O.W.E.R. OF HANNAH

By Shelby Frederick

"Seeds of purpose conceived in the bosom of God that are placed in the womb of your spirit require a spiritual catalyst to bring heaven on earth."

As we look at the life of Hannah and all that she embodied, she becomes a representation by which apostolic women of prayer should function. Every prayer starts as a blank canvas. There is a request but no instructions on how to get to the promise. Such was the case with Hannah. She was barren but believed God in spite of being taunted, shamed, and humiliated by Peninnah, Elkanah's other wife. Peninnah was referred to as her adversary because she provoked her sore. Hannah's pursuit of the promise of God left her misunderstood, even by Eli, the priest who was blind, both spiritually and naturally. But Hannah made a vow to the Lord! And she was relentless in her prayer until God brought it to pass! It is during these times that you must pull from the very essence of who you are and operate in **P.O.W.E.R.**

Hannah means "favored." She was surprisingly treated the opposite of her God-given name but continued to model the character of her name, even in the midst of humiliation and shame. Her barren womb was shut up by God. Why would God shut up her womb? Did He not know her heart's desire to birth a child? Did He not know that infertility was a source of humiliation and shame? Yes! But sometimes the Lord will close things up so that He can get the glory out of the opening! So God had a plan and Hannah understood the P.O.W.E.R. of her prayer. It is only when we are touched by our pain that we truly pray from our spirit. When you pray from the place of pain, you touch the heart of God and He remembers you throughout the process. Hannah's pain produced faith. And I believe this is why Samuel is listed in the *Faith Hall of Fame* in Hebrews 11. Samuel's name, "heard of God", is the response to Hannah's prayers.

Hannah's prayers can be referred to as call and response prayers. The call— "Bless me with a son." The response—"Samuel." The Lord will never give you a friendly visitation without leaving a blessing. Although Hannah gave Samuel (her promise) back to the Lord once he was weaned, the Lord didn't forget her sacrifice. Hannah delivered three boys and two girls after the birth of Samuel. She received grace after the sacrifice. We must always maintain our personal and corporate worship in birthing **P.O.W.E.R. Prayers**. When we do this, we are showing our remembrance of the Lord.

What is this P.O.W.E.R. That Hannah Harnessed?

- **P.O.W.E.R. Prayers** never change. You are never moved by time because you learn the art of *PERSEVERANCE*. People can misinterpret your perseverance for pain, but it is really a catalyst pushing you to receive the promise. Romans 12:12 says, "Be joyful in hope, patient in affliction, faithful in prayer." All of these characteristics are needed in order to persevere in prayer.

- **P.O.W.E.R.** prayers produce *OVERCOMERS*. Our emotional state must remain in balance even in the midst of great trial and suffering. By acknowledging her emotions and not suppressing them, Hannah was able to overcome and realign her negative feelings for continued effectiveness in her assignment to birth the promise through prayer. Ephesians 6:18

- **P.O.W.E.R. Prayers** produce *WARRIORS* (Exodus 15:3, Isaiah 42:13). A warrior is one who fights against an opposing enemy. In the case of Hannah, she had to become a warrior for the promise. She had to press past her fear and become mighty in the Spirit. She prayed until she looked like a fool for God! Warriors don't take down and they don't retreat until the battle is won.

- **P.O.W.E.R. Prayers** are *EFFECTUAL*. Hannah was graced to produce effectual prayers. Answered prayers will always be the response to those who know how to harvest the perseverance needed to overcome the enemy, including the thoughts of one's own mind. Effective prayers hit the target every single time.

- **P.O.W.E.R. Prayers** are *RESILIENT*. The inner fortitude that Hannah had to embody was that of resiliency. Every taunt, harassment, shame, and humiliating word caused a blow to the core of her soul. But she also used this negative situation to make her prayer and worship lifestyle like that of a buoy. No matter the pressure, she was about to bounce back with resiliency! This lifestyle was the anchor of her soul that allowed her to **P.O.W.E.R.** to the promise!

What is God Saying Now?

If there was ever a time for an understanding of how to **P.O.W.E.R.** pray, that time is now. Apostolic Women of prayer must envelop the intensity that is needed to see Heaven manifest on Earth through their prayers and they won't stop until it is evident in every sector of society. This is accomplished by the principle found in Isaiah 62:6-7, "O Jerusalem, I have posted watchmen on your walls; they will pray day and night, continually. Take no rest, all you who pray to the Lord. Give the Lord no rest until he completes his work, until he makes Jerusalem the pride of the earth (NLT)." The Kingdom is set forth with great power when we continually **P.O.W.E.R.** pray and give the Lord no rest. He has already promised to complete the work. And because of this promise, all things must start, be carried through to completion, and remain sustained through **P.O.W.E.R.** prayer. This is the sure foundation because **P.O.W.E.R.** prayers birth spiritual seeds in the natural, which return to their original spiritual state when manifested on Earth. Finally, **P.O.W.E.R.** prayers must be prayers of faith, favor, and future success. This is our charge and mandate!

Prayers and Prophetic Decrees

- I aggressively use the principles of **P.O.W.E.R.** to snatch back from the enemy's camp that which belongs to me. Matthew 11:12 NLT
- I **P.O.W.E.R.** pray until cities, regions, and nations have been uprooted, torn down, destroyed, overthrown, rebuilt and planted in

the image of the Kingdom of Heaven. Jeremiah 1:10

- When I am tormented by my adversaries, I **P.O.W.E.R.** pray until the mouth of every accuser is shut up for the reputation of the Lord. Psalm 109

- I pray through the spirit of faith which gives me the strength to **P.O.W.E.R.** to the promise. I will not faint in the day of adversity. Isaiah 40:31

- I know the promise of the completed work, therefore I **P.O.W.E.R.** pray until the mountain of the Lord's house is established on top of every mountain of cultural influence. Isaiah 2:2

Father God, in the Name of Jesus, we thank you that we can come boldly before the Throne of Grace and access the courts of Heaven during times of adversity. Pour out a spirit of prayer among apostolic women on the frontlines. We declare that You are our God and that our identity is found in You alone. We refuse to submit to the systems of this world but boldly proclaim that we will man our posts with continual prayer and we take no rest because our strength is found in You. We give You no rest until You complete Your work through us. Our prayers of faith, favor, and future success bring glory, honor, and praise to Your Name. Our perseverance is the catalyst as overcomers and warriors that allows us to hit the target every time with resiliency and we maintain this posture of **P.O.W.E.R.** until the promise is manifested. We will not back down or retreat because victory is already ours! And we give Your Name all of the glory, honor, and praise! In Jesus' Name. Amen!

References:

1. *Who Was Hannah in the Bible - https://www.thoughtco.com/hannah-mother-of-samuel-701153*

2. *5 Things You Didn't Know about Hannah in the Bible - https://www.crosswalk.com/faith/bible-study/5-things-you-didn-t-know-about-hannah-in-the-bible.html*

3. *All The Women in the Bible: Hannah and the Excellent Bargain – pages 220 - 222*

4. *Strongs Bible Concordance*

5. *Hebrew-Greek Key Word Study Bible*

CHAPTER 14

DR. LENA MAE JOHNSON MCLIN: THE HALF-PINT APOSTLE

By Michelle Thomas

"It is more blessed to give than to receive." **Acts 20:32 KJV**

She stands squarely on a firm foundation of small feet at 4'8" and packs a wallop. Her height would fool you, but her demeanor avers that "I'm a woman of God and I know Whose I am"! Her name is Dr. Lena Mae Johnson McLin.

Her most prominent apostolic quality is her governmental authority. She founded a church, Holy Vessel, 27 years ago. She balked at the idea, not wanting to be a female pastor, but soon found unrest until she obeyed the leading of the Lord. Lena attended divinity classes and was ordained as a minister in 1982. Since the church's inception, she has been the musician and choir director as well.

The sterling example of Dr. McLin's operating in the Judicial, Executive, and Legislative areas in the church is one of many vivid memories. A gentleman that had separated from his wife, decided to show up with his girlfriend one Sunday. Now, his wife was a choir member and was ready to sing in the service. After seeing this, naturally, she was a basket case and couldn't stop crying. Needless to say, she did not sing. Now, Dr. McLin knew the situation and did not remain silent, but she did not mention names. She just let everyone know that 'a fool' had shown up to church and should not partake of communion. The gentleman was indignant at this point and decided to take the cup anyway. Pastor unseated herself from the piano, calmly walked toward the gentleman, stood in front of him (about waist-high) and repeated herself. He huffed up and she *took* the cup from him and told him to leave. Everyone was shocked and slightly amused at her guts. And, of course, there were men there to enforce her decision, but they weren't needed. She had judged this man, by the leading of the Holy Spirit, to be found unworthy to share in the Lord's Supper. She laid down God's Law and executed the consequences of not recognizing the Law of taking Communion unworthily.

Lena is an International Marketplace Apostle because she is a "sent one, an Ambassador for Christ." Her love of music and for Christ have gone all over the globe, either in print or in person. A 'Google-YouTube' search will result in videos of choirs singing her music as far away as Japan. She has written and arranged many spirituals, cantatas, operas, and various musical pieces in several genres, published by the Neil Kjos Co. Her childhood was spent with her uncle, Thomas A. Dorsey (the "Father of Gospel"), as he desired to be around children after losing his family in a tragic accident. Being the eldest child and daughter of a minister and choir director, she was already an accomplished pianist at the tender age of five. Dorsey honed her gift and set her upon a course that would alter many musical lives. Her adolescent years would tell the story of a pianist who accompanied Dr. Martin Luther King, Jr. on many of his speaking engagements.

Lena attended college and garnered many awards in music before, during, and after her storied career teaching for the Chicago Public School System. She taught close to 40 years in prominent high schools, including Harlan and Kenwood. One of many examples of her *stick-to-it-iveness* was during a choral competition that was held annually for high school students. The accompanist did not show up to play under her direction. With her "never say die" personality, Lena quickly concluded that she would have to do both jobs: play and direct *from the piano*. Not to be undone, she succeeded in attaining a "Superior" rating for the choir as onlookers and students alike were astounded at the accomplishment. She did this and flew to the Peabody Institute in Maryland on some weekends to teach students in attendance there. She had developed a "get-it-done-regardless" mentality and strength.

Another one of Lena's apostolic qualities is her pioneering/enterprising acumen. She forged a successful early music career in the south during the tumultuous Jim Crow Era in America, and gained the respect of many professional musicians despite her ethnicity, although it wasn't easy. Traveling in the American south was dangerous, but God's favor was with her. She would not be swayed; she was determined and steadfast to complete God's calling on her life regardless of seeming adversity and in the face of fear.

Dr. McLin is also a powerful prayer warrior. She has prayed many out of harm's way, including herself and others. She became a widow at a young age and raised her two children alone for many years. God was with her through those years of forging ahead for her family. God's favor allowed a rich, Jewish woman to hear Mrs. McLin's students singing and wonder who had taught them. When Lena spoke up, this woman was so amazed that she offered and *gave* away her 4-bathroom, 5-bedroom apartment for $1. This lady was up in age with no small children and just wanted to downsize and move somewhere smaller. She didn't want to profit from the deal.

Lena's love for people and her students caused her to never turn anyone away who needed prayer and/or Godly counsel. One of her former students and my fellow classmate was once arrested for swatting a neighbor's little girl on the behind after this gentleman repeatedly reprimanded the child for swinging on his iron fence and gate. She would not stop, so he took a belt to her. The girl's mother saw this and called the police. He was facing a court date and prosecution when he called Mrs. McLin. Of course, he was nervous, never having been in any kind of trouble of this nature. She prayed for him and told him that everything would turn out in his favor. Sure enough, it did and the case was dropped. Because of her love for people, Lena has helped many on her job, in her church, and in her community. She has put action to her words by giving funds to those in need, providing shelter for some and networking for others in need of jobs, etc.

Lena's prophetic gift was most evident with a young married couple who desperately wanted a baby. She prayed and let them know that by a certain time, they would have a child and this came to pass. God uses her frequently in this area. Like John the Baptist, her main thrust for God is the prophetic message that Jesus is the Word of God and Holiness is His desire for us. The visions and prophecies that God gives her do not fall to the ground—they come to pass.

Lena's apostolic mantle is one that also pulls purpose out of those who God shows her. She has trained and worked with many notable talents, including Robert Kelly, Opera stars Robert Sims, Mark Rucker, and many others. Her talent has put her in association with Jerry Butler, Quincy Jones, and other African-American pioneers of the 60's and 70's who, more or less, had to forge their own ways in their respective industries.

These examples show us that a strong faith in God and being obedient to His calling, even in adversity, gives glory to Him. Whatever you are called by God to do, being willing and obedient will yield a rewarding life of many surprises. NEVER GIVE UP!

CHAPTER 15

MARY MAGDALENE: THE WATCHMAN, WOMAN, AND WONDER

By Ladonna Jackson

If we were distributing titles to every female leader according to how they are mantled in this anthology, Mary Magdalene would be deemed as "The Apostle Who Watches Over." In modern times, one may coin her as Overseer Mary Magdalene, as her very name, *Magda*, translates to "tower." Aside from being a watchman, we will discuss how Mary was also a woman and a wonder. She is an outstanding Biblical character who has an identity beyond what the base-level believer could see. The purpose of this piece is not designed to prove or disprove Mary's implied past life before her encounter with the Messiah, but rather to illuminate her many empowering strengths that I discovered during her earthly ministry.

As I mentioned in the introduction, Mary Magdalene, from Magda, translates from Hebrew as *tower*. In her name lay her prophetic destiny to be a tower, or watcher over her personal faith walk, people, events, and spiritual realms. If we assign a human quality to a tower, what may be contrived are the characteristics of a giant. As a giant in the spirit, Mary needed to be tall in stature. When one is tall, their prophetic purview changes because they can see more, and their responsibilities expand. They pray with keener vision, trust more, worship deeper, love deeper, respond quicker with apt listening abilities, and navigate better in the spiritual realm. We witness this giant predication as she shifts from being a faithful disciple to an apostolic believer in two ways: with an increase in faith, and through obtaining additional responsibility. Pre-resurrection, Mary shared a community faith in Jesus Christ with the 11 apostles, and a few other women as she traveled with them in ministry. Post-resurrection, she was alone when she encountered the risen savior, therefore, she had a mindset shift from being led by others' faith to being led by her own faith. Secondly, according to John 20:17-18 (KJV):

> **17** Jesus saith unto her...but go to my brethren, and say unto them, I ascend unto my Father, and your Father; and to my God, and your God.

> **18** Mary Magdalene came and told the disciples that she had seen the Lord, and that he had spoken these things unto her.

Mary was given the additional responsibility of not only conveying that Jesus was risen, but that he also would ascend into His Father's arms.

Subsumed in the spiritual acumen as an intercessor, or watchman, is the ability to climb up high in the spirit realm and sit between the inner and outer gates to detect, react, and protect their leader from a possible threat. A watchman demonstrates this ability in II Samuel 18:24-28 (NLV):

> **24** While David was sitting between the inner and outer gates, the watchman went up to the roof of the gateway by the wall. As he looked out, he saw a man running alone.

> **25** The watchman called out to the king and reported it. The king said, "If he is alone, he must have good news." And the runner came closer and closer.

> **26** Then the watchman saw another runner, and he called down to the gatekeeper, "Look, another man running alone!" The king said, "He must be bringing good news, too."

> **27** The watchman said, "It seems to me that the first one runs like Ahimaaz son of Zadok." "He's a good man," the king said. "He comes with good news."

> **28** Then Ahimaaz called out to the king, "All is well!" He bowed down before the king with his face to the ground and said, "Praise be

to the Lord your God! He has delivered up those who lifted their hands against my lord the king.

Mary clearly exhibits her protection of the Messiah in John 20:1-2 (KJV):

1 The first day of the week cometh Mary Magdalene early, when it was yet dark, unto the sepulchre, and seeth the stone taken away from the sepulchre.

2 Then she runneth, and cometh to Simon Peter, and to the other disciple, whom Jesus loved, and saith unto them, They have taken away the Lord out of the sepulchre, and we know not where they have laid him.

Marked to expand the Kingdom, Mary was sent out for a specific purpose. When preparing to be commissioned, in John 20:17, Mary was told by the Lord to "go to my brethren, and say unto them, I ascend unto my Father, and your Father; and to my God, and your God." This indicates that as an apostolic vessel, as Mary's responsibilities expanded, they also became more specific. As a result, after Jesus' resurrection, she was entrusted with the most significant event in history…preaching Christ's second coming. Another strong apostolic leadership attribute is decisiveness. As seen in Mark 16:9-10 (KJV):

9 Now when Jesus was risen early the first day of the week, he appeared first to Mary Magdalene, out of whom he had cast seven devils.

10 And she went and told them that had been with him, as they mourned and wept.

After Jesus appeared to her, she made the decision to go and tell the 11 disciples that she saw him, without being prompted by Him.

Many times, while attempting to unearth our purpose, we become disheartened and can even display a loss of identity and weakness. However, when we seek our Savior for answers, He will often times ask us questions in return to get us to ponder, rather than leave us aimless. In the end, once we have contemplated our responses concerning our callings and gifts, He reveals Himself and offers instructions. We see this in John 20:11,14-18 (KJV):

11 But Mary stood without at the sepulchre weeping: and as she wept, she stooped down, and looked into the sepulchre,

14 And when she had thus said, she turned herself back, and saw Jesus standing, and knew not that it was Jesus.

15 Jesus saith unto her, Woman, why weepest thou? whom seekest thou? She, supposing him to be the gardener, saith unto him, Sir, if thou have borne him hence, tell me where thou hast laid him, and I will take him away.

16 Jesus saith unto her, Mary. She turned herself, and saith unto him, Rabboni; which is to say, Master.

17 Jesus saith unto her, Touch me not; for I am not yet ascended to my Father: but go to my brethren, and say unto them, I ascend unto my Father, and your Father; and to my God, and your God.

18 Mary Magdalene came and told the disciples that she had seen the Lord, and that he had spoken these things unto her.

Mary had a paradigm shift, or identity restructuring, once she encountered the Messiah. In the midst of transitioning from being addressed by role (woman) to being called by name (Mary), she was given keys to a new territory. She is mantled for women and men issues. Her name was mentioned 14 times in the gospels, thus one would argue that she had major influence amongst the 12 apostles.

Mary was not only a faithful steward over people, events, and realms in the Kingdom, but also a financier in the marketplace. Luke 8:2-3 says that she and other women helped fund Jesus' ministry. They were builders. A ministry like His was worth the investment. The aforementioned Scripture states that Mary gave out of her substance. No matter how little or much she possessed financially, the word "substance" indicates that what she gave was significant. An investor builds on projects that they only find substantial. She invested into: (1) essence- every soul and system to be impacted by Jesus' ministry; (2) marrow- the core, or strength of a person; (3) groundwork- the beginning of a thing; (4) gravamen- the death of a thing, or a person's deliverance; (5) individuality- the uniqueness of a person; and (6) essentiality- what every person needs from the Messiah (wholeness, deliverance, prosperity, etc.).

Can an apostle be lazy and effective? My formidable opinion based on the following observations, says absolutely not! An apostolic leader must be willing to do the work. As a forerunner and a glory carrier, she literally and figuratively made power moves. With a forerunner and pioneer spirit, Mary was at the foot of the cross, catching the blood, sweat, and tears of Jesus. This also proved that she was willing to do something that no woman would do- get dirty. The following are additional examples of her other *firsts*.

1. First to see him resurrected
2. First to testify to the resurrection of Jesus
3. Led the way to share the news with the 11 apostles
4. Marked and chosen to be a primary witness despite being the least likely to do so

Nothing says "general" like administering orders, then executing them. In John 20:18 she says, "Sir, if you have carried him away, tell me where you have put him, and I will get him". As a literal and figurative "glory-carrier", Mary was willing to defy physical strength and carry Jesus' body.

Mary was a wonder! To comprehend the magnitude of what a wonder is, one would need to examine Mary's conversion process. Seven (7) is the number of devils she was bound by for years. Once she encountered the Messiah, she was freed of seven afflictions, [albeit emotional, physical, and spiritual]. Pre-encounter, I can imagine how void of purpose she felt. Someone who had never encountered the Messiah had been a hostage of Stockholm syndrome, where she had learned to live with her afflictions. However, destiny would have her change direction and leave a mighty legacy for generations that her bloodline may not have afforded her. Although, according to Acts 5:12, the apostles performed miracles, Mary *was* the miracle. Luke 8:2 was a living testimony of Jesus' miracle ministry.

2 And certain women, which had been healed of evil spirits and infirmities, Mary called Magdalene, out of whom went seven devils...

In an instant, she became a curse-breaker and miracle-maker!

Not only did Mary experience the supernatural pre-resurrection, but another supernatural encounter occurred post-resurrection. As demonstrated in Acts 9 with the Apostle Paul, a supernatural encounter with the Lord was a sign that one was called into the ministry of an apostle. Mary had an increase in sight, and the miracle now beholds miracles.

John 20:11-12 (KJV)

11 But Mary stood without at the sepulchre weeping: and as she wept, she stooped down, and looked into the sepulchre,

12 And seeth two angels in white sitting, the one at the head, and the other at the feet, where the body of Jesus had lain.

Bold and courageous as a lion, Mary risked extreme opposition against the religious rule of the early church in the following ways. One would be executed by the religious authority if they were seen publicly supporting Jesus. Amongst all-male apostles, she was one of a few female emissaries and disciples of Jesus Christ and traveled with him for three years. According to John 20:18- "…I have seen the Lord" proclaiming the Gospel, she risked being perceived as crazy and extreme.

Apostolic leaders are well aware of the supernatural faith it requires to climb any of the seven mountains. Mary Magdalene may not have been aware of why she was chosen to meet purpose through pain; however, her one encounter with the Messiah changed her life. She found destiny as a builder, watchman, glory-carrier, financial investor, wonder, forerunner, "sent one", and servant. She built a legacy that changed the course of how women "overseers" should lead.

References:

Higgs, Liz Curtis. *The Women of Easter*. Kentucky: WaterBrook Publishing, 2017

CHAPTER 16

THE BARREN WOMAN: AN APOSTOLIC REFORMER IS SHE A CATALYST FOR THE NEXT GREAT MOVE OF GOD?

By Jackie Betty

Hazel sits on a nearby tree stump with an exhaustion that seems to creep upon her small frame. "I will stay here for a moment," seems to be her thought. The sun had begun to rush in with its usual furious pelt this time of year. "Farming can be exhausting business," she muses…

Suddenly, a flicker of radiance flashes across her vision. "Am I…What's happening to me?" She wipes her hand across her eyes. "I'm more exhausted than I think," she sighs. "Oh, Lord! My eyes are playing tricks on me." … She blinks in startling wonder. A man stands in this radiance. "What's happening? Did he say 'don't be afraid'? I'm not sure."

"You are barren and childless," he says. She looks at him. "I'm sure the entire town knows this," she thinks. What he says next makes her gasp, "But you are going to become pregnant and have a son." In what seems like a moment, he is gone. She needs to regain her composure, but must run to Manoah now." "My Lord, my Lord!"
Hazel runs with unusual speed to her husband. "Manoah, Manoah," she shouts in excitement. "I will no longer be called barren!"

Barrenness today, as in ancient times, is still seen as a female problem. It is a humiliating social stigma which some believe was divinely imposed upon certain women by the gods says Dr. Noreen Jacks. The dramatized story of Manoah's wife's angelic encounter captures the shame barren women are made to feel. "Barren women were habitually taunted and ridiculed. Often, they were considered a public embarrassment to their husbands." Yet, as one studies the life of women who were deemed barren in Bible stories, one observes a pattern that our Creator uses to fulfill His divine earthly mandate. Sarah bore Isaac, Hannah bore the prophet Samuel, Elizabeth bore John the Baptist—all previously diagnosed barren. These stories relate a common theme in God's plan about barrenness.

God makes what seems unfruitful fruitful. She was barren; now she bears. Her song is like that of the barren woman who is urged to rejoice in Isaiah 54. This common Biblical theme reveals another type of birthing—the five-fold apostolic movement now in its fifth decade. She continues to take shape, but faces the challenge to produce new wine from her new wineskin. She yearns for something new and fresh. There must be new birth; this birthing must come through the one who often appears barren—the prophetic intercessor. She has interceded for many. At times, it seems like there are no answers, but her travail will birth and bear fruit. Like Samson's mother, stigmatized for her barrenness, the apostolic woman, through deliberate prophetic intercession, is the catalyst to pull the apostolic blueprint that will drive Christ's seemingly barren ecclesia into God's next great move.

Samson's Mother—Today's Apostolic Woman and the Church

Today's apostolic woman is like Samson's mother, Hazelelponi, in many ways. She carries a longing to birth answers to her many petitions. She often travails in tears and anguish, not taking rest until victory comes. Hazelelponi spent times of separation and quietness in the field, alone, where she could consecrate herself to the Lord. This practice caused an unexpected angelic visitation that brought the prophetic promise of a son. As he did for Samson's mother, this angel called Wonderful will meet the prophetic intercessor who separates herself and steps into the supernatural realm where she remains until Abba's messengers download supernatural codes for breakthroughs. The apostolic woman must see herself as today's prophetic intercessor. She is the *sent one*. She is the one who will go behind the ripped veil. Her divine access positions her to birth the yearnings of the apostolic movement. She must break the apparent barrenness of the ecclesia, where, for the most part, the glory seems to have departed. She must not allow religious stigma to keep her in spiritual lethargy, a condition that has held the apostolic movement in lower level prophetic acts and utterances. She must pull the apostolic blueprint for this era.

The Apostolic Blueprint: What Does It Look Like?

The apostolic blueprint in many ways will resemble patterns and activities of its current structure, being developed over the last 20 years. It resembles a pattern of takeovers and mergers as was common in the business arena in the latter part of the 20th and early 21st century. Local churches are being transformed into apostolic centers. An even more recent occurrence is the birthing of prayer and revival hubs. But this blueprint must take its pattern from the first apostles of Jesus Christ. Christ sent Mary Magdalene, the first apostle, to tell the other disciples of His resurrection (John 20:17). Therefore, this blueprint must make room for women who not only labor in prayer, but also are sent to evangelize regions through prayer and intercession. In the latter part of 2017, I had an internal vision while praying with an intercessor counterpart. As we prayed, I sensed a satellite connection that allows intercessors to see what is happening in the regions they are praying over. Acts 9:10-17 gives insight into this phenomenon. Ananias in a vision heard Jesus who sent him to Saul of Tarsus, who was praying. Ananias saw, and he went. This blueprint must not only include spiritual visuals, but must also plot strategic takeovers for intercessors' visions, which they can use in prayer. Today's visual expressions are spiritual tools to infiltrate and disrupt religious systems and demonic princes globally. If utilized effectively, such spiritual innovative acts of intercession will not be just "a significant rearrangement of intercession and prophetic forces" like Caron described, they now become disruptive to the forces of darkness.

God's Next Great Move

A peek into some of the acts of women in previous awakenings gives a panorama of Gods' next great move. Maria Woodworth-Etter was a spiritual dynamo in the Third Awakening. She is known for her extraordinary anointing gained through prayer and intercession. She "shut the mouths of lions" and put her mockers in trances that caused them to bow to the Almighty.

Lucy Farrow was another female apostle who Dr. Hyatt referred to as the "forgotten apostle." She was a black woman, born in slavery, who provided the initial spark that ignited the Azusa Street revival. William Seymour invited her to a prayer meeting. As she laid hands on people, they began to receive the baptism of the Holy Spirit and spoke in tongues as was done in the Book of Acts. Prayer and intercession catapulted her into a ministry of power throughout the southern United States and Liberia in West Africa. Despite the looming ghost of prejudice and injustice, she "became a powerful voice in the early Pentecostal Revival, and became the spark in Los Angeles that ignited and spread across the world and significantly impacted all of Christendom."

So, this new move, as illustrated above, is one of exponential spiritual revival, healing, deliverance, soul saving, and supernatural manifestations. It will dislodge, dismantle, and disrupt demonic forces over regions and territories. It must infiltrate the seven mountains and take them. Winning souls for Christ must be a hallmark event in this era. Other parts of the world like North Africa such as Libya are experiencing the awakening through miraculous encounters in dreams and visions.

Christianity has hit the Muslim world and is seeing an exponential shift on the mountain of religion, an act unprecedented in missions. A region, once hostile to the Gospel, sees tens of thousands of Muslims following Jesus, reports George Thomas. But the western world must also catch the vision and significantly impact these mountains. This awakening must spark and sustain the supernatural act of God throughout the globe.

The apostolic woman has a pivotal role in God's next great move for His Bride. This woman, in her intercessor capacity, cannot be intimidated by religious stigma that seeks to cloud the burgeoning revelation that she carries. As her prophetic womb expands in the spirit, she must press through the throws of her birth chamber and pull together her piece of the blueprint with divine exactness for vision, mission, and purpose.

- The apostolic woman must be intentional, purposeful, deliberate, and focused in intercession to see God's next great move
- She carries fervent hunger for the move of God and pursues the supernatural relentlessly to bring reformation
- She utilizes the apostolic blueprint to infiltrate her seven-mountain intercessory mandate
- She realizes her visions are no longer rare, so she activates them as spiritual tools to scale and capture these mountains
- She realizes, like Samson's mother, that her prophetic travail births more than a son; it births a deliverer
- Her prophetic acts of intercession usher in an unprecedented manifestation of authority and glory and forces Junia to arise. Hallelujah!

References:

Caron, Alain. "An Apostolic Blueprint for the 21st Century." *Hodos*, Hodos Apostolic Network, July 2012, hodos.ca/an-apostolic-blueprint-for-the-21st-century/?lang=en.

Hyatt, Eddie L. "Lucy Farrow: The Forgotten Apostle of Pentecost." *Charisma Magazine*, Charisma Magazine, 20 Feb. 2014, www.charismamag.com/spirit/revival/19805-lucy-farrow-the-forgotten-apostle-of-pentecost.

Jacks, Noreen. "Barren Women in the Bible." *BibleInteractcom Barren Women in the Bible Comments*, 29 Apr. 2014, bibleinteract.com/newsletter_teaching/barren-women-in-the-bible/.

Liardon, Roberts. *God's Generals: Why They Succeeded and Why Some Failed*. Whitaker House, 2003.

"Manoa." *Wikipedia*, Wikimedia Foundation, 17 Feb. 2018, en.wikipedia.org/wiki/Manoa.

Thomas, George. "Dreams and Visions: Revival Hits Muslim N. Africa." *Christian Broadcasting Network*, CBN News.com, 27 June 2016, www1.cbn.com/cbnnews/world/2014/April/Revival-in-Land-Once-Hostile-to-Christ.

"A Very Brief Introduction." *RESOURCE CENTER*, Apologetics Resource Center, 10 Nov. 2012, arcapologetics.org/comparative-religion/the-apostolic-and-prophetic-movement/.

CHAPTER 17

I AM THAT GIRL; I AM
THE VOICE OF ONE!

By Cassandra McKissack

"I am that girl" is an expression of camaraderie. It represents fellowship between people with mutual interests. Anna represents women, women who sacrifice for the good of all, just like the Apostle Junia. Paul said of Junia that she was outstanding among the apostles (Rom16:7 NIV). We are all called to be outstanding and to live a life of sacrifice as the voice of one. May we all lift our voices as one, that justice be exemplified. Sacrifice is the surrender of self to God; it's our reasonable service. We offer ourselves because we love the Lord.

So what exactly is sacrifice? It is giving up something for the sake of a better cause (Vocabulary.com). You give up something valuable to you in order to help another person or God (dictionary.cambridge.com). When you understand the cause of giving up, you understand it is worth your all. It reminds me of the song, "Lord, I'm available to you, to do what you want me to... use me Lord to show someone the way!" Me too, even me, Lord!

And Anna was the one, the voice of "that girl." Luke 2:36-38 says there was also a prophet Anna, the daughter of Penuel, of the tribe of Asher. She was very old; she had lived with her husband seven years after her marriage and then was a widow until she was eighty-four. She never left the temple but worshiped night and day, fasting and praying. Coming up to them at that very moment, she gave thanks to God and spoke about the child to all who were looking forward to the redemption of Jerusalem (NIV,

BibleGateway.com).

The author really makes a point of stating that she was very old; aren't you glad God uses people of all ages? A lot of people have in their mind that God only wants to use young folk. But when you look in the Bible, Moses was very old; hundreds of years old, as well as many others. I remember a pastor in his seventies stating, "People keep asking me when am I retiring…" And his reply was, "I'll retire when I'm dead; I'll retire when I'm no longer useful. As long as God wants to use me, I'll keep at what I love doing!" I see many people retire and die within a few years because they lack purpose and don't know what to do with themselves. God's plan is that we remain useful and productive. The goal is to die empty, as I have heard Dr. Myles Munroe say many times.

Anna was found living her life for the greater good of humanity. She lived a life of sacrifice in the Temple and was God's handmaiden, ready and available for service. Anna was the only woman in the New Testament explicitly described as a "prophetess." She stands in the line; offices like the judge, military leader and prophetess Deborah, and the Jerusalem prophetess Huldah, who in the days of Josiah was asked to verify that an ancient scroll discovered during Temple renovations was indeed the word of God (2Kings 22; Biblicalarchaeology.org).

Let me ask you…are you ready; are you available for service? Anna wasn't laboring over the fact that she wasn't in her *own* house and not tripping because she wasn't sleeping in her *own* bed at her house as many do today. Even Jesus said of himself, the son of man has nowhere to lay his head (Matt. 8:19-20). Are you able to *answer* The Call to the fullest extent? Why or why not?

Anna and Simon were the last Old Testament prophets who recognized Jesus as their Savior. They were at the Temple when Jesus was presented as was the custom (Luke 1:29). Anna bears witness to what she has seen. She is the **first** woman to understand fully and proclaim the good news (Biblicalarchaeology.org). So my question to you is, do you fully *understand* your call? If yes or no, what are you doing about it?

Get out a piece of paper and write the vision or possibly rewrite it according to what God is telling you now. And if you don't feel like you know, seek out a mentor or wise person to instruct you as you seek the face of God. There is nothing wrong with getting help.

"I am That Girl!" Empowerment Statements

The Scriptures are spoken in the first person so that you can feel the words for you personally.

I am that girl; a woman of inspiration, insight, and revelation and I do matter because God says in His Word that He knows the plans He has for me; plans to prosper me and not harm me, plans to give me a hope and a future Jer. 29:11. I believe I am on Earth to do Kingdom exploits and learn of Him and so I study to show myself approved (2 Tim2:15 NIV).

I am that girl and I am the Apple of His eye (Pro 7:2 NIV) and that speaks to my significance in Him. He knows every hair on my head (Matt 10:30 NIV), that's how much He cares, because I don't even know that and it's my head (smile). I am a woman who knows the joy of the Lord is my strength and I am being strengthened in him right now (Nehemiah 8:10 NLT).

I am that girl, the one God reveals his secrets to. The Bible says God communicates His secrets to His servants and just like Anna, I am His servant and I want to do all that I know to please God (Amos 3:7 KJV).

I am that girl and it's in my spiritual DNA to know the purpose that He created me to express on Earth. I know that because I spend time with Him. I seek His face, pray, and fast The Lord will fulfill His purpose for me (Ps 138:8 ESV).

Yes, I am that girl and God wants to use me like Anna to proclaim His word; and like Junia, I do outstanding work. I am that girl that God can use just as He used the servant girl who told Naaman's wife the truth, even if it cost her, her job (2Kings 5: 2, 3). I pray God would give me the audacity to know when I need to tell the truth so someone can receive their deliverance. I too, will tell the truth and be a person of integrity even though it costs me everything. #metoo

Yes, I am that girl, like the daughters of Zelophehad who stood up to Moses and told their truth. They were women of faith (Numbers 27: 1-11 NIV). I am a woman of faith and will stand for truth and tell it whether it is popular or not! And furthermore I won't back down or be afraid because God has not given me the spirit of fear, but of love, power, and a sound mind (II Tim 1:7). I know God got this, for me. And what's for me is for me! Just as God told Moses that they should be granted their father's inheritance, I will be granted what is rightfully mine.

I will establish new precedents like them; like Apostle Junia who was outstanding; like Esther who said if I perish, I perish (Es. 4:16), and didn't back down as many others who stood for what was right in the Bible. I, too will help lead the way in my own way as I am lead by the Spirit of God. I have God-confidence and boldness.

References:

Mary, Simeon or Anna: Who First Recognized Jesus as Messiah? Ben Witherington III, 11/ 18/2016

Bible History Daily (biblicalaracheology.org)

OpenBible.info/purpose

BibleHub.org/Zechariah2:8; Matthew10:30; Esther 4:6; II Tim 1:7;

Numbers 27:1-11

New Living Translation (NLT) and New International Version (NIV), BibleGateway.com/scriptures

CHAPTER 18

THE SAMARITAN WOMAN:
THE UNNAMED CITY SHAKER

By Carla Louis-Wallace

"Many of the Samaritans from that town believed in him because of the woman's testimony..." **John 4:39 NIV**

Evangelism in America has had a decline over the years, while Africa's evangelism has ranked high compared to other nations (T.Rainer). According to the Google Trends web search from 2004 through 2017 there is a noted loss of interest of evangelism in searches. Executive Director of the Billy Graham Center, Dr. Ed Stetzer states, "It's a sobering reality that nearly 80% of unchurched people say they will engage in a faith conversation but that only 30% of Christians are actually telling people about Jesus." The Samaritan Woman who was an evangelist, had no issue with telling people about a man she met at the well who was Jesus Christ.

The unnamed woman carried an apostolic anointing for evangelism but could not perceive it before her encounter with the Messiah. The encounter left her thirsty, which motivated her mission to gather people together to bring them to Christ despite her past. Because she testified to the people regarding what Christ had told her about herself, they became interested in knowing him, which produced many Samaritans for Christ (John 4:39).

In John 4:40-41 we can see how the Samaritan Woman was like a modern-day marketer in the marketplace. Marketers are used to getting the word out and grow a company through strategic approaches. This was an apostolic strategy used with the wisdom of God to establish truth to the believers. First, they believed in Jesus because of how she presented him to them. Once they encountered what she presented about Christ, they tried him for themselves. Then they believed in him because of what they heard themselves.

How do we get back, as a nation, the desire to evangelize like the Samaritan Woman did and reap the harvest? How do we overcome the notion that our broken past dictates our future? The Samaritan Woman was truly a sent one. She was sent to break ground in her territory despite the relationship between the Samaritans and the Jews. She was an ambassador, missionary, pioneer, and a representative for the Kingdom of God. There was no holding back after the encounter at the well.

No More Distractions

When Jesus asked for the drink, the Samaritan Woman quickly went into defeat mode. She first used an external factor (the social and political environment) as an excuse for not being able to draw the water. She asked Jesus, "because you are a Jew and I am a Samaritan, why do you want a drink from me because there are no dealings between the two?" (Pure Jews and the Samaritans who were mixed with Jews and Gentile) (John 4:9) Second, when Jesus replied to her, she responded by telling him that he had nothing to draw with and that the well was deep. Here we see that she used an internal factor that Jesus did not have anything to draw the water up with. She did not go after what was needed to draw the water from the well, no effort, no thinking out of the box to accomplish what Jesus had asked of her. Lastly, she makes an excuse that the well was too deep.

Obstacles and barriers are the biggest distraction to our destiny and calling. The negative internal and external factors of our strength, weakness, opportunities, and threats should be left behind like the Samaritan Woman left the water pot at the well to go and tell the people in the city about Christ (John 4:28). She did not allow the enemy to torment her mind and distract her from her mission to deliver the message despite her past behaviors, low self-esteem, and reputation after her encounter with the

Messiah. From her going to the well at odd hours to avoid people, to going into the city to tell people of the man she met at the well, we know that a transformation took place.

In Jeremiah 30:17 God said, "I will restore your health unto thee, and I will heal thee of thy wounds," because they called thee an outcast. Not only did transformation take place but also restoration did at the well and her new identity caused people to positively respond to her when she said, "Come, see a man" (John 4: 29-30). If she still had her old mindset she wouldn't have had the drawing power to draw and gather the people from the city of Sychar to allow Jesus to minister to them for two days. According to Berni Dymet, "over 50% of women in this world suffer from low self-esteem," which is unhealthy.

Arise and Move Forward

Draw: To cause to move continuously toward or after a force is applied.

Well: A natural source of water, which something may be drawn as needed.

Vertical aspect of a well: Damp, cool deep and dark

Almond: Hebrew meaning "the waker" "emblem of the Divine forwardness in bringing God's promises to pass" (Biblehub, 2017).

How many times in our life have we felt that Jesus didn't have anything to draw from us? We may have had feelings of shame, failure, inadequacies, negative feelings from rejections, etc.…

It is imperative to realize that he has the drawing power to draw from the vertical aspect of the deep, dark cool places in our life so that we may receive the Holy Spirit, the living water so that we may never thirst again on our journey in life. As the ground breaks and the water is released from the source of the well, living water will spring forth from you and you will begin to walk into the ordained authority that God has given you to release, heal, deliver and have true encounters of worship for the Kingdom of God. The living water will also sustain you and replenish you along your way as you pioneer new places in the spiritual realm and take new territory in the natural realm.

Principles

You may ask the question, "how can I become apparent and move forward, when I have a past? What type of faith do I need to become victorious in multiplying, being fruitful, and subduing?"

By raising your expectations, you can pioneer new territory through courage, being willing to take risks, removing all excuses, breaking old routines, and getting into a position to receive (Apostle L. Brown, Sr.).

- After breaking the old routine of the Jews not dealing with the Samaritans, she placed herself into a position to receive from the prophet the Son of God, after laying all of her excuses aside, the woman was able to courageously go back to the city, taking the risk of not being accepted because of her reputation and bringing her testimony to the people that motivated them to know and follow after Christ (breaking old routines to pioneer new territory).

Change your thinking, see yourself how God sees you, be alert to what the enemy wants to plant in your spirit.

- The Samaritan Woman was able to produce fruit once she bloomed out of her box. She was able to gather the people for the advancement of the Kingdom. In Jeremiah 1:11, Jeremiah was alert to the purpose of God for the fulfillment of God's promises unhindered.

Get over the fear of failure.

- Like the Samaritan Woman, we may avoid people and situations because of fear, but in Jeremiah 1:8 God declares, don't be afraid of men's faces because he has delivered you to be the deliverer of the good news. Strengthen your faith to go to the city and break new ground for the Kingdom.

Don't breathe in the toxic O2: Opposition and Offense.

- Walk in wisdom, humility, and love. The Samaritan Woman could have returned to the city boastful as she just had met Jesus. She went back to the same people she was avoiding to tell them to go and see a man; it was her season to bloom in the mist of the white harvest.

Apostolic Prayer

Son of the living God, I praise and worship you for taking away the sins of the world. Forgive me for being concerned with how man views me and not focusing on how you see me. For you are my deliverer and I thank you for saving me from the deep dark places of sin. Elohei Ma'uzzi, the God of my strength, equip me to stand strong before your people to witness and proclaim your Good News, impart in me wisdom, love, humility, and, most of all, compassion towards humanity so that my work will be effective in your Kingdom. This I ask, in Jesus' name, Amen.

Affirmations:

I am a sent one and am authorized by Heaven for my Kingdom mission.

I am a pioneer, a trailblazer who will break through barriers culturally and spiritually.

No more distractions from my past, I am an overcomer.

I am restored and transformed for the assignment on my life.

I am a world-changer through my testimony.

I carry will not stay hidden in a vessel, it will spring forth as living water.

References:

http://thomrainer.com/2016/06/seven-things-google-tells-us-evangelism-united-states/

Thom S. Rainer Seven Things Google tells us about Evangelism in the united states

http://www.evantell.org/blog/the-decline-in-evangelism-what-can-be-done/

Larry Moyer May 31, 2017

http://www.christianitytoday.com/edstetzer/2017/april/why-has-evangelism-fallen-on-hard-times.html

"Well." *Merriam-Webster.com*. Merriam-Webster, n.d. Web. 2 Feb. 2018.

"Draw." *Merriam-Webster.com*. Merriam-Webster, n.d. Web. 2 Feb. 2018.

"Pioneer." *Merriam-Webster.com*. Merriam-Webster, n.d. Web. 13 Feb. 2018.

https://christianity.works/adp/3714/

http://biblehub.com/sermons/auth/post/tree_emblems.htm

https://www.charismanews.com/opinion/the-pulse/45731-12-characteristics-of-the-new-apostolic-leaders

Apostle L. Brown, Sr. "Embracing A New Season", Feb 11th, 2018

CHAPTER 19

RAHAB: REJECTED BY MAN, BUT CHOSEN BY GOD

By Connie Strickland

As you come to him, the living Stone-rejected by humans but chosen by God and precious to him. 1 Peter 2:4 (NIV)

I remember a prophetic word that was released many years ago by prophetic voices concerning the emerging of women in the church. The prophecy revealed that there would be a great company of women from every culture and background who God would use to bring reformation and transformation to regions and territories. We are living in that time NOW as women have vital roles in leadership, ministry, and the marketplace. Their voices are being heard and they are being inspired by the Holy Spirit to empower a generation. The manifestation of this Anthology is evidence that God has something to say through women. The truth has been "unleashed" in God's Kairos timing as "JUNIA", the first female apostle, is now celebrated!

The Church is moving in completeness as the "sons of God" both male and female work together in unity to fulfill God's purpose and plans on Earth. Both the Old and New Testaments are full of powerful and passionate women who put their lives and livelihood on the line for the Kingdom of God. I am going to bring your attention to a woman named Rahab, who was not my choice for this Anthology. I am just keeping it real—my first choice was Deborah! Why? She was noted among all the other great women in the Bible. I began to have a dialogue with God and asked Him, "Lord are you sure? Rahab was a prostitute!" "Yes," the Lord said, "and don't forget you were a whore, fornicator, and adulterer and I made room for you!" God certainly has a sense of humor.

Everywhere Rahab's name is mentioned in Scripture, it is associated with her occupation. She is called "Rahab the prostitute" in Joshua 6:17 and 6:25. If that isn't enough, twice in the New Testament her occupation is mentioned: "By faith the prostitute Rahab" (Hebrews 11:31), and "Rahab the prostitute" (James 2:25). What God is conveying to you is that if He can use Rahab, He can use YOU! It does not matter who you were in the past, God can redeem you and make your future great!

As we delve into Rahab's life, we are going to observe apostolic qualities and virtues that she exemplified and God used them to bring her out of obscurity. Rahab's story began in Joshua 2. Joshua is now the leader of Israel, as his successor, Moses, is dead. God gives Joshua an apostolic commission in the first chapter to go and cross over Jordan to the Promised Land. You and I both know if we are going to possess what God has promised, there will always be an enemy to deter us.

Nevertheless, God affirms to Joshua as he prepares the people to cross over that He would be with them. Whatever assignment God has given to you, He wants you to know that He has given you the grace to complete it. Just like God told Joshua to be strong and of a good courage, these same words are relevant to you today. I want to challenge you to read Joshua 2 in its entirety so that you can observe the series of events that took place in Rahab's life that brought transformation to her and those connected to her.

Joshua sends two spies to Jericho and the first person they encounter is Rahab. History reveals to us that Rahab's house was situated on the city wall, providing an escape route. As it turned out, the spies' choice of a hiding place was God-ordained. Rahab took a great risk when she sheltered the spies and sent them out another way and when she refused to tell her own people where the two spies were and sent the soldiers on a wild goose chase on the road that led down to the Jordan River. Why would she do that? I am glad you asked that question. *There are two ways to answer the question, and they both lead to the same conclusion.* Joshua 2:9-13 tells us that she and all the people of Jericho had heard stories about how God had delivered His people through the Red Sea and how He had given them victory over the Amorite kings. Great fear came over the people and deprived them of their courage.

We see God's amazing grace at work in the life of Rahab. She heard about the God of Israel and in her conversation with the spies, Rahab declared her faith, saying, "The LORD your God is God in heaven above and on the earth below" (Joshua 2:11). Rahab knew that Jericho was under judgment and she did not want to perish with the city. This scenario sounds much like what we are experiencing in America. Just like Jericho, America is also under judgment and God wants to use apostolic people like you and I who will stand in the gap.

The Scripture also reveals to us that Rahab and the spies entered into covenant. Joshua 2:14 reveals this truth: And the men said to her, "Our life for yours even to death! If you do not tell this business of ours, then when the Lord gives us the land we will deal kindly and faithfully with you." Rahab presented an unselfish request to the spies to save her family. They honored their word and when the city was conquered, Rahab followed the instructions in Joshua 2:18 which depicts a picture of the Passover. By hanging the line of scarlet thread on the window, death passed over her family and they were all saved. It is imperative to note that this story is about God's grace upon a woman who was identified by her occupation. Rahab was justified by her works according to the Scripture in James 2:25. In my conclusion, I want you to observe the apostolic grace that was upon Rahab's life. We will identify some apostolic characteristics that we can apply to our own lives.

Rahab's Apostolic Qualities

- Rahab took a risk to identify with God's people that went against her own culture and put her life in jeopardy. She was willing to deny her culture to save another. What about YOU? Are you willing to take a risk even if it means putting your life in jeopardy to save someone else? Apostolic people are risk-takers!

- Rahab recognized an opportunity and seized it – an opportunity was presented to her and she made herself available to complete the task. She made a choice to protect the spies and not reveal their location to their enemies. God presents opportunities to us every day. Apostolic people don't have to seek opportunities, but they will be able to discern God-given opportunities and accept them.
- Rahab exemplified faith instead of fear – at a time when her city was under judgment she knew the only way to escape it was to believe in the God that she heard about. It is going to take bodacious faith to represent the Kingdom and eradicate religious systems that produce heresy.
- Rahab was obedient to the instructions given to her by the spies – I always say the anointing is in the instructions. When you are given instructions by God or your leader, you must follow them. Your obedience is the evidence that you heard the instructions.
- Rahab had a strategy that she implemented to protect the spies and sent them out. Her strategy led them out of the city without being captured. If we are going to be effective in advancing the Kingdom of God, it is going to take divine strategies. God releases divine strategies to those who know how to tap into His mind.

There's an epilogue to the story of Rahab. What happened to Rahab after the city of Jericho fell? She became an integral part of the children of Israel. God placed His honor on her. When you look at the book of Matthew and read the lineage of the Lord Jesus Christ, there's an interesting name that pops up: Rahab. Rahab is in the line of descendants for the Lord Jesus. Matthew 1 lists Jesus' genealogy and in Matthew 1:5 says, "Salmon the father of Boaz, whose mother was Rahab..." Rahab is listed in the Faith Hall of Fame in Hebrews 11:1; Rahab is noted in WIKPEDIA! She may not have been celebrated in her era, but she is certainly celebrated today! Are you convinced that God wants to use you to do great exploits? I have a great respect for Rahab! There are many other PROSTITUTES that God used in the Bible to fulfill His purpose!

Apostolic Declaration

I want to prophesy to you today that upon reading this book your life is never going to be the same. I decree and declare that God is releasing you into new realms of His glory and the apostolic and prophetic anointing is intensifying in your life. I decree and declare that you will not settle for complacency and you will be diligent in the work of the Lord.

CHAPTER 20

THE BIRTHING OF NATIONS AGAINST RELIGIOUS STRONGHOLDS

By Deborah L. Anderson

We are standing in the most pivotal time of history to witness the birthing of nations against religious strongholds! It is my honor and privilege to be given the grace to be amongst living epistles to be read of men who are on the frontlines of this Kingdom movement. This epic anthology will leave a legacy of Apostolic Women who were born to be for this time the voice to transform a faulty religious belief system that states that a woman should "keep silent in the church." This systematically imposed belief system was founded upon one main contextually misconstrued Scripture (just one) in I Corinthians 14:44 and upheld as absolute truth by prima facie evidence for justification. *"Prima facie"* is a Latin expression meaning *"on its first encounter, first blush, or at first sight,"* and its literal translation means *"at first face"* or *"at first appearance."* It is used in modern legal English to signify that on first examination, a matter *"appears to be self-evident"* from the facts[6]. In common law jurisdictions, prima facie denotes evidence that unless rebutted, would be sufficient to prove a particular proposition or fact and similarly used in academic and religious philosophy while masking a woman's calling and anointing through human ingenuity, thereby sentencing women to silence, especially in the pulpit.

However, there is a second revelatory examination emerging from the

---

[6](Black's Law Dictionary abridged 7th Edition)

sound arising in of 21st Century of Apostolic Women Birthing Nations that have broken the strongholds of silence and shattered the sound barrier of such prima facie interpretations of Scripture and passed down from generation to generation. The sound and the anointing of 21st Century Apostolic Women reveals a very unique mark of distinction between those who were held captive by the voice of religious systems past, and the apostolic and prophetic women who are on the frontline today. They have a Kingdom mindset towards their calling and unapologetically function walk in a Kingdom identity reality that:

> God has "raised us (women) up together, and made us to sit together in heavenly places in Christ Jesus: That in the ages to come He might shew the exceeding riches of His grace in His kindness toward us through Christ Jesus. For we are His workmanship, created in Christ Jesus unto good works, which God hath before ordained that we should walk in them. That you may understand the mystery of Christ (by relation not traditional information) which in other ages was not made known unto the sons of men, and is NOW being REVEALED through Apostles and Prophets by the Spirit to make all men see what is the fellowship of the mystery, which from the beginning of the world hath been hid in God, who created all things by Jesus Christ TO THE INTENT THAT NOW UNTO THE PRINCIPALITIES AND POWERS IN HEAVENLY PLACES might be known by the church the manifold wisdom of God". (Ephesians2:6-10, emphasis added)

Consequently, God is giving us a second glance into His manifold wisdom at what first appeared as truth concerning women by revealing His original intent characterized and echoed throughout history by two of my favorite apostolic and profoundly prophetic women written into Biblical and world history – Deborah, an Apostolic Judge and Prophetess; and an Apostolic Pioneer, Sojourner Truth.

Deborah exemplifies the type of apostolic and prophetic authority that emerged on the frontlines today, illustrating the dual dominion and power God gave to men and women for national deliverance of nations oblivious to the religious misinterpretation of their roles as leaders! Deborah characterized the nature of an apostle whose anointing has the grace to come alongside great men to fulfill the plan of God on Earth! She uproots religious systems' imposed belief that a woman is not supposed to lead or be over a man. Deborah takes the lead as a Judge and Prophetess to summon a military general who did not consider her gender, but relied on Deborah's anointing and governmental authority to be the one to help him carry out God's command to take out the Midianites! She steps into time as an Apostolic Judge, announces the time of the nation's deliverance, and prophetically declares: *"This is the day the LORD has given Sisera into your hands!"* Deborah was the key God used then and now who set Barak in order to break strongholds over an entire nation. It should be noted by those God is calling to the frontline, that Deborah is introduced in the Book of Judges not by examination of her degrees, what school of law or theological seminary she matriculated through, nor by a cross-examination by religious rulers who evaluate whose church or what leader, what mentor or manager she "came from under"; who licensed, ordained, confirmed, or affirmed her to this governmental and judicial apostolic office over her jurisdiction - she came from underneath a palm tree!

Mandates are not qualified by religious credentials! Deborah's mandate was qualified by the seed of authority in her womb that birthed out of her command when she pronounced the timing of God's deliverance. Barak responded positively to the Judge's summons beyond his personal dread of the army of Jabin, because he valued her influence and respectfully submitted himself to her seat of authority. Further, he was not going to battle if she didn't go with him, not to sit under him, or be silenced by him by the religious cultural norm to submit to male authority. His request for her to go to battle with him was heartfelt because he also knew Deborah as a true worshipper, a wise counselor, a prophetic intercessor who carried the anointing of the Sons of Issachar who are known to have an understanding of the times and seasons and knew what Israel ought to do (I Chron. 12:32). It was time for the rebirthing of the nation of Israel against religious strongholds.

In the midst of the birthing of nations against religious strongholds, God raised up another pioneering apostolic revelator by the name of *Sojourner*

Truth as an abolitionist against slavery who also was put to raise the voice of women's right to preach. In her most famous speech, *"Ain't I A Woman?"* (1851[7]), Sojourner Truth delivered a powerful message, standing tall in her oratorical defense to clarify God's original intent of a woman's power to carry the seed of deliverance in her womb and give birth to fulfill His purpose on Earth. Sojourner Truth (Isabella Baumfree) was born into slavery in New York and freed in 1827, and was about 6 feet tall and whenever she walked into a room, people would know authority walked in by observing her appearance and presence. Her message captivated and shifted an audience of religious mindsets with this statement:

> *"Some say women can't have as much rights as men, because Christ wasn't a woman! Where did your Christ come from? From God and a woman! Man had nothing to do with Him....If the first woman God ever made was strong enough to turn the world upside down all alone, these women together ought to be able to turn it back, and get it right side up again! And now they are asking to do it, the men better let them"*! Sojourner Truth: *"Aint I A Woman?"*

It was Deborah and Sojourner Truth as forerunners then, and it is the Apostolic Women who are on the frontline now, who are manifesting the glory of God's original intent and purpose for creating a woman specifically to give birth to His plans and carry out His mandate. Women have been kept silent until the time to fulfill their greatest mandate as written in their Genesis in the following excerpt taken from a book I published[8] that reveals:

GOD'S ORIGINAL APOSTOLIC MANDATE FOR WOMEN:

"And the LORD God said unto the serpent, Because thou hast done this, thou *art* cursed above all cattle, and above every beast of the field; upon thy belly shalt thou go, and dust shalt thou eat all the days of thy life: And **I WILL PUT ENMITY BETWEEN THEE AND THE WOMAN,** and between thy seed and her seed;

---

[7] "Aint I A Woman?" (1851) http://www.blackpast.org/1851-sojourner-truth-arnt-i-woman

[8] *"Apostolic Women Birthing Nations: A 21st Century Guide for 21st Century Ministry"* (2013)

it shall bruise thy head,
and thou shalt bruise his heel." - Genesis 3:14-15(KJV)

- The cause for your captivity has nothing to do with your gender *"as it has appeared"* to be the truth. The truth is you are the mystery that is destined to crush the head of the enemy!
- No one and nothing comes onto Earth except through the womb of a woman! Your womb is pregnant with seeds of deliverance for nations!
- You are God's delegated representative on Earth to walk with an apostolic and prophetic anointing and SENT to come alongside great leaders to win great battles!
- I DECREE AND DECLARE THAT the Issachar Anointing will be upon you to understand the time and the season to PROPHESY to Great Leaders facing Great Battles to Win Great Victories!

CHAPTER 21

FROM HOUSEWIFE TO MOTHER OF A MOVEMENT PHOEBE PALMER

By Kenna O'Flannigan

"Then Peter and the other apostles answered and said, We ought to obey God rather than men." **Acts 5:29**

Phoebe Palmer is an example of a great apostolic woman because she was confident in her identity in Christ and rose above societal prejudices of women in the 19th century to complete everything the Lord sent her to do. Phoebe challenged the tenets of her denomination and became the leader of the Holiness Movement during a time when women were not allowed to teach or speak publicly. Phoebe Palmer is known as the most influential woman in the largest, fastest-growing religious group in the United States during her time.

Phoebe Palmer is known as the Mother of the Holiness Movement. She was born as Phoebe Worrall in New York City on December 18, 1807. Her father emigrated from England in his early 20's and her mother was born in America. Growing up, Phoebe's family was devoutly Methodist. Her parents instilled strict Methodist values in her and her sister and conducted family worship services twice a day. She expressed a deep devotion to her faith in Christ at a very young age. As early as 11 years old, Phoebe began writing religious material that showed her strong commitment to Jesus.

The teachings of John Wesley, however, caused her to question her conversion, as she did not experience the emotional and even ecstatic conversion as described and expected by most evangelicals and specifically the Methodists at that time. Convinced in her heart that she was saved because of her belief in Christ despite not having the same experience described by so many, this caused her to seek the Lord for herself by searching the Scriptures and in prayer. Her conviction to devote her life to the Lord and teach what she came to understand as a "shorter way" to sanctification through grace surpassed what was taught by preachers at that time.

Phoebe married Dr. Walter Palmer, a homeopathic physician, at the age of 19. They had six children over the years but lost three of them in their infancy. What is remarkable to me is that the experience of losing three of her children at various times only caused her to draw closer to the Lord and seek out His will and purpose for these tragedies. For example, after enduring the loss of her second child, her journal entry showed that she found comfort in the conclusion that, "*Surely, I needed it, or it would not have been given.*" Each time she experienced the crushing loss of a child, she sought the comfort of the Lord and did not question His faithfulness, but rather, sought His purpose for such a trial. This led to her complete and passionate devotion to the Lord and fulfilling all He had purposed for her life.

Phoebe Palmer was a pioneer in the Holiness Movement because she did not allow herself to be trapped in the doctrinal trappings of religion, but followed the Holy Spirit in seeking out truth through study of Scripture and a personal relationship with God. In concert with her sister, Phoebe began Tuesday afternoon meetings in her home around 1835 to teach the Word of the Lord. These were weekly meetings, which her sister Sarah Lankford first began teaching, as Phoebe was not interested in such a platform. However, over the following couple of years, Phoebe began teaching and took over the weekly meetings, which lasted for nearly 40 years.

Phoebe Palmer was a trailblazer. During the 19th century, when Phoebe was holding the Tuesday afternoon meetings, women were not allowed to speak publicly or to lead, whether in secular circles or in ministry. But she was so convicted that the Lord had sent her, that she did not concern herself with the restrictions and opinions of others. As a lay person, she operated in her calling without concern or motivation for a title. She moved in wisdom with how she broke barriers and taught new doctrine so as not to offend those who she hoped to reach. The weekly Bible studies that she held in her home were her way of public speaking in an acceptable way. As her notoriety grew, besides the lay men and women who attended the meetings regularly, male university and seminary professors, as well as male clergy in the Methodist church and other denominations attended. The meetings grew so large that Phoebe and her husband had to build extra rooms onto their home and eventually moved to a larger house.

By the end of the 1850's, Phoebe Palmer was at the apex of her preaching career, as she was invited to teach at camp meetings and revivals around the country. Phoebe and her husband taught at over 300 such gatherings over the years. Her calling became one of international proportions, as she and her husband were invited to hold holiness meetings in Canada, the British Isles, and Europe. Both men and women viewed her as a leader. Phoebe had the ability to bring men and women together in worship and was graced to advance the role of female preachers. She had become a distinguished religious figure during a time when few women rose to positions of leadership in America.

Phoebe's humility and devotion to serving others were remarkable. In addition to being the wife of a doctor and a devoted mother, she was involved in many community outreach programs and ministered to prisoners, widows, and children, as well as freed slaves. Phoebe Palmer was instrumental in organizing numerous church plants in poor neighborhoods. Most notably, she established the Five Points Mission, which reached out to the economically, morally, and spiritually lost in one of New York City's most notorious slums. She also headed the Methodist Ladies' Home Missionary Society. These efforts grew out of Phoebe's belief that holiness was best shown by human service. She believed that people responded best to the call of God if they had food, clothing, and shelter. Phoebe served as a leader in the National Camp Meeting Association for the Promotion for Holiness; the corresponding secretary for the New York Female Society for the Relief and Religious Instruction of the Sick Poor; and was active in the Methodist Ladies' Home Missionary Society.

Palmer was also a prolific writer. She wrote letters, articles, and tracts. She was a member of the New York City Tract Society and was the author of many tracts about Christianity and holiness. Phoebe published a total of 18 books throughout her lifetime. Beginning in the 1840's, she published three works, *The Way of Holiness* (1843), *Entire Devotion to God (1845)*, and *Faith and Its Effects* (1848). Her published work in 1859, entitled *Promise of the Father*, outlined in detail with research and cogent arguments, using Hebrew and Greek etymology, why women can be preachers and public speakers. Acts 5:29 was her foundation to justify women preachers, to obey God rather than man. She also stated, *"It is always right to obey the Holy Spirit's command, and if that is laid upon a woman to preach the Gospel, then it is right for her to do so; it is a duty she cannot neglect without falling into condemnation."*

Upon their return from their four years preaching in the British Isles, Phoebe and her husband purchased the leading Christian publication in America, Guide to Holiness, of which Phoebe was also editor from 1864 until her death in 1874.

Phoebe Palmer's religious and civic activism influenced others to become active in what they felt the Lord leading them to do, such as Frances Willard, a leader in the late 19th century temperance reform; and Catherine Booth, co-founder (along with her husband William) of the Salvation Army. After Catherine Booth read *Promise of the Father*, she began studying the Word for herself and was so convinced that the Lord chooses who He wishes to preach, that she also began her own preaching ministry.

Apostolic characteristics demonstrated throughout Phoebe's lifetime are:

- She knew her identity in Christ
- Phoebe persevered through personal trials and was unrelenting in her calling

- She was courageous and used wisdom to move through the unknown and break barriers
- Phoebe was a pioneer for the Holiness Movement
- Phoebe was a trailblazer in her community and ministry
- She moved in authority to legislate her circles of influence to accomplish all she was sent to do.

Phoebe Palmer had the ability and wisdom to legislate within her realms of influence. She was able to move in circles of influence that other women of this era were not permitted. Because she was consistent and tenacious in her faith and beliefs, she was relentless in her pursuit of equality for women in the marketplace as well as in ministry. Phoebe Palmer moved with boldness and clarity. She moved in the apostolic realm to bring salvation and deliverance to tens of thousands of people and is known as the Mother of the Holiness Movement. May we all become the *Phoebe Palmers* of our own worlds to make a lasting impact for the Kingdom.

Affirmations for change agents

- My identity is rooted in Christ because I am made in the image of God.
- Because I have made Jesus the head of my life, I have been given the authority to walk in my purpose and calling.
- I choose to view all my life experiences, failures, and trials as lessons and examples of God's grace which are working for my good and I am pushing past any limiting mindsets and attitudes to Arise and legislate the realms of influence that I have been given jurisdiction over as a result of the challenges that I have overcome.
- I walk in wisdom without fear of man to be a trailblazer and pioneer in every area the Lord has gifted me and sent me to manifest His glory in the earth.
- I break through the barriers set by false teachings, limiting attitudes, small mindsets, low self-worth, insecurity, and critical thinking to walk in the power and authority of the Most High to be a change agent in my spheres of influence.

- I have favor with God and man to move in unchartered territory and enlarge my tent in every area that women are ordained to operate, including marriage, family, ministry, business, and upon every mountain that I have been gifted and called to rule and reign with authority.

References:

1. https://www.encyclopedia.com/people/history/historians-miscellaneous-biographies/phoebe- palmer
2. http://www.teachushistory.org/second-great-awakening-age-reform/approaches/phoebe palmer-1807-1874-holiness-theology
3. *The Life and Letters of Mrs. Phoebe Palmer,* Wheatley, Rev. Richard, (New York: Palmer & Hughes, 1876)
4. *The Way of Holiness With Notes by the Way*, Phoebe Palmer (1843)
5. https://www.christianitytoday.com/history/people/moversandshakers/phoebe-palmer.html
6. https://www.wesleyanholinesswomenclergy.org/phoebe-palmer-mother-of-the-holiness-revival/
7. http://www.gcah.org/history/biographies/phoebe-palmer
8. https://www.britannica.com/biography/Phoebe-Worrall-Palmer
9. https://margmowczko.com/phoebe-palmer/
10. *Promise of the Father*, Phoebe Palmer (1859)

CHAPTER 22

DEBORAH: A PROPHETIC GENERAL

By: Kierra Douglas and Donita Gordon

Woman of Illuminations

"Blessed is she who has believed that the Lord would fulfill his promises to her!"
Luke 1:45

In the Book of Judges, we find one of the most influential prophets of all time, Prophetess Deborah. This Prophetic General was one of the seven women prophetesses whose prophecies were accurately recorded in the Bible. Prophetess Deborah was widely known for her wise counsel and the support that she rendered to many despite their social or economic stances.

Deborah, the wife of Lappidoth, was one of the most distinguished leading ladies of her time. Her name in Hebrew signifies *"bee, "Spirit of Fiery One,"* and she answered her name with a double-edged sword. She could be found under the Date Palm Tree between Ramah and Bethel in the Ephraimite hill country. Here, she labored herself in making wicks for the lamps of the tabernacle. There was a strong gifting of hearing and knowing the voice of God in the spiritual and natural. Her extraordinary gift made room for the leading of the Spirit of God.

In the Hand of a Woman

"She sets about her work vigorously; her arms are strong for her tasks."
Proverbs 31:17

During a time of great awakenings and prophetic activations, we have come to the understanding that God speaks to His people at various times and in countless ways.

> Hebrew 1:1 *"God, who at various times and in various ways spoke in time past to the fathers by the prophets."*

Deborah was an oracle who gave judgment on various matters. She would listen and offer Godly words of wisdom. Jael was considered a woman who utilized the strategic instructions of God to deliver justice. The Lord sold Sisera into the hands of a Jael, just as Deborah had prophesied. Jael is an example of what can happen when God's promises are spoken into the earthly realm. He will provide weapons to defeat the adversary. Both Deborah and Jael shattered the expectations of society to land victory. Look in your hand and see that your right hand is full of power. God has not given you a spirit of fear, but power. For the Spirit God gave **us** does not make **us** timid, but gives **us** power, love, and self-discipline (2 Timothy 1:7)

Standing in Boldness

> *"Have I not commanded you? Be strong and courageous. Do not be afraid; do not be discouraged, for the Lord your God will be with you wherever you go."* Joshua 1:9

The body of Christ must understand when you're chosen by God for a special purpose, He will send you to people who are in perfect alignment with His plan. He will give you special favor for what He has designed to do in you and through you. There will be glorious times in which you may be admired by many. Your life may look stress-free, trial-free, and pain-free to those looking in from the outside. On the other hand, God may assign you to people who are obstinate, disobedient, religious, and oppressed. The environment may be entirely new to you but you are in total submission to God's will. In the natural realm, it can be hard to lead people under severe pressure, untimely circumstances, and being the first to ever do something.

Just as God proved Himself to prophetess Deborah, He can do the same for you. At Barak's request, Prophetess Deborah promised to go along to battle. Her boldness assured victory. (Jdg. 4:8): *"If thou wilt go with me* to direct and advise me, and in every difficult case to let me know God's mind, *then I will go* with all my heart, and not fear the chariots of iron; otherwise not." Warfare and oppressed conditions would scare the average person, but not Deborah! Deborah was bold for God, and showed her boldness in her actions. The time has come for you to stand in **BOLDNESS!** The only way to release the Boldness anointing in a greater magnitude is to hear God's directions. You should expect to rise up with a great manifestation of power to defeat the enemy and win the battle. In this season, we must stay close to God through intimate encounters. Prayer and fasting will help you to stay in the face of God. Our boldness should not include fear. Barak was chosen to lead the men, but because of his fear, God had to use Jael. We must be bold and fearless!

Prophetic Principles

"She speaks with wisdom, and faithful instruction is on her tongue."
Proverbs 31:26

It's time for women to take their rightful place in God's Kingdom here on Earth. He is raising up an army of prophetic generals. A prophetic general can best be defined as someone of chief ranking in God's spiritual army using the prophetic gifting of inspiration, interpretation, and/or revelation to speak wisdom and faithful instructions into the Kingdom of God. Deborah said to Barak, "spring into action for this is the day the LORD is handing Sisera over to you! Has the LORD not taken the lead?" Barak quickly went down from Mount Tabor with 10,000 men following him (Judges 4:14). Barak obtained victory with the spiritual inspiration and guidance of the prophetic general. The following principles will shift you to the next dimension in providing prophetic guidance.

- *Circumcision of the Heart:* God will only release authoritative guidance to those who He trusts. He will search out for those who have the heart of God to go out and do mighty exploits for His Kingdom. Rebuild your intimacy with God.
- *Living in a Manna Moment*: Expect God to manifest during the most unpredictable moments. "You gave your good Spirit to instruct them. You did not withhold your manna from their mouths, and you gave

them water for their thirst." Nehemiah 9:20

- *Encounter the Lord of Host:* Believe the encounters you've had with God through life experiences have prepared you for such a time as this. You will encounter Jehovah Sabaoth. "Jehovah, the God of the armies of Israel, the Giver of the victory in battle, of the stars and of the angels."

Empowering the Prophetic Voice

Praise the LORD. Sing to the LORD a new song, his praise in the assembly of his faithful people." Psalm 149:1

Remember, after we experience victory, God will give you a new song to sing. The famous Song of Deborah is in many ways similar to the Song of Moses, which he and Israelites sang after the miracle at the Red Sea. There is something special about the connection between God and music. The Hebrew word *"Bara"* means "to create." Look unto the Heavens to activate the prophetic sound. It is imperative to set your affections on those things above when using your prophetic voice.

When Deborah and Barack defeated Sisera, God gave Deborah a new song to sing. Psalms 40:3 The glory of the victory belonged to a woman, not to Barak. Deborah was recorded in the Bible "Song of Deborah." You can also note how she praised the brave Jael for having with her own hands killed the worst of Israel's enemies. She concludes her song of praise to God with these words:

Blessed above women shalt Jael be,
The wife of Heber the Kenite,
Above women in the tent shall she be blessed . . .
At her feet he sank, he fell, he lay; At her feet he sank, he fell;
Where he sank, there he fell dead . . .
So perish all Thine enemies, 0 God;

We must produce a sound of victory that will empower those enlisted in the army of God. Go forth and prophesy (foretell the word of the Lord), build up, and bless somebody through the work of your hands and the sound of your voice! Stay focused on what God has called you to voice. Use your voice activation to call into being the things which were not.

Prayer and Prophetic Decrees:

"God is within her, she will not fall; God will help her at break of day." Psalms 46:5

Heavenly Father, I come to you now in Jesus Christ's holy name. I ask you Lord to multiply me and impart every blessing and prophetic gifting into full activation. I have received Jesus as my personal savior and I freely give myself to be used by You.

1. I listen to the voice of the Lord. Exodus 15:26
2. I am built upon the foundation of the apostles and prophets, Jesus Christ being the Chief Corner Stone. Ephesians 2:20
3. I am God's workmanship created in Christ Jesus for good works. Ephesians 2:10
4. I will earnestly remember the Lord my God who gives me power. 2 Tim 1:7
5. I have a right to come boldly before the Throne to find mercy and race. Hebrew 4:16

References

http://www.Chabad.org

http://www.womeninthebible.net/women-bible-old-new-testaments/deborah-and-jael/

https://www.biblegateway.com

CHAPTER 23

MIRIAM: AN ORACULAR APOSTOLIC PROTOTYPE FOR THE 21ST CENTURY AND BEYOND

By Cecilia Davis-Jackson

Women Apostolic Leaders

Contributions and the critical roles of women are being recognized more extensively in the world today. Included, is the authentic Biblical truth that women of God functioned as apostles historically and function as apostles today. Although still highly debated by some, there exist progressive Biblical scholars, philosophers, change agents, prophets, apostles, and leaders globally who concur that women apostles helped, and are still helping, to shape the Movements of God throughout the Earth. Miriam is one of those exemplary, unsung female apostles.

Genesis, a Seed Archetype

Prior to contemporary female apostles, were those who set examples throughout secular and Biblical history. Many did not hold the title "apostle"; but their accomplishments, manners, and ethics were indeed archetypal of the office of the apostle. Genesis, the seed book of beginnings, sets the foundation and template for Christian faith, its government, leadership, and lifestyle. Miriam's life is an example from Genesis that sets the foundation for governmental leadership as a female apostle. Every female apostle today can proudly stand upon this foundation lifting her voice, proclaiming the Word of God without fear or compromise! Miriam's narrative in Genesis supports our contemporary story! She is an oracular apostolic prototype for the 21st century and beyond!

Miriam the Apostle, Her Story

When glimpsing into Miriam's story and garnering present truth from it, we realize this woman was intelligent and brave even in her youth. Both Jochebed, Miriam's mother, and Miriam conspired to keep Moses (Miriam's younger brother) safe during a time when an Egyptian king imposed fierce commands upon the Hebrew people, demanding the slaughter of their youngest male children. Miriam is identified as the young Jewish woman who watched over her younger brother who was hidden among the reeds along the Nile River bank escaping the Pharaoh's decree to kill the newborn Hebrew males. Since death was inevitable, Jochebed made an ark for her son and Miriam bravely stood in the face of death as a guard, protector, and nurturer of a future generation, Moses!

It was Miriam's predisposition as an apostle then, and it's our predisposition as female apostles today. We reach and impart into future generations! Moses' Nile River did not look like our Nile today; nevertheless, the treacherous possibilities of the death of the seed of families by drug addiction, prison, suicide, and the hijacking of the true Church and Kingdom doctrine we face today are as treacherous as death by reptiles and amphibians of the Nile. Arise, women apostles, and embrace what the Lord has predetermined in you; affect future generations.

Miriam saved Moses' life by watching for him during the building of his ark and his journey down the Nile until he landed in the hands of the Egyptian princess, who would raise him as her own child. Miriam also strategically connected her mother, a Hebrew woman, to the Egyptian princess. The Apostle Miriam was the instrument God used to position Jochebed to be the nursemaid of her own son, Moses who would be the deliverer of the nation of Israel, yet nurtured by the Egyptians. Miriam was an early personification of the apostolic characteristic of bridging nations! Rejoice sisters! Female voices are still going forth confidently, bridging nations for the Kingdom of God.

Further examination of Miriam's story reveals her as a woman of distinction and courage. Her parents, Amram and Jochebed, were unique in Israel's history. They produced three great leaders who served the nation at the same time: Moses, Aaron, and Miriam. Thus, Miriam (an unmarried woman) had an exceptional calling, being part of church government with Aaron and Moses, co-leaders of one of the greatest movements of Biblical history - the exodus of God's people from Egypt to Canaan.

Though elderly when the miracle of the Red Sea occurred, Miriam was also a leader of women in dance and worship for God's triumphant victory at the crossing! She was the first female prophet, a born leader for whom leadership came easy and as an early apostle, Miriam understood team leadership while serving with two men. Her carriage of merit was daring and full of faith. Having this calling, an equal with her brothers, confirms this unmarried woman's gift was not just for a few small families, but for governing an entire nation. This is another prototype for contemporary female apostles. Break free from the chains society and Christian "religious" individuals have placed upon your life. Open your mouth and speak as an apostolic and prophetic oracle of the Lord who is fearfully and wonderfully made to be what God has called you to be.

Surely, Miriam made mistakes regarding Moses' decision about marriage. Maybe she was upset because he married a Cushite woman from the region of Ethiopia (Numbers 12:1). Perhaps Miriam was attempting to protect the Israelite women who desired marriage. Was she upset because Moses by-passed the cultural practice that the eldest would marry first? Was Miriam concerned about how his marriage would affect the people of their nation? Did she simply misunderstand her apostolic authority and overstep her boundaries as a co-leader of Israel?

Regardless, Miriam was a mature, chosen spiritual leader who exercised poor judgment and was plagued with leprosy then put out of the camp of Israel. This was a harsh punishment. God's real plan was to use her as a proton apostle who would implement a new movement of God (with Moses) to end traditional ethnic and racial division in God's camp. This was a huge apostolic appointment that would shape the ages! Miriam struggled and missed fulfilling the assignment. Only because Moses pleaded with God for his sister's life did God reduce a death sentence of leprosy to a brief seven-day chastisement. More importantly, despite the magnitude of her failure, the almighty God healed the apostle and fully restored her into the camp (Exodus 15, Numbers 12)! The Lord forgives downhearted, misguided female apostles and reestablishes them into Kingdom (Romans 11:29)! This is your inheritance as a female leader, no matter how hard or how far you feel you have fallen. Your weakness is not beyond His forgiveness and repair.

Many of Miriam's actions were rich with strong apostolic characteristics:

- Initiator of cross-generational ministry
- Bridge-builder between nations
- A type of redemptive work for Israel
- Watcher and caretaker for leaders
- An Old Covenant shadow of an intercessor and worshipper
- A fruitful "sent" one even during old age
- A first of her type, a foreshadowing design and vision casting
- A picture of achievement for unmarried women as leaders
- A picture of an apostolic woman who fell, but was fully restored
- A leader of a movement in church government
- Daring and full of faith
- A model for female apostles to come

These same apostolic characteristics are resident in women who are called to apostleship today. Miriam's narrative is our contemporary story! Be courageous, stepping forward in sure anointing and Kingdom authority.

Father, I pray that female apostles hiding in ignominy because of discouragement, past failure, or error will be lifted to a place of honor, accepting that they are called as apostles and ministry gifts for the perfecting of saints and the work of the ministry. Reveal the magnificence of Your deep love and forgiveness that will lift women to their appointed places of strength and valor for advancing the Kingdom of God on Earth.

We decree that each one reading this chapter will come forth into the light of her calling and soar above every obstacle also seeing Miriam's narrative as her contemporary story and will build arks of safety for those of another generation.

We declare that apostolic women today will bridge and impact the deliverance of nations throughout the world.

We decree that women and girls will propel positive changes in neighborhoods, villages, cities, and churches, impacting crime, racial, and economic shifting for Kingdom.

We decree that female apostles and leaders will stand in ongoing travailing prayer and worship so the supernatural power of God will wreck ancient religious practices, bringing strongholds down while Kingdom culture arises in greater measure in the churches of the world.

We decree the spirit of the Lord will reign through His female apostles and subdue every system that challenges the authority of the King and the culture of the Kingdom designed in His Word!

We decree that female apostles will take on the apostolic characteristics of Miriam and be leaders alongside men, vision-casters during times of crisis, and those who embrace the interminable love and forgiveness of the Father.

In a conversation of indictment of the Lord, the prophet Micah confirmed that God sent and placed Miriam into ministry along with two other men (Micah 6:4). Women leaders of God stand assured that Miriam is one of the historic *Oracular Apostolic Prototypes for the 21st Century and Beyond*! You too are "sent" as apostles into ministry alongside men today. Miriam's narrative is your contemporary story!

CHAPTER 24

RAHAB: A WOMAN OF APOSTOLIC BOLDNESS

By Jeannette Connell

By faith Rahab the harlot did not perish along with those who were disobedient, after she had welcomed the spies in peace. (Hebrews 11:31)

In the book of Joshua chapter 2, we find a heroine whose name is Rahab. Rahab would be described as a shameful woman of her day, a harlot. Rahab was a Canaanite, an enemy of Israel. But we find her name recorded in the beginning of the book of Matthew, chapter one verse 5 in the lineage of our Lord Jesus. It reads that Salmon was the father of Boaz by Rahab, Boaz was the father of Obed by Ruth, and Obed the father of Jesse. One might ask how a harlot got to be a part of bringing forth our redemption, but this speaks prophetically of how Jesus opened wide the way for all to be redeemed. The lineage of Christ speaks not only of the great men and women of God, but also of sinners with a colorful past. The name Rahab in the Hebrew *raw-khawb* means "proud," the root word of her name means to make room in any or every direction, broad, large, to open wide. This speaks of her destiny as an example of the Lord making room for the vilest sinner and those considered outcasts. Rahab was a businesswoman and had an inn according to the historian Josephus, and it was not uncommon for an inn to function as a brothel within the same building. She is noted in the books of James 2:25 and Hebrews 11:3, as a harlot who was justified by her faith and action. Jesus identified himself with humanity to such an extent that it reads in Mark 15:28; *And the scripture was fulfilled which says, "And He was numbered with transgressors."* Ephesians 2:14 says, *For He Himself is our peace, who made both groups into one and broke down the barrier of the dividing wall.* So, we see that there was purpose in including a woman such as Rahab to reveal the love and kind intentions of the Father for all humanity.

Let us consider the life of Rahab and see her story as revealed by Scripture and recorded history. Rahab lived in the land of Jericho and she probably grew up there as her whole family was also dwelling in the city. They were Canaanites and history records that the Canaanites practiced polytheism, which was the belief in multiple gods. Some common gods of their worship in Rahab's belief system would be Baal, El, Asherah, Dagon, and Moloch to name a few. She and her people were idolatrous and had multiple gods they worshiped and called upon for any and every need imaginable. They lived with household gods and goddesses and erected gods on the high places for worship. The Canaanites were a people who were greatly influenced by Mesopotamian and Egyptian practices. This was the cultural practice by which Rahab was influenced and the religious practice that she participated in along with her business in prostitution.

When God spoke to Joshua to send in the spies to Jericho to check out the military strength in the city, the spies lodged at Rahab's house, which was built into the city wall. (Joshua 2:1-7) The soldiers of Jericho were sent out to capture the spies when they heard that the men were lodging there. But while they were in pursuit, Rahab had a conversation with the spies and clearly, she had a change of heart in her belief system. Rahab had heard of the victories of the God of Israel and she appealed to the spies not only for her life, but for her whole house before hiding them from the apparent danger of the soldiers. Her confession to the spies was that she knew Israel served the living God, that Jericho was without courage, immobilized by fear, and that they would surely take the land. She asked them for a sign that she and her house would be spared from death. (Joshua 2:9-13)

Hebrews says Rahab welcomed the spies in peace, meaning she had confidence in the revelation she had received personally concerning Israel. Rahab was a bold woman, full of courage; she had a plan in place with a strategy not only for herself but also for her family and the spies. She seized the moment of her deliverance and took a risk. Rahab lies to the soldiers of Jericho of the whereabouts of the men and sends them in another direction, working in cooperation with the purpose of God to possess the land. She was told to hang out a scarlet thread from her window as a sure sign that she and her family would be spared. This is a perfect symbol as the Israelites were accustomed to the practice of Passover of applying the blood of a lamb over the door of the house, so death would pass over. How poetic a scarlet cord hanging from a harlot's window as a lifeline of safety and a sure sign of the redemptive blood of Jesus saving through the salvation of the God of Israel. In the days ahead, Rahab would learn of this much more intimately as she dwelled among Israel as her people.

Rahab was a woman radiant of apostolic virtue in many senses of the word. She was discovered out of a life of sin and obscurity into divine purpose and destiny. She was a woman of influence, being a successful business owner. She had to demonstrate an authority to lead for the spies to trust her to keep them safe. She was a woman of strategy, giving them directive on how to remain safe after their departure and where to hide in the land to outwit the soldiers. She also empowered the spies with more courage that they were well able to take Jericho. Rahab was a pioneer as the forerunner of her family, clearing the path for their wellbeing and later moving into the camp of Israel. She would live among her new people, learning a new culture and way of life. She changed the course of her lineage by bringing deliverance to generations after her. They came out of bondage due to her noble act of faith. She truly lived up to her name as being a broad place, making room in every direction for her family to thrive and flourish with Israel. She finds love, forgiveness, and acceptance and is married to Salmon, becoming the mother of Boaz who is recorded in the lineage of our Savior. The reproach is rolled away of her former life and she becomes a woman of faith and valor by her righteous acts recorded for all to see. We can understand through this heroine that the grace of God can and does make any sinner clean and it is God who chooses who He will to inherit blessing and eternal life.

In Rahab's story we see that her apostolic traits were uncovered and used to bring forth God's plan and purposes. These are clearly seen and demonstrated.

- Rahab was a woman of faith, taking a risk and going against the rules of her traditions.
- Rahab was a deliverer, saving her whole house from death.
- Rahab was an entrepreneur of her day, owning and operating a business successfully.
- Rahab flowed in revelation as she heard the news of the God of Israel and acted according to it by faith.
- Rahab operated in the spirit of wisdom with a strategy of victory concerning the spies' safety.
- Rahab was an intercessor as she pleaded for her whole house to be saved.
- Rahab was a pioneer as a forerunner for the generations after her to inherit the promises of the Living God.

If one finds themselves with a past tainted by sin bondage and the reproach of misguided direction, there is hope through Christ. There is a new beginning and an acceptance in him that no one can take from you! Today we will shut the door to the past and open the door to a new beginning.

Declaration of Destiny

I decree and declare that today is the day of salvation in my life. I say that old things have passed away and all things become new. I choose to take on the new mind of Christ Jesus and I declare the reproach of yesterday has been rolled away by the blood of Jesus! I decree and declare that I will walk in newness of life and I receive the call and destiny of God upon my life. I will not allow the past to dictate my forward faith! I am a chosen vessel of the Most High God called to expand the Kingdom of Heaven on Earth. I too will, as Rahab, through fearless faith action and intercession, change the course of generations to come to inherit the promises of God!

References:

Unless otherwise indicated, Scriptures come from the YouVersion Bible app the NASB From the Lockman foundation

Greek and Hebrew references come from Strong's Exhaustive Concordance of the Bible 2001 by Zondervan.

Jesus' great grandmothers' blog by Dr. Claude Mariottini, Professor of Old Testament at Northern Baptist Seminary

https://claudemariottini.com/2015/03/09/jesus-great-grandmothers/

Rahab: Harlot, Liar, ancestor of Jesus blog by Ray Pritchard @Keep Believing Ministries

http://www.jesus.org/birth-of-jesus/genealogy-and-jewish-heritage/rahab-harlot-liar-ancestor-of-jesus.html

Rahab article from online Wikipedia

https://en.wikipedia.org/wiki/Rahab

CHAPTER 25

MIRIAM: THE HEART
OF A PROPHETESS

By Josiah Lane

"Clothed in strength and dignity, with nothing to fear, she smiles when she thinks about the future." - **Proverbs 31:25**

Who was Miriam?

Miriam—A name that means "rebellious." She is one of the most highlighted, and also forgotten, people in Scripture; a woman after God's own heart, who led the people across the Red Sea and one who advised Moses along with her brother, Aaron. In Scripture, and according to various theologians, she was considered to be the first prophetesses in Scripture. Many also attribute her to being a key leader in the crossing of the Red Sea, as she is ascribed by Phyllis Trible as an unnamed sister of Moses in Exodus 2:1-10 who helps deliver him and his people at the Nile River. She becomes, one could say, the central archetype of the female prophetic tradition.

How did Miriam Influence as a Leader?

Miriam's influence as a leader and a worshipper touched the heart of God.[9] If it had not, then God would have chosen not to include her through the hand that penned down this book in the Bible. Essentially, the prophet Micah lists Moses, Aaron, and Miriam as the three leaders in the Exodus.

---

[9] Micah 6:4

Micah's statement reflects an ancient tradition that would affirm Miriam to play a very significant role in leadership in early Israelite history,[10] a role that is very much downgraded due to promoting Moses as the main "dominant" leader of Israel, as he is known to be the most mentioned in the Biblical text. Her influence as a leader also stemmed from her song of victory, that many attribute to Moses. However, she is the one that began to sing and dance because of their victory, and in this she led a nation to WORSHIP. In her song of victory, she led an ascription to God for the victory;[11] because without the grace and hand of Yahweh on their side, the Egyptians would have killed them, and thus the line of Israel would have never been what it is now known as today.

What is a "Miriam Anointing" and How Can Women Today Walk in it?

A "Miriam anointing," is an anointing that rises up within a woman that starts with ascriptive worship. When God had told me this, I was under the impression that God was reminding me of the fact that whatever a woman goes through, that He will continue to prepare them for further ministry and destiny. But that was not all. It was also this, God has allowed for the enemy to "make his first move" on women being in the "shadows." THE ENEMY HAS MADE HIS LAST MOVE, AND APOSTOLIC WOMEN SEEKING THE HEART OF GOD ARE RISING INTO A MIRIAM ANOINTING, and will experience the love of Jesus in a whole new way that they have never seen before! Even though the oppression was there, GOD IS BIGGER. To walk in a Miriam anointing is to lead the people of God to the heart of worship. THE ACTIVITY OF PRAISE IS THE BLOODLINE OF THE SUPERNATURAL.

---

[10] T. Desmond Alexander, "From Paradise to the Promised Land: An Introduction to the Pentateuch 3rd Edition," Grand Rapids MI: Baker Academic Pub. 2012, 189.

[11] Exodus 15

Apostolic Principles

INITIATIVE: The apostolic principle that I kept hearing over and over again from God was that Miriam CONTINUED to take initiative. She took initiative when it came to leading the people of Israel through the Red Sea; she took initiative when she led the nation of Israel to worship and ascribe praise to God. She was responsible for carrying a weight like Moses, and thus took initiative to remind him of the leader that he is supposed to be. What God specifically was telling me concerning this one word was that, "If my women wish to lead, then all they have to do is say 'yes'. When they say 'yes', they must accept the responsibility of INITIATIVE throughout everything they do." The Lord revealed to me that night that He has anointed women for a position and a season that men will find it very hard to lead in without women leading with them in the Body of Christ. The God of the universe will confound the minds of those who denied those women the right to lead by placing them in areas where they see the love of God like never before![12]

Practical Steps

1. Miriam took initiative to lead the nation of Israel, while keeping them focused on what God had promised for them.
2. Women today must take initiative and authority over the enemy; rebuke the prince of the air!
3. Worship like Miriam worshipped. Recognize who you are in God.
4. Just as Miriam recognized the victory through Yahweh, so must you.
5. Just as Miriam stepped out of her "box" to check Moses, it is okay for you to step out of your "place of contentment" and be the leader God has called you to be.

Empowerment Declarations

1. You have been anointed to preach the good news and set the captives free!

---

[12] See Isaiah 60: 21b-22

a. "Arise, shine, for your light has broken through! The Eternal One's brilliance has dawned upon you." (Isaiah 60:1)

2. YOU ARE EMPOWERED TO LEAD FAR MORE THAN YOU REALIZE! THAT'S THE RECKLESS LOVE OF GOD.

    a. "He (Jesus) cannot be distracted from his late-night prayer in Gethsemane." --Alex Early, The Reckless Love of God: Experiencing the Personal, Passionate Heart of the Gospel

3. YOU ARE VICTORIOUS!

    a. "Whatever you don't speak, you won't see, and it will never change until you CHANGE YOUR LANGUAGE." –Pastor Judy Jacobs-Tuttle (Pursuit Women's Conference)

4. The enemy has no hold over you. YOU ARE A STRONG, POWERFUL, ANOINTED WOMAN OF GOD.

    a. "I've given you true authority. You can smash vipers and scorpions under your feet. You can walk all over the power of the enemy. You can't be harmed." – Luke 10:19 (THE VOICE)

5. THE FATHER CALLS YOU BEAUTIFUL!

    a. "You are beautiful, my dear, as beautiful as Tirzah, as lovely as Jerusalem, as regal as an army beneath their banners." – Song of Songs 6:4

Prophetic Prayer

Father God, I pray the peace of Your presence rests over me right NOW. I pray that the fire of my altar would never be blown out or burnt out. May the understanding and strategy of God begin to flow naturally within me. MAKE ME A LOVESICK WARRIOR. I pray that the old wounds from the bondage of insecurity do not keep me back from going forth in my destiny. I REBUKE THE SPIRIT OF FEAR, THE PRINCE OF THE AIR, AND I SAY YOU MUST LOSE ME IN THE NAME OF JESUS, AND LET ME GO. I release the fire of God over myself and may the peace of God surpass all understanding as I seek to be a worshipper like Miriam when she was victorious over her enemies in dance, in singing, and even in instrumental praise. May I be so on fire for the word of God that it drips off of my tongue like honey when I preach, when I lead, when I discern, and when I begin to see the face of God through my prayer walk. I pray the spirit of prophecy from Heaven to reach down to me RIGHT NOW, and that the leadership qualities, THE APOSTOLIC AND PROPHETIC QUALITIES, be released over me now, in Jesus' name. AMEN!

CHAPTER 26

APOSTOLIC WIDOW
STARTS AN OIL BUSINESS

By Michelle J. Miller

Now one of the wives of a man of the sons of the prophets cried out to Elisha [for help], saying "Your servant my husband is dead, and you know that your servant [reverently] feared the Lord; but the creditor is coming to take my two sons to be his slaves [in payment for a loan]." [2] Elisha said to her, "What shall I do for you? Tell me, what do you have [of value] in the house?" She said, "Your maidservant has nothing in the house except a [small] jar of [olive] oil." [3] Then he said, "Go, borrow containers from all your neighbors, empty containers—and not just a few. [4] Then you shall go in and shut the door behind you and your sons, and pour out [the oil you have] into all these containers, and you shall set aside each one when it is full." [5] So she left him and shut the door behind her and her sons; they were bringing her the containers as she poured [the oil]. [6] When the containers were all full, she said to her son, "Bring me another container." And he said to her, "There is not a one left." Then the oil stopped [multiplying]. [7] Then she came and told the man of God. He said, "Go, sell the oil and pay your debt, and you and your sons can live on the rest." - 2 Kings 4:1-7 (AMP)

Many people have read 2 Kings 4:1-7 and felt sorrow for this widow (and single mother) who was in debt. I initially felt sorry for her and I identified with her plight as a mother. Then one day God spoke to me and told me that she was not just a damsel in distress, she was an apostolic entrepreneur. This indebted widow's desperate situation became the catalyst that God used for her to experience personal and business breakthrough.

> *"In this distress the poor widow goes to Elisha, in dependence upon the promise that the seed of the righteous shall not be forsaken....[h]e did not give her some small matter for her present provision, but set her up in the world to sell oil, and put a stock into her hand to begin with."*
> (https://www.biblestudytools.com/commentaries/matthew-henry-complete/2-kings/4.html)

The product (a vessel of oil) that this widow had, was multiplied supernaturally. The widow's obedience to Prophet Elisha's instructions resulted in a business enterprise that paid off her debt, kept her sons out of bondage, and provided sufficient profit for her family to live without worry. This woman could have simply submitted to the Levitical Law concerning debts (Leviticus 25). However, she did not submit to the status quo, she was a pioneer that went to the prophet for help.

> *"To pioneer means to advance, progress, gain ground or conquer territory. Pioneers and pioneering people will eventually succeed, flourish and prosper. Pioneers are usually men and women of extraordinary talent, vision and ability"*
> (John Eckhardt, Moving in the Apostolic, Pg. 52, 1999).

It is evident that this apostolic widow had a vision that if she had an encounter with God through His prophet, her situation would change, and it did. This apostolic widow had a vision that if she followed the instruction of the prophet, she would succeed in paying off her family's debt, saving her sons from the yoke of bondage, and she did. The bible word "widow" appears in the King James Version of the Bible 82 times, so these women are important to God. In fact, the Lord watches over the fatherless and widows (Psalms 146:9). I am sure other women knew the plight of this widow and observed what was happening in her life, but at the same time, the Lord was watching over her and sent her out on a marketplace ministry mission.

I believe other women were watching this widow as she humbly went from house to house collecting empty jars. I am sure women were wondering what she would do with the empty jars. After she boldly followed the prophet's instructions, this widow was going to show other women that they could sell items in the market even if they didn't have husbands. This indebted widow gave hope to other women, her obedience to God through the prophet revealed the miraculous work of the great I AM. This widow had an apostolic breakthrough anointing and she demonstrated that women could be champions for change in their communities if they pressed past obstacles and stepped out in extreme faith. This widow is an apostolic example that women need not be bound with debt and distress. On the contrary, women can put their trust in the Lord and pave a way for women to prosper in the marketplace. This woman did not sell just any kind of oil in the marketplace, she presented a special miracle oil to the market, so I am sure she received a great price.

> *"She must sell the oil to those that were rich, and could afford to bestow it on themselves. We may suppose, being produced by miracle, it was the best of its kind, like the wine (Jn. 2:10), so that she might have both a good price and a good market for it."* (https://www.biblestudytools.com/commentaries/matthew-henry-complete/2-kings/4.html)

By the Spirit of God, I know that this widow's situation ministered to other widows and women.

God is raising up female apostles and apostolic women in the marketplace that will minister to other women. Women who are in a state of despair are going to arise and ask God for apostolic strategies to transform the financial circumstances of orphan girls, single mothers, and widows around the world. Female apostles and apostolic women are arising as ministers and as marketplace leaders.

Traditional Bible teachings have surrounded around the conclusion that an apostle must leave their position in the marketplace to start a full-time ministry. The indebted widow, like many today, must care for their families. While many people are called into full-time ministry, people are not exempt from holding an apostolic office simply because they have careers and businesses. In other words, you are not disqualified from your apostolic office because you work. Many women feel as if it were virtually impossible for them to walk in their apostolic calls because they are mothers, widows, or even entrepreneurs. I believe some of you reading this book believe that you are called to be an apostle, but the burdens of life and religious patriarchal paradigms count you out of your calling. Well, do not fret because your day is coming and God is going to use your situation to demonstrate that He can use you as an apostolic example in society. In fact, there is a new breed of apostolic women arising that God will use to obtain the treasures of darkness and hidden riches in secret places (Isaiah 45:3). God will use them as marketplace ministers, church investors, and Kingdom advancers. The Bible has several examples of apostles and apostolic people who were used powerfully in ministry and in the marketplace.

Peter and Paul are examples of men who were apostles that also operated in the marketplace. Traditional Biblical teaching concludes that when Peter was casting his net into the lake and instantly stopped fishing to follow Jesus, it meant that Peter quit his fishing business (Matthew 4:18-20). However, when Jesus appeared again, Peter stated that he was going out to fish (John 21:2-14). In one scenario, Peter's net was already in the lake, while in the other instance, Peter was getting ready to go fishing; he did not instantly quit his business. Peter was an apostle and businessman. Paul was also an apostle and he had his own business; tent-making (Acts 18:2-4). Paul worked to supply his own needs and the needs of his team, in addition to receiving offerings (Acts 20:34, 35). Paul also asked the Corinthians if only he and Barnabas must work for a living (1 Cor. 9:6). Paul was an apostle, businessman, and philanthropist. The widow in 2 Kings 4 was used in ministry and eventually in the marketplace. Her husband was a prophet and if you are married to a prophet, you must participate in the work of the ministry. She continued her honor of the prophetic ministry by going to the prophet for advice and obeying his instructions; as a result, she went from broke to breakthrough. This widow is not the only example of women being used in ministry and society. Deborah was a prophetess and a judge (Judges 4:4, 5). The virtuous woman is described as a woman who has God-like compassion for people, buys real estate, saves her money to start business endeavors, and makes fine linen for women to buy (Proverbs 31: 10-31). Lydia was an intercessor, a worshipper, and a dealer in fabrics (Acts

16:1-15). God is about to use the apostolic call on your life to take you from distress to destiny. The widow identified her trouble and unbeknown to her, she became an apostolic model to demonstrate that women have the ability to go from broke to business owner.

Recap of Apostolic Traits:

- *Apostolic women obey God despite religious traditions.* The indebted widow did not accept the religious mandate that her sons had to become slaves to pay off a debt in accordance with the Levitical law; she went to the prophet because she wanted to do something different.
- *Apostolic women are bold and courageous.* The indebted widow boldly went from house to house, borrowing jars not knowing how she would use them, but believing that she would receive a strategy to remove her financial burden.
- *Apostolic women are marketplace pioneers.* The indebted widow explained her dire situation to the prophet and after following the prophet's direction, she had the product she needed to start a business.
- *Apostolic women have a breakthrough anointing.* The indebted widow was able to break through religious laws, poverty, and even concerns about what other people may have thought about her.
- *Apostolic have balance in life.* The indebted widow had to first balance supporting her husband in prophetic ministry, while also being a mother. After her husband died, she had to balance financial stress, maintaining a respect for the prophet, and being a mother alone.

Prophetic Prayer:

Father God, ignite the apostolic call on my life and position me to be a pioneer for Your glory. Give me apostolic strategies that will take women from debt and poverty, to destiny and purpose. Awaken the apostolic entrepreneur within me and give me innovate breakthrough business ideas that will provide resources to women around the world. Make me an apostolic model for women around the world to see that you are a God that delivers women out of debt, depression, despair, and distress. Give me the courage to overcome obstacles to walking in my apostolic call and use me mightily to minister to nations of women and to be a wise master builder in the marketplace.

Declarations & Affirmations:

- I am an apostolic entrepreneur and I develop strategies to get women out of debt.
- I am an innovator and I will initiate trailblazing tactics that will trigger an outpour of blessings and favor on the lives of women around the world.
- I am a pioneer and I will plow through obstacles, obstructions, and any mountain that tries to keep me from moving forward.
- I am called by God and I will courageously arise my bleak circumstances because a breakthrough anointing is being ignited over my life.
- I am a catalyst and God will use me to bring about change.

CHAPTER 27

THE DAUGHTERS OF ZELOPHEHAD: THE FIVE WOMEN WHO CHALLENGED THE STATUS QUO

By Loria M. Morrison

The Introduction

Throughout history, God used women to birth nations, kings, and to lead Israel into victory. In the beginning God, created Heaven and the Earth (Genesis 1:1) and according to Genesis 1:26, God said, Let us make man in our image, after our likeness, and let "them" (emphasis) have dominion over the fish of the sea, and over the fowl of the air, and over the cattle, and over all the earth, and over every creeping thing that creeps upon the earth, (27). So, God created man in his own image, in the image of God created them; male and female. From these Scriptures, I believe God always intended for women to have dominion and to rule on Earth, however, because of the fall of mankind in the Garden of Eden, women have struggled to take their rightful place in the Kingdom and society. God is raising up 21st Century women to push, pioneer, to blaze trails like never before, these (YOU) women refuse to be marginalized, alienated, and oppressed, as they have been given a charge by the King of the Kingdom (the Lord Jesus Christ), they will lead with confidence, assurance, and faith in the one who sent them.

It is my hope, as you read the story of the Daughters of Zelophehad, that you will rise to new heights, with a fresh impartation of courage, strength, stamina, resilience, and understanding you have been accepted and are His beloved and that you will do and be all He has intended for you since the beginning of time. And lastly, may you receive a deeper revelation of what it means to be seated in Heavenly places in Him. Shalom!

The Petition that Shifted Israel's Laws of Inheritance

One day, a petition was presented by the daughters of Zelophehad: Mahlah, Noah, Hoglah Milcah, and Tirzah. Their father, Zelophehad, was a descendant of Hepher, son of Gilead, son of Makir, son Manasseh, son of Joseph. These women stood before Moses, Eleazar the priest, the tribal leader, and the entire community at the entrance of the Tabernacle. They made their petition before Moses and said, "Our father died in the wilderness, he was not among Korah's followers, who rebelled against the Lord, he died because of his own sin. But he has no sons. Why should the name of our father disappear from his clan just because he has no sons, give us property along with the rest of our relatives". So, Moses brought their case before the Lord and the Lord replied to Moses, the claim of the daughters of Zelophehad is legitimate and right. You must give them a grant of land along with their father's relatives, assign them the property that would have been given to their father, and give the following instructions to the people of Israel: if a man dies and has no son then give his inheritance to his daughters. And if he has no daughter either transfer his inheritance to his brothers. If he has no brother transfer it to his father's brothers. But if his father has no brothers give his inheritance to the nearest relative in his calm. This a legal requirement for the people of Israel, just as the Lord commanded Moses. Numbers 27:1-7 (NLT)

Apostolic Courage

Here is the story of five women named Mahlah, Noah, Hoglah, Milacah, and Tirzah, who decided to challenge the status quo of their day. Their father died, and during this time, the law was written that if a man died without sons, his inheritance would be given to his male relatives despite having daughters. This is a powerful example of courage, tenacity, and resilience.

147

These women lived in a time where women were not considered equal and certainly did not speak or advocate for themselves. The law was written were women were overlooked and not considered in their father's inheritance. This compelling story demonstrates desperation, a drive to be considered and to be heard. Throughout the Scriptures in the Old Testament, women were considered inferior to men. For example, Genesis 3:16 God says to Eve, "I will greatly multiply thy sorrow and thy conception; in sorrow thou shalt bring forth children; and thy desire shall be to thy husband and he shall rule over you." This is the connotation that men will have dominion over women and there is not much you can say and do. However, our God is a just God, He is a God of equality and fairness and He will always hear the cries of His children. I could imagine the desperation of these women, realizing all that their father had worked for would be given to others and more likely than not, they had financial needs. Scriptures does not tell us that they were married, so that gives their case even more legitimacy of their right to an inheritance. These women stepped out of time into the apostolic and prophetic grace, they dared to challenge the system and pioneer a movement of equality. They dared to speak up! They petitioned Moses to intercede on their behalf before God, they were desperate, they realized they had nothing to lose because the law stated that if a man died and had no sons, his inheritance would bypass his daughter(s) and go to his brethren. Their act of faith moved the God of Abraham, Isaac, and Jacob! God spoke to Moses and said, "The daughters of Zelophehad speak right!" Could it be that God is waiting for women to catch that revelation that He created them to rule and reign! I can imagine God saying, "Ah at last, my daughters are taking their rightful place into what I created for them before the foundation of the world, they have stepped out of normalcy and asked me for what seemed impossible."

The Significance of *FIVE*

These five women represent the Apostolic and Prophetic grace, they changed the trajectory of Israel's history in that women would now receive an inheritance from their father. God showed Grace (5) and through these five women, the five-fold ministry showed up by being a voice, hands, feet, eyes, and ears. These women risked their reputations, they could have been ostracized or labeled *Jezebellic* in nature. However, they yearned for change. They understood they had nothing to lose and everything to gain. Faith is what moved God; these women believed. This is the hour where God is raising women to new levels, dimensions, and heights in His Spirit. These 21st Century Apostolic Women will be armed with faith and revelation of Jesus Christ in their hearts and minds. I believe revival is coming, just as it did for the daughters of Zelophehad. Can you imagine the joy and burdens that were removed because these women dared to believe? God spoke to Moses and declared from that day until now women would have a legal right to their fathers' inheritance, Hallelujah!

Women of God rise, the Master has heard you and has declared you blessed, to rule and to reign. As you petition Him, he is delighted to declare, "Give them what they ask for, for they have spoken right!"

CHAPTER 28

THE TRUTH ABOUT MARY MAGDALENE

By Adrienne Sumler

The story of Mary Magdalene is one of intrigue and societal transformation for women. She gives hope to the hopeless but also revelation of how our Lord and Savior loved, cared, and restored women into their proper place. Mary's story is so profound for so many today who are enduring the same scenario, it brings great clarity and hope. It gives the full interpretation of the Scripture while we were yet sinners, Christ died for us in Romans 5:8. So it doesn't matter who we are, where we come from, or what our sins were; He died for us. Historically, we have been taught various things about the nature and character of Mary Magdalene versus who and what the word of God says. So, my question is, where in the word does it say Mary was a prostitute? It was recorded she was a disciple, or even an apostle to the Apostles. But, where does it say a prostitute?

Mary comes into scene born in "Magdala" on the Sea of Galilee. She was given the nickname "The Magdalene" to distinguish her from other Mary's and her place of birth. Mary in Greek means "strong". Magdala means "tower" or "castle". It is a fortified structure rising to a considerable height to repel a hostile attacker or to enable a watchman to see in every direction. This is who she was destined to become. To rise above or surpass others. And lastly, a person who can be relied on for support, aid, or comfort, especially in times of difficulty. In 14 passages of Scripture, she is connected to other women and her names always appear first. 8 out of 14 times her name appears with Mary, Jesus, Mother, and aunt; she was close to them and even closer to Jesus.

When she met Jesus, he cast 7 devils (demons) out of her, which speaks of the extreme violent, chronic nervous type of disorder, and the severity of her bondage. He doesn't speak of what they were, but speaks of deep affliction of the mind, body, and soul similar to Legion in (Mark 5:1-5,9) she also lived by the sea.

Jesus set her free, she was clothed and brought back in her right mind, but it was never stated that her affliction was one of prostitution. The Jewish Talmud spoke of Mary practicing harlotry and had a reputation of reproach. Then the Roman Catholic Church was guilty of slandering her in Naples in 1324, as they established "Magdalen House" for fallen women.

In western European art and literature, Mary Magdalene is most often portrayed as a repentant prostitute the Christian model of female sexuality redeemed (King, Gospel 149). A forgiven prostitute is the wrong image and wrong message. But Jesus gave Mary the right image and message. Even artists in that era would paint her in galleries as a loose, voluptuous female. Why was the woman who was caught in adultery's name never named by theologians or Christian Fathers? But Mary's name was "denigrated." It means she was criticized unfairly, belittled, attacked, and defamed. To go deeper, it is a Latin word meaning an attempt to blacken their reputation or to treat or represent as lacking in value or importance. I believe this was part of the enemy's plan to discredit her character because of the plan of God for her life.

Jewish culture in the first century was "patriarchal". Jewish men would pray, "Praise be God that he has not created me a woman" (Jesus Extraordinary Treatment of women 2017). This is the way society treated women. As property with no voice, i.e. as a slave. The finality of this was to spread negative or hurtful information about a person or situation. Like believers using her past of mental illness against her when Jesus healed her and other women with infirmities and evil spirits (Luke 8:1,2). There is no proof of her being a prostitute. She was a sinner needing a savior like the rest of us.

But the Bible does speak of her commitment to follow Jesus. She was always found at his feet; anointing them or kissing them. Mary was devoted through deliverance and when she realized what she was, as opposed to who God created her to be, a mighty devotion and covenant was formed with the Lord. She became an Apostolic Seal (an authentically transformed woman) for Christ. She and the other women were devoted all the way to the cross. After deliverance, she became a disciple (Luke 8:1). She is also listed in commendations and greetings in Romans 16:1-6, 7. In Romans 16:6,7 "Greet Mary, who bestowed much labor on us. Salute Andronicus and Junia my kinsmen and my fellow prisoners who are noted among the apostles, who also were in Christ before me."

She was a single woman of means who supported, aided, and traveled from place to place with Jesus on his missionary journeys. Her and other women knew what the needs were and were willing to help evangelize and serve. They were fully submitted in their hearts and service to him.

Luke accounts their strong support in:

1. Traveling – Luke 8:1-3
2. Finances – Luke 8:1-3
3. Prayer – Acts 1:14
4. Loyalty unfeigned

There was a very negative cultural view of women in Jesus' day, but he treated them with love, respect, and compassion. He went around healing and liberating women despite cultural and societal bondages, bringing restoration and dignity everywhere he went. Mary was the "strongest" of the women and the closest to Jesus besides his mother.

Because of the relationship with Jesus and her deep-seated love for him, it would place her at risk with some of the other disciples. At risk for:

a) Jealousy
b) Sexism
c) Competitiveness
d) Greed
e) Anger
f) Hatred
g) Murder

Matthew's and John's account differ a little. When Jesus was being anointed at Bethany things began to surface among the disciples (Matthew 26:6-13; John 12:3-8). Mary took a pound of ointment of spikenard and anointed the feet of Jesus, and wiped his feet with her hair and the house was filled with the odor of the ointment.

Then Judas the betrayer, one of the disciples, wanted to know why wasn't this very costly ointment sold for three hundred pence, and given to the poor. Not because he cared for the poor, the Bible says but because he was a thief and had the bag "and bare" what was put therein. "And bare" means through the idea of removal; to lift literally. Judas would take his cut off the top. To bear away and carry off, for he was a thief.

Jesus is prophetically speaking that she is anointing him for his burial. And that this one act should be a memorial unto her wherever this gospel is preached. He entrusted her with the gospel when she anointed his feet. Memorial translated, "a record for all eternity." Because of this, we should all speak well of her for all eternity (Matthew 26:12*13).

Then Jesus is arrested, crucified, and dies. Meanwhile, in Matthew 27:55-56; 61 many women far off followed Jesus, from Galilee with Mary Magdalene, Mary the mother of James and John, and the mother of Zebedee's children.

In Matthew 28 is the account of the resurrection. Mary Magdalene and the other Mary return to the sepulcher where an angel appears, rolls back the stone, and sits on it. The angel said, "I know you seek Jesus he is not there, He has Risen."

The angel commissions her and tells her to "Go" and tell his disciples that he has risen from the dead. They departed with fear and joy and Jesus meets them. They came and held him once again by the feet and worshipped him. Then Jesus said unto them "Go" and tell thy brethren…. Finally, in verses 16-20 he sends them all in verse 19 to "Go" and commissions them all. "Ye therefore and teach all nations baptizing them in the name of the Father, the Son and the Holy Ghost." Mary was the first to see him resurrected, the first to be commissioned, had the honor of anointing him for his burial, and trusted to first bring the gospel.

She was in my opinion an Apostle, also the first to see him resurrected she fulfilled the Scriptural and spiritual qualifications with the memorial Jesus spoke over her, Mary Magdalene, and Mary his mother were placed above all others by God the father and Jesus himself.

What Can We Learn from the Ministry of Mary Magdalene?

- You can be called, discipled, and apostolized (sent) by God the Father, God the Son, and
- God the Holy Spirit.
- You can be empowered, entrusted, and commissioned with the gospel by Jesus today.
- Follow Christ, die daily, and work with your strong apostolic giftings and assignments.
- Support the Kingdom mandate with your substance, married & single alike.
- Bring societal transformation via the 7 mountain mandates in your communities, cities, and regions to bring forth change.

References

Author, G. (2017, July 03). Jesus' Extraordinary Treatment of Women. Retrieved February 15, 2018, from https://www.franciscanmedia.org/jesus-extraordinary-treatment-of-women/

Evans, G. (n.d.). A memorial to Mary of Bethany. Retrieved February 5, 2018, from http://www.icogsfg.org/ge-maryb.html

Meyer, M. W., & Boer, E. D. (2004). *The Gospels of Mary: the secret tradition of Mary Magdalene, the companion of Jesus.* San Francisco, CA: HarperSanFrancisco.

The Woman Who Had Seven Devils. (n.d.). Retrieved February 10, 2018, from https://www.biblegateway.com/resources/all-women-bible/Mary-Magdalene

Tolbert, B. (n.d.). Mary Magdalene: Apostle to the Apostles. Retrieved January 16, 2018, from https://www.lagrange.edu/resources/pdf/citations/religion/magdalene.pdf

CHAPTER 29

MIRIAM: A WOMAN OF GREAT RESILIENCE & POWER

By Jacqueline R. Simmons

For I brought you up out of the land of Egypt and redeemed you out of the house where you were bond servants, and I sent before you Moses, Aaron and Miriam. **Micah 6:4 (AMPC)**

Arise, Mighty Woman of Valor, Arise, shine, for your light has come and the glory of the LORD has risen upon you. Isaiah 60:1 (ESV) Just as Miriam, whose name (Mar) meaning "bitter" and/or "water" arose during an oppressive time in Egypt. In grievous times, the Lord rose up a prophetess, a prolific leader among leaders to war against the familiar enslavement and fatal obscurities of the Egyptian pharaoh which first appears in the book of Exodus. Miriam was the firstborn of her father Amram, a leader of the Jewish people and of her mother, Yocheved, as Wikipedia states, who was so righteous she was exempt from the curse of Eve. She was also the oldest sister of Aaron and Moses according to (1 Chronicles 6).

Miriam, a bondswoman of Egypt, served as a midwife to the Hebrew women by saving their babies from the vicious decree of the pharaoh and healed all who were brutally beaten at the hand of Egyptian soldiers with herbs. According to the word of God, Scripture lets us know that Miriam's apostolic DNA, "sent one" was affirmed by God (Micah 6:4). She was a pioneer for women that educated them on their assigned duties and motivated them not to give up hope because God would soon bring deliverance to their captivity.

By faith, she led the women in honoring Yahweh through worship with songs and dancing with timbrels after crossing the Red Sea. At age five, little prophetess Miriam, very bold and mature for her age, went against the status quo by speaking words from the heart of God which could have brought her to a death sentence if her mother had not intervened. During the demands of Pharaoh making the decree of getting rid of all baby Hebrew boys by throwing them into the Nile River, her father, Amram, also sent forth a gruesome request. Miriam was disturbed in her spirit by her father's motion of divorcing his wife (Yocheved) and all the men who followed him did the same. The power of influence almost destroyed not only the future of today but also the effect of what was to come for the next generation. Prophetess Miriam simply told her father that his decision was an injustice and worse than King Pharaoh's decree and that he must make things right openly because a son would be born to bring the Israelites out of Egypt.

Even though opposition was at hand in the life of Miriam, she didn't allow the many tests that came her way to hinder her mission. She leaned on the God of Abraham, Isaac, and Jacob to see her through the many adversities that came into fruition at the time of oppression. Therefore, as I mirror my life after Miriam, a prophetic voice of nations, I believe I can share my personal testimony of perseverance through the enslavement of life circumstances, which brought me through by the power of deliverance, prayer, and petition.

The Lord says in Psalms 34:17, "When the righteous cry for help, the Lord hears, and delivers them out of all their distress and troubles." Yes, he delivers you from things that you didn't know that you were bound to until you call out to Him. Before coming to Christ, I had a dream that I was in a big sanctuary surrounded by people full of love and unity. There was a woman of God who was so beautiful; her face was full of light, who loved me into the Kingdom of God by a life she lived before me. She led me to Christ in her home and invited me to the exact same church in my dream. As I walked into the Pentecostal holiness church, everyone was filled with the joy of the Lord and praises. I felt at home because of all the love and comfort among the believers; it was more than what I received from the pleasures of the world.

As time went on I grew in knowing the power of faith, healing, prayer, and deliverance as the leaders in the ministry taught the word of God. As a new believer, my first duty was an usher that stood on the wall with greeting cards wearing my favorite red lipstick. The Lord did a quick work in me from being filled with the Holy Spirit to an intercessor and deliverance minister of the gospel. Many low valleys occurred in my life as my former Pastor proceeded in her death twelve years ago. She was a trailblazer that went against the status quo in the south. Many leaders persecuted women who proclaimed to be pastors, and she was one among them who were persecuted.

It was always said that women should be silent in the church, to which she always said, "It's the God in me that I will obey, not voices of men!" She never let the many words of slander and gossips stop the blueprint that God had placed on her life. She was a mother, teacher, and prophet that helped anyone that was in need in and outside of the four walls of the ministry. She was my Miriam who taught me the importance of seeking the heart of God, but then she died during the summer of her vacation twelve years ago. By this time I had grown so strong in the Lord that I began to teach other women the power of prayer and intercession. She gave wise counsel, direction, and teachings on the many things that a woman needs. As a dreamer, I studied the word of God to understand what was troubling me, and one service night the same week, she taught on dismantling generational curses.

I can go on about the many breakthroughs I encountered while receiving her tutelage as the Holy Spirit led her. She was the one who birthed me into the leader I am today. When being placed in a position of authority, one can grow a spirit of importance if not prayerful due to the praises of people.

The Lord says in Proverbs 16:8, "Pride goes before destruction and a haughty spirit before a fall." As God used me as a vessel, the spirit of pride took me to places while in ministry that I didn't bargain for. The best thing a fallen leader can do is step down from position and that was what I did. It took me to the place Miriam was in Numbers 12:10, "And when the cloud departed from over the Tent, behold, Miriam was leprous, as white as snow."

After being restored from my cave experiences, the Lord asked me a question," Would I be His intercessor for the broken hearted and bring liberty to the captives?" The many God encounters of sweet communion with Him dismantled the markings of the religious spirit, church hurt, rejection, witchcraft, legalism, spiritual adultery, and liberated me out of those familiar places. In the Kingdom of God, the power of prayer and intercession will take you to new realms of the Spirit, reveal who you are, and cause you to rise above any obstacle of opposition. My whole life, through fervent prayer and intercession, brought me out of familiar enslavement, only to embrace living an undiscovered freedom in Christ Jesus.

Summary:

1. Teaching indicates that women who experience bondage through life circumstances bring change by prayer.
2. You will discover that the power of influence can transform a life, whether good or bad.
3. Allowing a position or praises of men will bring you to a place of pride and open shame.
4. Praise and worship to God give you a merry heart and freedom during trying times.
5. Leaders are like trees; they inspire those around them and live their lives on the cutting edge and against all odds.
6. Even though there are difficulties leaving a place where legalism abides, God can still break every chain that binds you.

Uplifting Poem: Arise Miriam Arise

Arise O' Miriam great woman of Power
I'm calling you to do a work for me in this very hour
You thought that I left you because hearing me changed

I was with you in the beginning of the world that I ordained
You kept the faith, with praise you blessed me
Your reward is so great because you served so diligently
The FIRE of God thrust you to survive through your Red Sea
You acknowledged my presence when surrounded with resilience and plea
Be steadfast, unmovable, and planted as a tree
Your Redeemer stands with you and has made you free.

References:

Chabog.org, https://www.huffingtonpost.com what women leaders can learn from Biblical Miriam, Wikipedia

CHAPTER 30

RACHEL: A MARKETPLACE APOSTOLIC LEADER

By Uloma Chinwe Obi

Rachel is the first woman in Scripture to be linked with the role of a shepherd, setting the pace for work outside the home front. Other women mentioned in Scripture before Rachel were spoken of in the light of their careers as wives, mothers, and homemakers. Rachel sets the pace as a single woman working tirelessly to build an empire both or herself and for her father. The next set of women who kept their father's flocks were the daughters of Jethro.

Unlike the daughters of Jethro, Rachel enjoyed an amiable work relationship with the other male shepherds. The daughters of Jethro on the other hand, could not effectively thrive as shepherds because they were constantly being harassed by the male shepherds. There were seven of them, in contrast to Rachel who served alone in a male-dominated industry and yet she still thrived. The shepherds Rachel interacted with were ready to wait for Rachel to come with her flocks before they watered the entire flocks. Everyone knows that success requires successorship and that great leadership is the product of a great team.

Laban, Rebekah's brother and Jacob's uncle, was a man of great wealth and repute. So much so that when Jacob arrived in the east as he fled from the rage of Esau, his brother; the shepherds at the city gates knew who Laban was, as well as the state of his affairs. When the shepherds spoke about Laban, they also knew as a certainty, that as a matter of diligence and routine, Rachel his daughter, the shepherdess, would show up in the course of carrying out her daily business.

The first encounter we have of Rachel in the Scriptures is not on account of her beauty or lineage, but on account of her industry. The shepherds were so certain that Rachel would show up on the day and hour that they made bold to declare the same to Jacob; and true to their words, she showed up.

2 key traits that distinguished Rachel as a marketplace leader:

1. **Reputation and integrity** – We have been told that your character is who you are when you stand alone, while your reputation is who you are when others are watching. Your reputation is your 'front man' – it arrives before you eventually arrive. Take note that the shepherds spoke about Rachel on the basis of their encounters with her and nothing derogatory or malicious was said in her absence. Many profitable transactions have been aborted as a result of a lack of integrity. This is an irrefutable truth that our lives are like open books which many read.

2. **Consistency** – It is the seconds that make up the minutes; minutes make up hours; hours give way to days; days to weeks; weeks to months, and months to years. Yet, as miniscule as our seconds are, they have the capacity to derail an entire destiny. Seconds which are abused produce a lifetime of insignificance. It is the routines that we follow through consistently that eventually produce a life of significance and worth.

Rachel was not a 'once in a while' shepherdess. Her routine was consistent and predictable. She carried out her role in season and out of season. She did not show up at the well with the sheep occasionally. She did it every day. The shepherds assured Jacob that Rachel would show up with the sheep and she did.

It is one thing to look after your own enterprise and another to look after what belongs to another, as if it were yours.

The Bulldog Persistence that Gets Things Done!

"Women received their dead raised to life again: and others were tortured, not accepting deliverance; that they might obtain a better resurrection." Hebrews 11: 35

When God began to teach me about the women who received their dead back to life again, He spoke of this in the arena of prayer. He said prayer is such a potent force and likened it to the doggedness and persistence of a bulldog. In the place of prayer, strategic destiny exchanges are made. The word 'impossible' becomes non-existent as ungodly decrees are overruled and the unimaginable is turned into a reality. Prayer makes a mockery of sicknesses and diseases and turns negatives to positives.

Go Big or Go Home!

Jacob serves Laban for seven years in the hope that he would be given Rachel as a wife but instead, through the trickery of Laban, he is given Leah. He lives with Leah for seven years until he completes his week of service to receive Rachel, the one he truly loved. Then, the battle for destiny begins.

There is interplay of the spiritual and the physical. To the physical eyes, it is mere sibling rivalry, envy, and jealousy, but to the learned in the spirit, it is a battle for inheritance and territories. The two contenders – Rachel and Leah, are aware of the dynamics and are battle-ready.

From the interactions between Rachel and Leah, it was a battle for the heart (affection) and hand (inheritance) of Jacob. They both knew that there couldn't be true dominion without the presence of a seed. A seed guarantees a harvest and ensures that the cycle is preserved. Your seed is your access to your future. Considering the rage and the contentions that occurred between Rachel and Leah, it does seem to say, and rightly so, that the battle was for the production of a Joseph – the seed which would preserve Israel in the time of famine.

Things continued the way they were until Rachel said 'ENOUGH IS ENOUGH'!

It did appear that Leah was triumphing for a season until Rachel decided that the end to all contention and strife had come.

"And Rachel said, with great wrestlings have I wrestled with my sister, and I have prevailed..." (Genesis 30:8)

Next Steps

- Your destiny is under fire. Time will not change things in your favor until you arise and take charge. With time, you grow old, but by faith and prayer, you go up. Rachel did not arrive to a glorious ending by whining. Remember, she complained to Jacob about her inability to conceive and Jacob told her that he was not the one who had withheld conception from her. She had to take her case to the court of Heaven if she truly wanted to see any change, and she did just that.

- There is no vacant territory in life. You either plant the seeds you want to see germinate in your life, or expect to harvest weeds. Leah continued to prevail because she was not just involved in this battle; she was committed. Don't ever think for once in your life, that Satan is a passive investor, because he is not.

- It takes wrestling to prevail in life. One key lesson the Lord taught me was that any generation that refuses to engage in spiritual warfare, will ultimately produce dwarfs. Our lives on Earth are regulated by activities in the realm of the spirit. There is an active spirit realm. As spiritual beings, we have authority and access to trade in this arena and to prevail.

- You can develop a strong work ethic. The anointing should not be an excuse to condone laziness and mediocrity.

- Dead situations and circumstances can be made to come alive via the vehicle of prayer.

Apostolic Prayer

Father, I come to you through the blood of Jesus. I declare that my portion in life is secured by the word of God. I uproot any plant which you have not planted in my life. My life is not regulated by the whims and caprices of the enemy. I forcefully take back all that Satan the devil has stolen from me. I recover lost opportunities and profitable relationships. Thank you for my restoration in Jesus' name.

Apostolic Traits of Rachel

1. Rachel was a pacesetter, being the first woman in Scripture to be recorded as a shepherdess.
2. She was a builder of wealth and homes. She contributed immensely to the prosperity of Laban and is recorded in the book of Ruth as a builder of the home of Jacob.
3. She was a strong spiritual force. She prayed earnestly for children and God hearkened to her.
4. Rachel commanded the attention of both men and God.
5. She prayed until she saw the change she desired.

Affirmations

1. I declare that I enjoy the favor of both men and God.
2. I receive strength and grace for my God-ordained purpose and assignment.
3. Nothing dies or diminishes in my hands. I declare that everything I touch prospers.
4. I will be faithful with my little so I can receive much from God.
5. I speak an end to all strife and contentions around me. My inheritance is secured by the blood of Jesus.

CHAPTER 31

JUDITH: MENORAH OF LIGHT

By Karen S. Williams

"The time came to observe the winter Feast of Renewal in Jerusalem. Jesus walked into the temple area under Solomon's covered walkway when the Jewish leaders encircled him and said, "How much longer will you keep us in suspense? Tell us the truth and clarify this for us once and for all. Are you really the Messiah, the Anointed One?" Jesus answered them, "I have told you the truth already and you do not believe me. The proof of who I am is revealed by all the miracles that I do in the name of my Father." (John 10:22-25, The Passion Translation).

"Rescue us every time we face tribulation and set us free from the evil. For you are the King who rules with power and glory forever. Amen." (Matt. 6:13, The Passion Translation)

THE BEAUTY OF HANUKAH

During traditional winters, in the depths of December, Christian, Hebrew, and Messianic Jewish women can be found, during the Hebrew month of Kislev (December), lighting an eight-flamed menorah to commemorate Hanukah/Chanukah. The feast, known also as the Festival of Lights, annually celebrates the miracle of a lamp being lit by a continuous flow of pure olive oil within the Maccabean Temple once the temple was rescued from the Syrian-Greek army and rededicated to God in 186 B.C. A hallmark of these women's celebration of Hanukah included the annual re-telling of

165

the legend of a God-fearing Maccabean heroine named Judith (Jdt 8:6-8), a stunning widow and daughter of a Hasmonean priest whose exceptional sense of stratagem led to the defeat the Assyrian army.

Due to the centuries of debate regarding the historicity of the Judith legend, many contemporary Christian women know nothing of it. To date, the story has been relegated to the Septuagint, the Apocrypha's Book of Judith, and other extra-Biblical documents studied predominantly by Christians engaged in study of the Hebrew roots of Christianity, Eastern Orthodox Christianity, Catholicism, Judaism, and Messianic Judaism, particularly during the Hanukah season. A Wikipedia entry on the Book of Judith also indicates that some scholars even believe the Judith legend is a "parable of the first historical novel" to have been written. Still, the story is so popular it has spurred considerable study as a predecessor story and parallel to that of Jael and her victory over the Canaanite general, Sisera, in the Book of Judges.

Has the legend of Judith peaked your interest yet? If so, to follow is the story in a "proverbial nutshell."

THE LEGEND OF JUDITH

According to the legend and literature, during the second century, BCE, Nebuchadnezzar's army, led by the evil General Holofernes, waged siege against Bethulia, a town some scholars consider to be a pseudonym for Shechem. If felled by Assyria, the overtaken town would serve as the gateway to give Nebuchadnezzar control over Jerusalem. However, Judith, a respected community leader, was so concerned about the siege, she entered a season of fasting and prayer so that God would give her a strategy to deliver the town from Holofernes and his forces. (Jdt 13:7). Consequently, the legend says that Judith, after praying for God's strength, takes food and wine into Holofernes' tent and gets him so drunk, she's able to decapitate him with his own sword (Jdt. 13:8). Her feat is so surprising and daunting to the Assyrian army, the Israelite army is positioned in return to wage siege against Assyria and utterly defeat them.

JUDITH AND JESUS: AGENTS OF SUBVERSIVE SPIRITUAL WARFARE

In the initial Scripture passage in the beginning of anthology entry, we find Jesus confronting his Hebrew detractors while standing in the expansive colonnade and worship center that is Solomon's Porch, the same site where the healing of the lame man would take place during the Book of Acts. But the fact that I find most fascinating about this Scripture passage is that Jesus, during Hanukah, perhaps unbeknownst to himself at the time, was engaged in an act of subversive spiritual warfare during Kislev and the season of Hanukah, just as Judith was. Her wintry footsteps, entwined with his before the foundation of the world, and similarly themselves against Holofernes, the evil detractor of her day. Therefore, with that being the case, what can a contemporary Christian woman learn from the Judith legend? Consider the following practical Scripture-driven points below for that answer.

SEVEN PRACTICAL TAKEAWAYS FROM THE LEGEND OF JUDITH

- When your spiritual or natural winter is at its darkest, with Jesus, you can always dream again. Kislev in Hebrew culture is considered the month of dreams. It is also considered the month of visions. Therefore, whenever you need to find God within a dark and cold season, remember a woman sets her dreams in motion with her tongue. "And God said, let there be light, and there was light. God saw that the light was good, and he separated light from darkness" (Gen. 1:3-5).

- Holofernes in the Judith legend represents the culture of worldly evil. But the culture of the Kingdom has the surest cure or medicine for this. Take it. "Look, I give unto you power to tread on serpents and scorpions, and over all power of the enemy, and nothing shall by any means hurt you" (Luke 10:19).

- Captivity seasons may come, but they *come to pass*. There is always the opportunity for captivity to break in your life if you're a Believer because the spirit of the Lord is upon you and you are one of God's sent ones. "The Spirit of the Lord is on me, because He anointed me... He has sent me to proclaim deliverance to the captives..." (Luke 4:18).

- The hostility that Nebuchadnezzar, Holofernes, and the Assyrian army represented can enter your life if you open any door that encourages you to set your mind on your flesh. "... the mind set on the flesh is hostile toward God, for it does not subject itself to the law of God, for it is not even able to do so" (Rom. 8:7).

- Judith was a wise, prayerful, and fasting woman. She mourned the pending condition of the environment. During times of spiritual warfare in or outside of your home, God invites you to be and do the same. Your prayers are powerful. They can break through. "Thus, says the Lord of Hosts: Consider, and call for the mourning women to come; send for the skillful women to come" (Jer. 9:17).

- The evil Holofernes displayed and championed can wreak havoc on a woman's body as well as her current and future lifestyle if she chooses to embrace it. "Don't you realize that your body is a temple of the Holy Spirit, who lives in you and was given to you by God? You do not belong to yourself" (1 Cor. 6:19).

- Judith was known for her stunning beauty born of righteousness. You can be known for the same. Be sure to adorn yourself in the following and you will be just as beautiful. "I will rejoice greatly in the Lord, My soul will exult in my God, for He has clothed me with garments of salvation. He has wrapped me in a robe of righteousness... and as a bride adorns herself with her jewels" (Is. 61:10).

SEVEN PROPHETIC DECLARATIONS TO SPEAK OVER YOURSELF

- I am a menorah of light. Darkness can't overcome me. I bring the light of Jesus with me wherever I go.
- The walk Jesus has given me is a supernatural and subversive walk. Wherever I go, Jesus is with me. And wherever he is, Jesus always reigns.
- I am a prophetic and an apostolic woman. I can see that I am God's sent one. Where He leads, I follow. And I follow without hesitation.

- I refuse to entertain the ways of the flesh because I choose not to walk in ways of the flesh.
- My prayers are powerful. They carry the Breaker Anointing (Micah 2:13) in me. Jesus breaks open the way and always goes before me.
- My body belongs to God. I will not abuse it. Nor will I let anyone else abuse it.
- My souls rejoices in God. He adorns me with love. He is my precious Bridegroom. I am His precious Bride.

A SEALING PRAYER

Father, in the name of Jesus, I worship and adore you. Thank you for sharing with me the legend of Judith. Let me be as she was, a menorah light. Let me help my community to conquer evil's assault. But mostly, let me use my natural and spiritual gifts and talents to usher in your Kingdom wherever I go. For you are the Kingdom and the power and the glory forever and ever, Lord Jesus. Amen.

References:

Briffa, Salvino. More than You Imagine: A Journey with People of Faith. Alba House. New York. 1989.

The Book of Judith. The New American Bible with Study Helps. Thomas Nelson.

Manela, Jakir; Weinberg, Jessica; and Aromin,Noah. Gan HaShana. The Hebrew Calendar Garden: Grounding Ourselves in Jewish Time. Retrieved from the entry author's files.

Rocker, Simon. The Woman Who Cut Off A General's Head. Retrieved from https://www.thejhc.com

Wikipedia. The Book of Judith.

Jewish Women's Archives. Judith and the Hannukah Story. Retrieved from https://jwa.org/discover/throughoutheyear/december/judith.

BiblicalArchaeology.org. Judith: A Remarkable Heroine. Parts 1 &2. Retrieved from https://biblicalarchaeology.org/daily/people-cultures-in-the-bible/judith-a-remarkable-heroine.

NPR.Org. A Hidden Hanukkah Tale of a Woman, An Army and Some Killer Cheese. Retrieved from https://www.npr.org/sections/thesalt/2012/12/04/166486095/a-hidden-hammukah-take-of-a-woman-an-army-and-some-killer-cheese.

Bible Odyssey. Judith. Retrieved from https://bibleodyssey.org/en/people/main-articles/judith.

CHAPTER 32

JOCHEBED "YAHWEH IS GLORIOUS"

"Progression; Do not focus on present stature, but groom them for their future."

By Crystal Billingsley

"Soon I will die, "Joseph told his brothers, "but God will surely come to help you and lead you out of this land of Egypt He will bring you back to the land he solemnly promised to give to Abraham, to Isaac, and to Jacob." Genesis 50:24 NLT

The Israelite descendants clung to this promise…even after Joseph and his brother's generation ended. Rulership changed. A new king had taken the throne in Egypt, *"who knew nothing about Joseph or what he had done."* Exodus 1:8 NLT. Where did the information get dropped? How could this new king not know about Joseph's favor, administrative skills, and God-given wisdom that preserved the Egyptians as well as the Israelites from catastrophe? Did he take the time to read the hieroglyphs written on the stone tablets and walls? According to *Knowing the Bible* (written by Theologian Cory Baugher) - *"The statement "who did not know Joseph" means that this pharaoh has no knowledge of Egyptian history… This suggests that something of great significance in history has caused Joseph's acts to be erased and forgotten or that the current Pharaoh did not come from a traditional Egyptian background."*

The Israelites were flourishing and in the pharaoh's view of the future, this was a threat to his kingdom. Something had to be done. A plan was put in motion and executed quickly. The mission to revoke liberality and genocide was declared for all Hebrew male infants! What was a place of refuge soon transformed into a place of oppression.

Without notice, A woman named Jochebed, makes the choice to not allow her baby to be a victim, but to stand as an unflinching catalyst of change! Her story demands our attention to embrace the need for women who have apostolic strategies on how to protect prophetic seeds within God's "next" from spiritual genocide for generations to come.

A Fearless Heart!

> *"Oh, how great are God's riches and wisdom and knowledge! How impossible it is for us to understand his decisions and his ways! ... For everything comes from him and exists by his power and is intended for his glory. All glory to him forever! Amen."* Romans 11:33,36 NLT

Any mother facing such a decree that places her child in harm has two options…allow that child to become a victim of despair, or take self-action by becoming an unflinching catalyst of change for them and generations to come. This national threat of genocide was out of Jochebed's control, but NOT out of her jurisdiction…allow me to explain. As long as this male infant was still in her care, she still had her legal rights-she just had to be strategic. The Bible says, "She SAW that he was a special baby and kept him hidden for three months" (Emphasis added) Exodus 2:2 NLT.

We are in a time where God is calling fearless Apostolic Women to stop listening to the sound of threats knocking at our church doors and feeling hopeless! We must allow it to be the inspirational adrenaline needed for us to tap into a deeper grace level to get this generation through this securely. Jochebed could have allowed the threat on the outside to come into her home, but she utilized every minute she had to strategize an exit plan that only could be whispered by God into a fearless heart.

This is the inspiration that all apostles must carry when given the authority to protect God's "next" when it's in infancy, and a spiritual genocide is released—a fearless heart! Spiritual genocide is *a methodical massacre against a particular human race, religion, economic status or other distinctiveness.* Expect legalism, jealousy, mind control, and hatred against the change you carry in your house to show up at your doorstep. Each generation, or what I call, "special baby" added to the church comes with a different fight. We as women must use cutting-edge discernment on how to cradle "this" special baby and keep it hidden until due time. You must open your spiritual eyes; investigate what's within your "special baby" that God has called you to lead. Don't get caught up in everyone else's give-up…close your eyes and tap into your maternal instinct:

"There is no fear in love; but perfect love casteth out fear: because fear hath torment. He that feareth is not made perfect in love." 1 John 4:18 KJV

Whether you're a Woman Apostle or a woman in leadership, the church needs a rare apostolic trait: the GRACE TO STEWARD THE MYSTERIES OF GOD!

The Blueprint

"Blessed be the LORD my strength which teacheth my hands to war, and my fingers to fight…" Psalm 144:1

"But when she could no longer hide him she got a basket made of papyrus reeds and waterproofed it with tar and pitch. She put the baby in the basket and laid it among the reeds along the bank of the Nile River." Exodus 2:3 NLT

Jochebed is a solutionist. She teaches us how to handle generations: when they become too big to hide anymore, it's time to execute transition. This can be an entryway to fear, but you must have this as your mindset: Progression.

Time to start building with:

Papyrus Reed- *This was a resource which grew along the Nile River that the Egyptians used for writing material. Studies show that the papyrus reed can grow up to fifteen feet tall* (Holman Illustrated Bible Dictionary p.g. 1243). What shocked me is the cutting process: *Each reed was cut into twelve-inch sections and laid vertically and horizontally to make a sheet of paper* (Holman Illustrated Bible Dictionary). What does this reveal? That we must write apostolic decrees that are saturated with the blood of Jesus Christ, which renders protection. This is the basket that will carry our spiritual sons and daughters into purpose. What we write will have to be honored by the adversary.

Tar- When looking up this word, you will find *Bitumen*, which is asphalt. It is used as mortar when laying bricks during the building process and stands in as a binding agent (Holman Illustrated Bible Dictionary p.g.222). We must take prophetic promises from God towards His "next" generation and use them as mortar so that they will be unshakable in times of agitation sent to disrupt their faith during transition time.

Pitch- *This dark-colored substance can be viscous! It's a mixture used for waterproofing and extremely flammable!* (Holman Illustrated Bible Dictionary p.g 1301). We must waterproof the next generation with heavy fervent prayer so that it cannot be penetrated by anything else on the outside, as well as cover what has already been prophetically decreed!

Once using this blueprint to build the basket to their transition, you must do as Jochebed did-release it into the Nile river!

> *"She put the baby in the basket and laid it among the reeds along the bank of the Nile River... Soon Pharaoh's daughter came down to bathe in the river, and her attendants walked along the riverbank. When the princess saw the basket among the reeds, she sent her maid to get it for her. When the princess opened it, she saw the baby. The little boy was crying and she felt sorry for him. "This must be one of the Hebrews children," she said."* Exodus 2:3,5,6 NLT

Jochebed made an apostolic move; the grace to release one into purpose! She carried the grace to release God's vessel into his divine calling with the anointing as a resistant for where he was treading, and was an expert in knowing the timing.

Jochebed also placed this basket right where it could be seen; along the reeds, right where the pharaoh's daughter bathed in her devotion time to her goddess of life and healing (which to the Egyptians is the Nile River). Jochebed displays how apostles are to position sons and daughters into their place of training called "Purpose."

Jochebed challenged culture without saying a word!

"Then the baby's sister approached the princess. "Should I go and find one of the Hebrew women to nurse the baby for you?" She asked.

"Yes, do!" the princess replied. So the girl went and called the baby's mother. "Take this baby and nurse him for me," the princess told the baby's mother. "I will pay you for your help." So the woman took her baby home and nursed him. Later when the boy was older, his mother brought him back to Pharaoh's daughter, who adopted him as her own son. The princess named him Moses, for she explained, "I lifted him out of the water." 2:7-10 NLT

Jochebed teaches us the foundation of an apostle's heart-humility. She exhibits how to never become bitter when it's time for your "special baby" to go into their next level of training without you. The Bible says, *"Train up a child in the way he should go: and when he is old he will not depart from it."* Proverbs 22:6 KJV

And Moses did just that…

Summary:

1. When a life-threatening notice is given, decide to become the unflinching catalyst of change for generations to live.
2. Possess a fearless heart! This is the vessel needed for God to pour in the unmeasurable grace to steward the mysteries within your "special baby".
3. Seek God for cutting-edge discernment. Open up your eyes and be a destiny investigator.
4. Know when hiding season is over and start building with these spiritual materials: Apostolic Decrees, prophetic promises of God, and heavy fervent prayer.
5. Consistently carry the grace to release at the right the timing.
6. Position them for purpose.
7. Don't be bitter when they move to their next stage of training…they won't forget!

Prophetic Decree

I prophesy that you will rise up now, oh woman of God, and become passionate about the generation you are called to General…I dismantle the life-threatening decree that has been sent out against your mission and speak to your spirit to be strengthened and unflinching! I command fear to remove its grip from your heart and I speak to it and say, "Be fearless!"

For the Lord will give you cutting-edge discernment and spiritual instinct to protect destinies in infancy. I decree that you will make Apostolic moves by developing breakthrough decrees, pull down Heaven's bowl of prophetic promises to be poured out for generations to come, and cover your seeds with intense prayer so that they will be firewalls of protection against Satan's army—Be courageous.

Resources:

Scripture quotations marked KJV are from the King James Bible Version. Copyright© 1908, 1917, 1929, 1934, 1957, 1964, 1982, 1988 by Frank Charles Thompson. Used by permission. All rights reserved.

Scripture quotations marked NLT are from the *Holy Bible*, New Living Translation. Copyright© 1996, 2004, 2015 by Tyndale House Foundation. Used by permission of Tyndale House Publishers, Inc., Carol Stream, Illinois 60188. All rights reserved.

Baugher, C. (2004-2017). The Pharaohs of the Exodus. Retrieved from https://knowingthebible.net/the-pharaohs-of-the-exodus.

Holman Illustrated Bible Dictionary (pp. 222, 1243, 1301). Copyright© 2003 by Holman Bible Publishers. Nashville Tennessee. All rights reserved.

CHAPTER 33

MOTHER TERESA: SUBMISSION TO THE CALL

By Robinette D. Cross

Women have served as revolutionary figures in every society known to humankind. They are incubators of knowledge and forces of change who supplant regimes and lay new foundations. Mother Teresa's commitment to education, the establishment of a new religious order, and Godly confidence, anchor her as an apostolic woman. She galvanized Christians to take action in India and served, despite what pressures surrounded her in the slums of Calcutta or in the Church.

Mother Teresa's enduring spirit did not go untested. As she sojourned new paths, she was faced with pressures from both believers and non-believers. Her sisters in the convent could not understand why she chose to live amongst the poor when there was safety within their walls. Those who lived in the slums were initially unable to comprehend why a white woman would settle in their community and offer nothing but her assistance. Her commitment to demonstrating God's love propelled her into unfamiliar territory, but she maintained a posture of service. Mother Teresa is an example of what it looks like to submit to the call and firmly stand in a "nevertheless" positioning.

The Explanation

Most believers understand the sacrifice of submitting to purpose because we are all made to exact God's will on Earth. We are called to occupy mountains of influence for the Kingdom, but the assignments are tailored to individuals' gifts and talents.

Fewer are familiar with the "nevertheless" positioning. This is a posture that one must assume as they walk in Christ and are led by the Holy Spirit. It is something that must resonate in your soul and spout up when your flesh is overwhelmed, for it was the posture that Jesus donned in the Garden of Gethsemane. The twenty-sixth chapter of Matthew explains that, facing abuse and death, Jesus was consumed by sorrow and pleaded with God to take the bitter cup from him. However, in the same moment, he said, "...nevertheless not as I will, but as thou *wilt*". [13] The term "nevertheless" connotes an imperturbable spirit; one that will remain steadfast and not succumb to emotions. Likewise, Mother Teresa adopted a "nevertheless" positioning because her assignment transcended any sorrow she encountered.

The Experience

Mother Teresa of Calcutta was born Agnes Conxha Bojaxhiu in Skopje, Macedonia in 1910.[14] At the age of twelve, she was called by God, and answered without hesitation. She went to Ireland and joined the Sisters of Loreto, a convent that was known for its missions to India. It is no coincidence that she took her vows in India instead of Europe. She taught girls in Calcutta at St. Mary's High School for seventeen years.[15] It was there that she saw and heard the sufferings of the unwanted and oppressed; the sounds that vexed her continually, until she was called to meet their needs with God's help.

She decided to leave the convent and lay new foundations in the slums. Previously, she was protected by the walls of the school, but she needed to be a touchpoint for aid in the city. The decision was difficult because, to

---

[13] Matt 26:39.

[14] "Mother Teresa – Biographical", *The Nobel Prize Foundation*, last modified 2014, http://www.nobelprize.org/nobel_prizes/peace/laureates/1979/teresa-bio.htm.

[15] Ibid.

Indians in the slums, Mother Teresa resembled the oppressor. Initially, she was unwanted, even by those who were dismissed by their own society. India, for most of its existence, legally operated under a caste system and those who fell below the lowest level were considered "untouchables" and dismissed to live in slums.[16] They were the forgotten poor who were often left behind as society progressed. Moreover, India was still a colony of Britain when she arrived, and the hue of her skin looked like those who had subjugated its inhabitants for nearly 200 years.

Compounding her physical difference in an unwanted place, Mother Teresa also angered her sister nuns because she defied authority, usurped hierarchy, and refused to follow the protocol of the convent. Having lost the support of many of her sisters, surrounded by others who neither understood nor wanted her, and essentially penniless, Mother Teresa firmly stood in her "nevertheless" positioning to aggrandize the faith.

Although later findings in her personal letters and journal entries revealed how lonely she felt, Mother Teresa understood that the assignment superseded her emotions, even if she questioned it at times. The same is with us; although we may question God's plan in a particular season of our lives, the Word reminds us that *all* things work together for the good of those who love the Lord and are called according to *His* purpose.[17] Even when life seems like a whirlwind, remaining steadfast and in a "nevertheless" positioning assures that our circumstances must bend to the will of God in our lives. It is a byproduct of our reasonable service.

Upon moving into the slums, Mother Teresa started teaching children how to read. She used her medical skills to help heal and improve the lives of those who once hated her. She operated from a position of equanimity that

---

[16] The caste system was legally abolished in 1950. The abolition was greatly inspired by the persistence of Mahatma Gandhi in his lifetime, however, the social ramifications persist to this day. Hindus believe that people are born into one of four major castes and that those social statuses are fixed until they are reborn into a better or worse caste. The level of treatment and respect vary based on the caste into which one is born.

[17] Rom 8:28.

was so spiritually elevated that it broke down the walls of misunderstanding and mistrust. Her redoubtable acts were so infectious that former students began to follow her example of servant leadership.

Ultimately, Mother Teresa broke with the Sisters of Loreto and founded her own convent entitled the "Missionaries of Charity" in 1950. It garnered local and international support, enabling her to ensure that people who were cast aside were cared for and the terminally ill did not transition alone. Although she did not proselytize, her benevolence encouraged some Hindus to ask for salvation before they died, which was groundbreaking. The momentum that Mother Teresa created was so potent that the "Missionaries of Charity" was made an international society by decree of the Pope in 1965. [18] The Christian presence, although not dominant, is stronger in India because of her seminal actions.

Notwithstanding the notoriety of her work, Mother Teresa is a controversial figure because her letters and journal entries reveal that she questioned God and her mission. There were moments when she felt out of synch and bemused. This is neither uncommon nor unrealistic, as it happens to everyone. There are numerous examples in the Bible that discuss how people began to lose stamina, but God will restore your faith. The angels of mercy will tend to you and you will be replenished. Nevertheless, despite what she *felt*, Mother Teresa was resolute and carried out her assignment with a level of excellence that earned her a Nobel Peace Prize during her life, and elevated her to sainthood in death. She was canonized in 1997 and the "Missionaries of Charity" continues to amass support.

Substance

Mother Teresa was the paragon in this chapter to demonstrate that the call on your life may take you to places that you have never before seen.

- You will have to launch into the deep, and people may not like or agree with you. This must not stop you because there is a tsunami of

---

[18] "Mother Teresa – Biographical".

glory that awaits your "yes" to walk with God.

- You are created to reproduce God's excellence on Earth and to establish firm foundations.
- Your calling must resound and echo in the hearts of those who encounter you.
- Do not be afraid to challenge the established order if God has called you to complete something.
- Maintain a "nevertheless" positioning. Let everything that God asks of you be "yeah" and "amen". Petition the Holy Spirit daily for your assignment and do not fear. God will never task you with something that He has not already graced you to complete.
- If you are asking God for vision and direction, you must work while you wait and listen for the assignment to come. Habakkuk said, "I will stand upon my watch, and set me upon a tower, and will *watch* to see what he will say unto me…"[19] Mother Teresa always included what the Lord told her in her correspondence with the Church hierarchy. You are dispatched to keep your watch and work while you await the strategy. You are fit, equipped, and well-able to carry out the task.

Decrees & Affirmations

Spiritual decrees are legal affirmations that adhere to the thing, space, or being to which they are assigned, including you. I exercise my Heavenly authority and release the following decrees concerning you:

- Your prayers and deeds shall change the hearts of leaders.
- You shall not subdue your intellectual acumen for the benefit of others, but you will submit your mind and understanding to the knowledge of Christ and walk surefootedly in the path that God has set before you.
- You shall, without hesitation, sever the enemy's deception against you

---

[19] Hab 2:1. Habakkuk was a praying prophet who was a watchman (an intercessor). Many Christians are familiar with Habakkuk 2:2, which includes the phrase "write the vision and make it plain upon the tablets so they might run with it."

or those called to serve in the army of the Lord with the sword of the Spirit.

- You shall adopt a "nevertheless" positioning and submit your flesh to burn as a sweet aroma unto the Lord as you walk out His purposes and plans for your life daily.
- The vicissitudes of life cannot displace the anchoring of your soul.

CHAPTER 34

MARY MAGDALENE: HAVE YOU CONSIDERED THE COST?

By Bessie Foster

It hit my spirit this early morning about Mary Magdalene. Why did Jesus appear to her first (Mark 16:9)? Think about it! Beside serving and supporting the ministry like the other women (Matthew 27:56), Jesus didn't go see about his mother first. Why is Mary Magdalene different from the others or, even to say, what made her stand out more than the rest?

As we take a look at Mary, she was demon-possessed and suffered from infirmities (Luke 8:2). Then we see Mary as a servant. Even though this is part of Mary's makeup, what has my attention the most is that, in spite of all she went through and came out of, she rises to the position of an Apostle.

Mary could have stayed the way she was: demon-possessed and sickly, but she knew there was more to her life than what she saw and all that she had experienced. She could have stayed upset with her life, but something kept tugging at her heart. She decided it was more! She had a deep desire to surpass all the demons she was possessed with and decided to go beyond her circumstances. Do you have a desire to go beyond no matter what life has handed you? Do you have a desire to excel? If so, just as Mary made a conscious decision to go beyond, you can do the same.

She pushed past all the hurts, pain, rejection, and feeling sick in her body. Even as she would listen to Jesus' messages and watch him, she knew in her heart that he was different. She knew she needed to be free. She hungered for true love and for someone that wouldn't keep throwing her past up in her face. She needed someone to believe in her and to not take advantage of her. One that could give and show genuine love to her. Someone different! That was Jesus Christ; her Lord and Savior.

After being saved, Mary was bold even in the midst of persecution. Willing and knowing that by following Jesus there was no telling what could happen to her, yet she was willing to take that chance. She was so in love with him, that it didn't matter wherever Jesus went, she would follow even if it could cost her, her life. She would say "where you go, I will follow". Mary wasn't afraid at the crucifixion while his disciples disappeared out of fear (John 19:25). No matter the cost, she was not leaving Jesus.

I wonder how many of us would have kept following Jesus or if we would be like his disciples. Not Mary! I feel like she would follow him to the cross. She loved Jesus so very much. She worshipped him and adored him. She longed for him so, that Jesus stopped for a moment to see about her before going to his Father. He heard Mary's cry. He knew the cry of a true worshipper. She cried out for him with all of her heart. He knew how she longed for him. She told the gardener to just tell her where his body was. She didn't care if she needed to go by herself to get his body. All she wanted was Jesus.

Ask yourself and be honest. Do you want him more than you want anyone or anything else? Do you long for him in such a way that when you rise in the morning all you want and desire is him? Or do you just have him for Sunday morning service? Or as a quick fix for the problems you're dealing with. Not Mary! In spite of all life laid before Mary, all she wanted was Jesus.

She weeped so, that Jesus stopped and called her by name. She knew his voice and said "Rabboni". She knew it was her teacher, her Lord. At that moment she had so much peace and joy in her heart. To her surprise, he came just to see about her before going to his Father.

When we truly cry out to him, he will come to see about us. He will turn his ear to his worshippers and to those who really love him. Those who really love him want him for himself and not for what he can give and do for them. Love will make you rise in the morning for him. Taste and see how good he is at lunch. Then lay your head on his chest at night time to sleep. This is what Mary did. So yes, Jesus came to see her first and not his mother. Mary was now commissioned and sent on the Lord's assignment.

Mary was sent in Luke 24:10 to go tell the apostles (John 20:18) that he'd risen. Jesus knew he could trust Mary to do what he asked. That alone should make you think! You're asked to go handle some business, but find yourself making pit stops. You didn't go straight to handle the situation at hand, nor come straight back. Hm!

Mary continued to serve after Jesus died on the cross in spite of her pain and longing for him. She knew deep inside he was the Son of the Living God, the Messiah. So Mary kept serving, even in opposition. It didn't matter who accepted her or who rejected her. She kept on serving.

Even in times of opposition, rejection, hurt, and pain, we have to keep it moving through the Kingdom of God. We cannot stop because of people, things, nor opposition. At the end of the day, we have no excuse why we couldn't serve or, needless to say, why we couldn't do what was asked of us.

Obedience is very important! Mary heard the call and was obedient to him no matter what the cost was. She was commissioned and sent to do the work of an Apostle. She continued to minister to the unfortunate, the hurt, and wounded. She helped many and shared the Gospel of Jesus Christ with love and compassion that was pouring out of her heart—the love of Jesus Christ.

I feel many souls were saved. Many were delivered from devils and those that were oppressed. Many were healed and made whole. She was the vessel of his outstretched hand—a vessel of love, compassion, and peace that was given to her. She gave this back, which Jesus gave unto her.

I want to leave you with this one thing I loved the most. In spite of being demon-possessed and sickly, Mary still went beyond measure. She looked for her Deliverance and kept pressing toward the mark of the high calling in Christ. Even when she didn't understand why she went through all that she did and why her life seemed so meaningless. Mary along the line set her face like flint. She was determined that there had to be more to life than this. It didn't matter what Mary had done in her past, but she was coming out.

You need to know that regardless of what life has dealt you; you can come out and walk into your destiny. This is not your end! All you need to do is repent of your sins and return to your first love, Jesus Christ. Or even make him your Lord and Savior, be born again. Allow the Holy Spirit to lead you into destiny and stop driving the vehicle of your life. Let him take the steering wheel and drive you right down the correct path into destiny. He has the roadmap for your destiny.

And another thing, please forgive yourself. To be an Apostle of Jesus Christ, Mary had to walk in forgiveness. Know that whatever you have done in life, God still loves you.

Mary's Character Traits:

1. Determination to not stay in her circumstances.
2. Compassion she had for others.
3. Love that she showed toward others.
4. Boldness to share the Gospel of Jesus Christ.
5. Fearless to stand in the face of opposition.

My Prayer for you:

Is that I command your emotions and body to line up with the Word of God. That you are healed, filled, and sealed by the Holy Ghost. You are no accident, for you live and move and have your being in Him alone. For He has set your life up for the miraculous. You are God's workmanship, created in Christ Jesus unto good works which God has ordained that you should walk therein. Now be determined to press to the mark of the high calling of Christ. In Jesus' name, Amen!

CHAPTER 35

MARIA WOODWORTH ETTER: GRANDMOTHER OF THE PENTECOSTAL MOVEMENT

By Alandis Porter

"I have been in great dangers; many times not knowing when I would be shot down, either in the pulpit, or going to and from meetings…But I said I would never run, nor compromise. The Lord would always put His mighty power on me, so that He took all fear away, and made me like a giant…If in any way they had tried to shoot, or kill me, He would have struck them dead, and I sometimes told them so."
- Maria B. Woodworth Etter

In The Beginning

This powerhouse world-changer's life started off very humbly, filled with many trying moments that would prepare her for the walk ahead. Maria was born on July 22, 1844 to Samuel Lewis and Matilda Brittain Underwood. She was not initially raised in a Christian home, until 1854, when her parents became members of the Disciple church. Her childhood had been a bit tumultuous, but she suffered her greatest childhood loss when her father passed away from sunstroke in 1857. Her family's heart was a bit comforted when they found that he died in prayer for his family. Life now was extremely difficult in that, all old enough to work, they were no longer schooled and required to obtain jobs to help support the family.

Conversion and Call

As Maria continued attending services, at age thirteen, she gave her heart to the Lord and soon after, she received the call "to go the highways and hedges and gather the lost sheep". She did not realize at the time, the impact of the prayer of the minister that day for God to make her a shining light. Maria saw early on that this call was met with opposition in that the disciples did not allow women to work in the ministry. Maria, in the search to obey God, determined that her only way to answer His call was to marry and work in missions with her husband. So, she finished her education and then married Philo Harris Woodworth, with whom she bore six children. They fervently began farming. Then, the greatest of all tragedies hit their life, as in a few years Maria's health begin to fail as well as her children's, of whom five of the six ended in death, leaving her only with Elizabeth, "Lizzie".

Through it all, Maria still felt God was calling her to preach.

After a call to speak at a friend's meeting, Maria saw a vision from the Lord seeing many souls lost. That moment changed the course of her ministry. In the days that followed many in her meetings, many were led to the Lord and she planted two churches. This was not only a history-making moment for women, but her first Apostolic work.

From Pain to Power

As time passed, the farm failed and the couple decided to start a traveling ministry. However, the grief the couple suffered proved too much for Philo to bare and he began to look outside of their marriage. Maria journeyed on and became licensed as an Evangelist in 1884. This was rare for a woman, Maria continued to preach all over the Midwest and, once again, was led by God to begin to pray for the sick. This powerful move yielded crowds of up to 25,000. Her reputation also grew as her meetings became known places for power, healings, visions, and trances. She had truly become a pioneer of the faith! "But to whom much is given much is required". 1890-1900 were trying years for Maria.

The meetings made her life controversial because many had never witnessed

God's power in such a way. She was arrested after a Massachusetts meeting for claims of her healing people. She had to be released after many came forward with proven testimonies. Between 1890-1891, local psychiatrists filed suits against her after she experienced these "trances" as they called them, and said she saw visions and heard from God. More heartbreak came when her marriage ended in divorce in 1891 because of the continued public infidelity. Her ex-husband turned bitter and slandered Maria's name. He died a year after their divorce. The worst of it was when her denomination turned on her and pressured her to stop the meetings. She finally grew tired and gave up her Evangelist license and was left on her own.

A New Joy

This general never let trouble stop her from obeying the work God called her to. She started traveling wherever He opened the door. Maria was once again blessed to marry in 1902 to Samuel Etter. They worked together for several years and experienced one of the greatest moves in Pentecost history at a meeting in Dallas that lasted five months. She had become a true trailblazer for the Kingdom. Her latter years were spent at the Indianapolis Church Conference Center, which she started, and continued preaching well into her seventies. She went home to be with the Lord on September 16, 1924.

This Woman of God changed church history forever. She was 20 years ahead of the Pentecostal move worldwide, making her a true Apostolic example for all servant leaders to follow. I am honored to be one of those women, picking up the mantle, blazing the trail today.

(Here are five earmarks that made Maria's life and ministry apostolic)

5 EARMARKS OF APOSTOLIC PREACHING

1. Apostles do not promote their personal agendas, ministries, or ambitions when they minister. (2 Corinthians 4:5)
2. Apostles minister in fear, trembling, and weakness because they refuse to depend upon their wisdom or ability to speak eloquently to change lives. (1 Corinthians 2:1-3)

3. Apostles are completely obsessed and fascinated with the person of Jesus Christ and release revelation concerning his life, death, burial, resurrection, ascension, and second coming. (1 Corinthians 2:2)

4. Apostles minister in a demonstration of power, not so they can get rich, fill up a travel itinerary, and become drunk on their own pride and arrogance, but on the contrary, the signs, wonders, and miracles manifest so that people's faith and trust will not rely upon the apostle, but in Jesus Christ! (1 Corinthians 2:5)

5. Apostles consider themselves bondservants of Jesus Christ and walk in humility as they steward and minister the mysteries of God. (1 Corinthians 4:1)

Prayer

Father, we pray that every woman reading this anthology will be inspired and empowered to do Your will, Your way. Let them not be moved by any word or deed, no circumstances nor audience response to them.

Father, keep them by Your love and allow it to cover their every action and reaction. Let peace be their portion day by day. Grant them wisdom to care for their first ministries, their family, as well as caring for themselves. Father, let faith always be their guide and may they always be convinced that You will never fail and with do the impossible in Jesus' name, Amen.

It is my continued prayer that the army of Apostolic Women God has called for this season will stand boldly without compromise and declare:

1. I am a vessel and mouthpiece of God, governed by His Love.
2. I am not only obedient to God's command but also surrendered to His will.
3. I am not moved by my circumstances, but remain focused and faithful to my call.
4. I will remain humbled by God's grace and will allow Jesus to be at the foundation of all I do for Him.
5. I will always know that it is not by might nor by power, but only by God's spirit that the work is accomplished.

References:

Biography Maria Woodworth-Etter - Healing and Revival Press 2004
WWW,HEALINGANDREVIVAL.COM

God's generals – Maria Woodworth-Etter – YouTube/October 13, 2013

Signs and Wonders Maria Woodworth-Etter originally published: 1916

CHAPTER 36

APOSTLE MOM:
DR. ANNIE B. CAMPBELL-PITRE

By Cynthia Bolden Gardner

Introduction

Petite, delicate, soft-spoken, oozing the appearance of fragility and vulnerability, Apostle Mom was far from it! A virtuous woman, who can find, indeed! Proverbs 31. A portrait of grace, love, humility under fire, joy, patience, cross-bearing is this Apostle. Yet, she never lost sight of her femininity, character, and Adonai Jehovah.

She was a bundle of pure dunamis/exousia. Mother could dance, shout, lay hands, slay, run, preach, teach, sing, prophesy until the gold dust fell from Heaven's floor and not forget that she was a servant (Luke 17:10) and an heiress, in that order.

As demonstrated below, her most pronounced influence was in the Mountains of Religion, trailblazing from 1951 forward; Family, raising elders everywhere, and becoming a national ministry from a one-woman storefront; Economics, lifting the heads of the homeless, addicted, and prison-released everywhere, while establishing local ministries and businesses to service and elevate them; and Government, where she demonstrated the wisdom of Daniel and Joseph, as she was privately called and consulted by local and nationally-recognized officials.

Mother was born on September 21, 1924, in Longview, Texas. She landed in California, working in the aircraft industry and accepted Christ under

Bishop J.A. Blake, serving as his Pastor's Aid President at Greater Jackson Memorial COGIC in 1951.

She married her beloved Lawney Campbell, Jr. on January 25, 1952, and had one devout son, Minister Rodney Campbell and a revered godson in Bishop Carlton Pearson. Widowed in 1993, she remained single and celibate until she met and was courted a year by her second Lonnie, Bishop Pitre, who married her in 2005. He preceded her in death.

An avid learner and advocate of education, Apostle Mom absorbed every piece of educational material she laid sight on. Then Evangelist, 1976 birthed a Charles H. Mason Bible College teaching certificate; 1979 a Bachelor of Arts via Crenshaw Christian Center, San Diego, while earning various certificates from San Diego Evening College, San Diego City College, and the Educational Cultural Complex.

Extremely spiritually grounded and civic-oriented, she served as a traveling revivalist, led shut-ins, regularly fed the homeless, and brought many home. Mother's Board President for Bishop George McKinney, Deaconess, President of the Young Women's Christian Council, Prayer and Bible Band, Purity Class Sunday School Teacher, and State Representative.

Apostle Mom became District Den Mother for the Boy Scouts, active in the Urban League, voter registration, PTA President, and recipient of the J.F.Kennedy Award.

In September, 1983, Mother birthed Giving and Living for others Ministry, where her outreach included a thrift store as an avenue to meet and counsel alcoholics and addicts and feed children in 2005 with Lord's Gym. This was the same year she was consecrated Bishop. 2006 ushered in the founding of National Regeneration Christian Fellowship, and in 2014, after much wrangling, she was finally convinced to acknowledge her apostleship.

LESSONS FROM APOSTLE MOM'S LIFE

Apostle Mom filled the Apostolic Metron of Grace (God's favor). Though starting in ministry at 27, the Lord was indeed her light and salvation and she was not afraid (Psalms 27). She faithfully worked her way in subservience and God quietly caused her to rise from obscurity to a spiritual force with which to be reckoned.

The Leadership Metron (influence without complaint or competition) came at a tremendous price as she juggled work, her family, and fought using only prayer, the sword of the Spirit, and the shield of faith to gain the ascendancy (Ephesians 6). She never sought elevation. She never sought titles. They did not matter, as long as she was doing the will of the Lord.

In the area of Church & Apostolic Metrons, Mother strategically impacted San Diego on all economic levels through her various posts, stores, and ministries. Her regional and national levels' impact was far-reaching as she studiously developed and consecrated Bishops, while ordaining and/or mentoring hundreds of prophets, pastors, evangelists, and teachers, hosting revivals and conferences, especially for women.

Apostle Campbell-Pitre was no stranger to pain and ostracism. Yet, she knew God called her to raise nations through the giftings and offices of ministry (Ephesians 3-4), and nothing or nobody could dissuade her, not the Sanballats, Tobiahs, or Gershoms, to come down from 'repairing the wall' to which this female Nehemiah was assigned.

Insofar as the Movements Metron, Mother was uncharacteristically skilled at convincing men from all denominations to come together, create a Board or Council of Regional Bishops, and work together towards common goals that benefited the community.

She simultaneously mobilized our Bishops Council and churches throughout the United States, while infusing the regions with revivals, trainings, online education through ABC School of Ministry and School of Evangelism, impartations, ordinations, and starting new missions.

With regard to the Movements Metron, Apostle Mom implanted Apostolic DNA in women from all walks of life, empowering them, nurturing small, established, struggling churches and bolstered men, who craved her knowledge and guidance, respected her leadership, and loved her like a mother. Rodney and Bishop Carlton had more brothers and sisters in the 'shoe' than they could shake a stick at.

1. HOLINESS: Psalms 93:5; Luke 1:75; 2 Corinthians 7:1

Apostle Mom was far from judgmental. Sin was not tolerated. I John 1:8-10. Condemnation was not the route to salvation. Romans 8. She would grab you, scrub you down with the Word, and set you ablaze with the vision as she backed you up with constant intercession (Zechariah 3).

2. LOVE PERSONIFIED: Mark 14:1-9

Apostle's life was highlighted by a remarkable capacity to genuinely love those no one else would fool with. She reminded me of Christ's dealings with the woman taken in adultery. The old adage 'once bitten twice shy' never touched her.

Verbally abused and frequently maligned, Mom would simply dust herself off and go back into fellowship with her detractors, disarming, confusing, and eventually winning them over (John 7).

She embodied the selflessness of Christ and Paul, dying daily and gladly spending and being spent for the Kingdom. IF THE SHIP WAS SINKING OR BREAKING UP, SHE WOULD NOT CRY OUT (John 5, Luke 5, Acts 27:21-44). If Jesus didn't come, she didn't mind drowning because he knew what was best for her! Her love and trust were unconditional.

3. PERSISTENCE: Acts 21:1-13

Intractable, rugged, dogged determination was her holiness hallmarks. THE NATIONAL REGENERATION FELLOWSHIP OF CHRISTIAN CHURCHES was birthed after years of Apostle Mom sitting in a storefront alone, worshipping, praising God, and faithfully preparing and delivering Bible studies and sermons to an audience of one, 'because God said so.'.

Nothing caused her to waiver or quit. She was like the woman beseeching justice from the unrighteous judge (Luke 18: 2); Elijah demanding the widow's last supper (I Kings 17:8-16); the neighbor knocking to borrow bread, who received it because of his importunity; Elijah praying until the cloud showed up (I Kings 18:44-45), and the disciples toiling all night for fish (Luke 5), until she did.

4. RESILIENCE: Matthew 5:34; John 3:13; John 7

Mom was an army of one, letting her 'little light shine, shine, shine' at a time when there was tremendous resistance to women preachers, blacks, and black women in power in the church. She knew how to forgive. She completely leaned and depended upon God to open doors that no man could shut and shut doors behind her so the world could do her no harm.

She never responded to or retaliated in kind to her detractors (I Corinthians 4:12). She simply prayed for them (Matthew 5:44). If she saw or heard that her enemy was fallen, ill, broke, bereaved—she would be the 'First Response Team'. She would give her two fish and five loaves to the enemy with the same love and compassion as breaking her alabaster box for Christ's eventual burial.

Her compassion was as genuine as her laughter with the hecklers who criticized her for being so 'gullible'. Her love was contagious. David refused to fight Saul (I Samuel 26:9).

5. DEPENDENT HUMILITY: Mark 10:42-45; Mark 10:22-26

Apostle Mom was never self-reliant. Sometimes she 'counted the cost' in advance and still came up short (Luke 14:28). She would sigh, chuckle, and keep it moving.

She always communed, consulted with, leaned, and depended upon God. Her bed was ALWAYS covered with Bibles, books, and study aids, with her sitting up in it (Luke 18:10; John 13:23); She was Ruth in her reliance upon the grace of Boaz.

6. EXTRAORDINARY COMPASSION: Matthew 25:1-46

She had an indomitable Spirit for the downtrodden, rejects, homeless, youth, drug addicts, alcoholics, prostitutes, unwed mothers. She started a 'feed the children' program at Lyon's Gym and opened a thrift shop as a means to reach the underserved and by others' accounts, the undeserving. She was akin to the Good Samaritan and Abigail, the wife of churlish Nabal (I Samuel 25:3).

7. LOYALTY/DEVOTION: Acts 20:17-30

Apostle was 'ride or die' and loyal to a fault all of the way. Once she received you, no one could steer or jeer her away from supporting you. She was Jesus being ridiculed for hanging with the tax collectors, winebibbers, and harlots, and conversing with the woman at the well (John 4:14).

Apostle Mom knew that He that hath begun a good work in you will see it through until the day of completion. Most don't have the patience or stamina against ridicule to wait that long, but Mother did. She would never flee like the *John 10* hireling.

8. PRIVATE POWER PLAYER: John 3 Nicodemus; Acts 23:35; Acts 24:24-27; Acts 26

She worked in tandem with the Bridegroom in stealth mode in and out of positions of power as a prayer partner with many notables. Few were even aware she made the acquaintance of these high public and religious officials.

Many would send gifts, donations, show up when she preached or gave a conference, or suddenly drop by when they were in town. No one had a clue she was in their sphere of influence. Lives of millionaires were spared through her prayers and intervention, some knowing and still thankless. This was her legacy of Love.

CHAPTER 37

FROM DEMON-POSSESSED TO APOSTLE

By Joyce Stevens

History

Proof-texting female apostles, in the early church, requires paying attention to intricate Scriptural details. The interpretation of many Scriptures, although interesting, can be both complicated and controversial. We are learning from many writers of the Synoptic Gospels, as well as Paul's writings, that women played a very important role in the early church.

This is the case of our subject, Mary Magdalene. Mary lived in a small affluent town on the west bank of Galilee. Although the town was prosperous, she did not reap the benefits of that prosperity. Instead, she was locked in a world of oppression and delusion, being controlled by seven spirits. Even though the spirits are not specifically identified in our text, (Luke 8:2), I believe the seven spirits were low self-esteem, rejection, shame, resentment, religion, blame, and scorn. We see these spirits still in operation today as women of every age and race struggle while being exposed to a "cultural prison," of religious brainwashing, unhealthy relationships, and gender bias. Mary Magdalene also had other unspecified infirmities. Her life was probably one of daily turmoil. She wanted to fit in, but couldn't due to the daily disturbance of her constant companions. Her life was on hold and had no significance. She simply existed. She was WOMAN! Born in an era where a Jewish prayer, recited by men, stated: "Thanks to God that I was not born as a woman, dog or Gentile." Men would have rather been anything but a woman.

Historically, Mary Magdalene was assumed to be a prostitute, even though Scripture simply describes her as the woman delivered from seven demonic spirits. The writer of the Holy Scriptures did not omit this important fact, even though it is contrary to how Biblical writers typically reported their stories throughout Scripture. As an example, Rahab, the prostitute who ran a house of ill repute (Joshua 6:22-25), is an Old Testament character, who is listed among other faithful servants in New Testament Scripture. Most importantly, it is not the assumption that Mary may have been a prostitute that is of significance, but the reality of her healing from the seven spirits. She met a man from Galilee, who showed her the ultimate of respect. When he approached her, he called her by her name, Mary! Even the simple act of recognition was unfamiliar to her and warmed her heart. She probably, throughout her life, had been referred to by many names, instead of her given name.

As a matter of fact, she did not even have a patriarchal name, but was named after the town in which she lived. Who was this stranger that approached her so warmly? His approach gave her an unexpected feeling of self-worth.

Prayer of Thanksgiving:

Father, we thank you that we have not given up our hope. We're thankful that our love is the motivating factor to keep us following you. Father, you are our guide and keeper. We will stay with your Word which says you will never leave nor forsake us...Amen.

Women are Valid Witnesses

According to Webster's, "apostle" is defined as "one who is sent." Apostolos (Greek) "messenger," is someone sent out to do a specific task: Apostles are commissioned and sent.

Let us consider the writing of Paul, in Ephesians 4:11. *"It was He (God) who gave some apostles, some to be prophets, some to be evangelists, and some to be pastors and teachers, to prepare Gods people for works of service, so that the body of Christ, may be built up."*

Apostle Paul instructs us that it is God who gives some apostles. The Scripture very clearly explains why the five-fold ministry is so necessary. Its purpose is to prepare God's people for service; to build them up until they come to the unity in the faith, and in the knowledge of the Son of God, and become mature; attaining to the whole measure of the fullness of Christ.

It has been determined by Bible scholars that women during this era were not as important as their male counterparts. They were voiceless and powerless. However, these women had been with Jesus as he traveled, performed miracles, taught great teachings, and spent time in the synagogues. They also supported him financially.

Their dedication to Jesus was apparent through their acts of benevolence. Jesus treated them with respect and love despite cultural and societal norms.

Mary Magdalene was present with Jesus in this select group; listening to him teach the disciples, telling them of his impending death. It is no surprise that after the crucifixion, on resurrection morning, we find that Jesus appeared first to Mary Magdalene, of whom he had cast out seven demons. There are several accounts of this same event noted by the various Synoptic writers (Mark 15: 40-41, Mark 5 :1-11, Luke 24:1-11, Matthew 27: 56). These accounts all demonstrate that Mary was sent by the Master to tell of the resurrection.

Some of the qualifications of an apostle include:

a. Having a servant's heart
b. Being clothed with humility
c. Being an example of a leader to followers
d. Having spiritual authority
e. Being revelatory

Apostle to the Apostles

The apocryphal Gospel of Mary Magdalene chronicles Mary's appointment and establishment as an apostle over a large portion of the early Christian church. The Gospel of Thomas cites her as an equal to Peter who saw her as a rival. (Quotes from Dr. Lee Ann Marino, PHD; D.D) *Females in history.*" One might conclude, based on these qualifications of an apostle, that Mary was indeed, an apostle; one sent by Jesus. She shared the message of his resurrection with her fellow disciples, later known as The Apostles. Additionally, she had a servant's heart, as evidenced by her service to the Master.

Based on Scripture, we see a woman, delivered from demonic obsession, who used her healing to pour out to others in response to Jesus' extravagant grace. She was grateful to be a part of the band of followers who accompanied Jesus during his three-year ministry. The Mary Magdalene story reassures female apostles of the twenty-first century that God does not consider us subservient to our male counterparts, but uses our wounds and afflictions to make us great Kingdom messengers.

Women Arising

In recent months, the "Me Too" movement has emerged, causing a crippling effect in the universal marketplace, tearing down barriers which have been established for centuries by male-dominated thoughts and behaviors. Over the years, women have been viewed as sex objects, being maneuvered by lustful, thoughtless, male dominance, and exploitation. The movement has exposed the treatment of women and the plan of institutional manipulation. Men had not realized that women had finally reached a point of no return; a place where our history was not just our story, but was that which would be a catalyst to push us forward to a place of destiny and purpose. After decades and decades of standing in the shadows, living with the pain and wounds of degradation, someone had to break the silence.

Although the "Me Too" movement is a secular event, I believe many of the same behaviors have occurred from within the institution of the church as well. Women are fighting for their rightful place in the Kingdom, allowing their scars to be their greatest motivation. These women have chosen not to disgrace the church, but to unfold their wounds into a masterful work for the Master. In all these things, God receives the Glory!

Prayer

Father, I pray for women across this country and countries beyond our borders. I pray that we will arise and share the good news of the Gospel without fear or intimidation. Help us to speak your word with a sharpness that sets captives free. Help us to break the bondages that often shackle our minds and hinder our giftings from springing forth. I also pray that we recognize that we are a liberated group who are in place for such a time as this. Our gifts and ministries are now elevated and accelerated. Father, we pray for a humble heart and a transformed mind to fulfill our God-given destinies—In Jesus' name.

Declarations

I decree and declare I am the chosen of God.

I decree and declare that no spirit of darkness shall block or hinder my walk in Christ.

I decree and declare my life shall reflect my apostolic call.

I decree and declare that I have great grace and boldness to perform my task as an apostle.

I decree and declare that there is a finishing anointing on my life.

CHAPTER 38

HARRIET TUBMAN: AN APOSTOLIC PIONEER

By Apostle Paula R. Hines, D.D.

She was born Araminta "Minty" Ross on the plantation of Edward Brodess of Dorchester County, Maryland in 1820. Like many who God uses, Harriett Tubman had a name change later in life and became known as Harriet, after her mother. This would not be the only change of name for Harriet for, as she grew older, she would be known as General Tubman, the conductor of The Underground Railroad and affectionately called Black Moses. Like Moses, Harriet had a unique call and assignment from God. While history records her as an Abolitionist, even a blind man can see the Apostolic oil all over this Woman of God's life.

As with most Apostolic and Prophetic leaders, hindsight is the best view to witness the sending of God in Harriet's life for surely He was with her. The Christ-like attributes can be detected early in her life as she suffered beatings and cruelty at the hand of her slave master along with undue judgment. History has noted that one time she chose to wallow in the pen with pigs for five days to avoid the task master's whip. The violence that Harriet suffered young in life caused her permanent physical and emotional injuries. In one day, Harriet stated that she was whipped five times before breakfast. It is a well-known truth that Harriet Tubman incurred a head injury as a young woman when a slave owner threw a piece of metal at a runaway slave and it hit Harriet in the head instead. Others write the slave owner struck her in the head when she refused to help him restrain the runaway slave. Harriet experienced headaches and seizures from this injury, and she also began to receive dreams and visions from the Lord. I believe these dreams and visions were the beginning of Harriet's call, sending, and commission to secure freedom for herself and others.

Over the years, it is said that General Tubman secured freedom for over 300 slaves during a 10-year span. While other accounts say 70, I am certain that half have not been told. Harriet Tubman led many men, women, and children from the darkness to the light while risking her life and freedom. She had no regrets when holding a pistol to the head of double-minded slaves who wanted to return and jeopardize the freedom, well-being, and lives of others. As I prayed and spent time with God, the Holy Spirit allowed me to see Harriet Tubman's journey through dry and rugged lands. As God led and guided her path, the Lord connected her with allies He chose. The Lord taught her Kingdom strategies and warfare tactics to accomplish His work in her. God gave her Scriptures to quote like Psalm 119:105: "Thy word is a lamp unto my feet…", 2nd Tim 1:7: "For God has not given us a spirit of fear…", letting FAITH be the evidence of what she could not see.

The Gift of Healing was at work in and through Harriet to keep herself and her passengers well. The ability to hold fast and keep what the Lord had entrusted to her was a priority as she proudly told Fredrick Douglas, "I have not ever lost a passenger." My God!

Harriet understood the economy of the office she walked in. Not only did others give into the work, but she used her gift of cooking to make and sell chickens to aid her God-given efforts. When all else failed, Harriet Tubman operated under the pretense "the Lord will supply."

Harriet increased in these gifts during the Civil War and became a nurse and spy. General Tubman sold Union soldiers gingerbread, pie, and root beer, which she baked at night after her day's work. Harriet purchased a 25-acre piece of land in Auburn, NY where she built and founded a home for the elderly. Harriet learned early in life the blessing of collaboration and teamwork working with many to fulfill her God-given mandate of obtaining social equality, freedom, ensuring equal rights for women, and fighting against poverty.

While history has not shown us that Harriet found and led her own church, it has definitely witnessed to us that Harriet collaborated with other churches and supported work of the Lord. We can also reasonably assume the preacher in Harriet, as she encouraged and empowered those she led out of their Egypt when their faith was low, bodies tired, and bellies empty. One cannot teach faith without first having faith, and faith has come the same way throughout all generations, by hearing of the Word.

Like the Apostles in the Book of Acts, Harriet Tubman had freely received and freely she gave. Harriet had a sincere love for God and his people. She understood that God created mankind to be free to serve Him. The grace and favor on her life was evident to all.

Harriet's nurturing spirit gave peace and spiritual growth to many. After leading slaves to freedom, she mentored and counseled many as they acquired jobs, businesses, and income to support their families. She was a no-nonsense leader. Harriet changed the culture of a generation while educating slave owners who thought they could dictate the outcome of a people that were not their own. Like all good apostolic leaders, Harriet decoded the Scriptures to show men the error of their ways.

Harriet had a "such a time as this" anointing that will last throughout all time. Harriet's anointing would speak to this generation and compel a nation to honor a Trailblazer whose apostolic acts are current and remain relevant today. This General called Tubman who once was sold into bondage with this nation's currency will now be the face of that currency by the grace of God.

A Faithful God has spoken to a nation founded under Him, a nation who was asleep. The Lord has awakened concerning this servant that history calls "The Black Moses."

This "such a time as this" anointing is yet alive in the Earth today. This apostolic oil is ready to be poured out among the Lord's elect. Will you arise, oh, great woman of God, and stand under the spout of His horn? Will you position and posture yourself for this "such a time" anointing? Harriet did and you can too!

Harriet's Apostolic Traits

1. SENT ONE
2. Trailblazer/Pioneer
3. Her warrior spirit and faith in God
4. Changed the culture
5. Understood the power of collaboration
6. Spiritual Mother and Mentor
7. Founder and Establisher

Confess these Affirmations and Proclamations Over Your Life:

1. I affirm and proclaim that the blood of Jesus Christ has washed me, cleansed me, and propels me in the path of righteousness.
2. I affirm and proclaim that I am a WOG with apostolic purpose and destiny in Christ Jesus.
3. I affirm and proclaim that I walk with power, authority, grace, and favor.
4. I affirm and proclaim that the church of the Lord Jesus Christ is alive in me and on the rise for His glory!
5. I affirm and proclaim that wealth and riches are in my house to economize the work of the Lord.
6. I affirm and proclaim that FEAR will have no place in me and that nothing or no one will hinder me from finishing strong in the Lord.
7. I affirm and proclaim that the Love of Jesus Christ is the motivating factor of all I say and do.

Pray this Prayer of Faith:

Father, I thank you that you are no respecter of person. I thank you that this day I am empowered, encouraged, and enlightened in the things of You, I pray that Your will be done in me as Your Kingdom purpose, principles, methods, and mandate be made manifest in my life. I pray a divine hedge of protection around and about me. I come against all words of crop failure that have been spoken over my life and I receive a harvest of total success in You. I command all darkness and every unclean spirit to cease and desist from maneuvering against Your plans and intent for my ministry, family, and faith in the church and marketplace. Father, may the authentic Apostolic and Prophetic anointing be alive in and through me for Your glory. May the realization of Your word which declares that there is no male or female, no Jew or Gentile, nor slave or free, become a revelation in me today as never before. I will arise in You to the heights and depths of Your love now and forever more in Jesus' name I pray!

CHAPTER 39

THE MAKING OF AN APOSTOLIC QUEEN

By Bonnie Scott

Many are the afflictions of the righteous:
But the Lord delivereth him out of all. **Psalms 34:19**

Hadassah arrives on the scene playing the hand dealt her by God as an orphan of both parents being deceased. Taken in by the cousin Mordecai; raised as his very own daughter. Being thrust into the fire of spiritual affliction and suffering at a young, tender age in life; served for all intents and purposes the shaping and forming of becoming an apostolic woman met for the Master's use. Hadassah was fair, beautiful, and pleasant to look upon. Marked by the God-given distinctions to fulfill her allotted assignment to become Queen Esther. In view of the fact that Queen Vashti had refused to come before the king at Ahasuerus at this request; Memucan said to the king "let there be fair young virgins sought for the king." Immediately, King Ahasuerus agreed. Queen Vashti was ordered never to be brought before the king again.

Declaration/Affirmation

- Before you formed me in the belly, you knew me and you loved me more than anything or anybody, so I thank You, Father.
- Moreover whom He did predestinate, them He also called: and whom He called, them He also justified: and whom He justified, them He also glorified.

- But now, oh Lord, You are my Father, I am the clay, You Are the Potter; I am the work of Your hand.
- Many are called, but few are chosen. Thank You for choosing me and I totally surrender my life to You, Father.
- I will praise thee; for I am fearfully and wonderfully made; marvelous are Thy works; and that my soul may knoweth right well.

Prayer

Father, I thank you for having Your divine hand upon my life. You chose me before the foundation of this world and I am grateful for that. I yield my will to You. Take my body, soul, and spirit. I'm all Yours! Use my life as You see fit. I decree that You may increase in my life; thank You for loving and choosing me. Cause the apostolic anointing to flow in my life so You may be glorified. Amen.

The Apostolic Traits of Being Yielded to Holy Spirit.

Psalm 141: *8 But mine eyes are unto thee, O God the Lord: other is my trust; leave not my soul destitute.*

After King Ahasuerus remembered what Vashti had done and the decree against her; the gathering up of all the fair young virgins was set in motion. Esther, showing one of her strong traits of being a being an Apostolic Woman, simply yielded herself to the situation. But before departing her cousin/father-figure in life, Mordecai, charged her not to reveal her true identity as a Jew.

Thus, he called her by the name Esther. Strong's definition: H635 of Persian derivation; Ester, the Jewish heroine: Esther. She was one among the young virgins captured and brought into the custody of the king's chamberlain. He was keeper of the women. Most apostolic identities are concealed and hidden by God until He decides to manifest Himself through them. We are His workmanship; Strong's definition G 4161 a product; i.e. fabric (literally or figuratively): things that are made, workmanship. Another strong trait or characteristic of being apostolic is living in the understanding of the Revelation of Ephesians 1:5

Having predestined us unto the adoption of the children by Jesus Christ himself, according to the good pleasure of his will. Surrendering your life and will to your Heavenly Father is much easier because you are now walking in the Revelation that is His good pleasure that He delights in your yielded pliable will to Him. During certain seasons, you must remain humbly hidden lest you hinder His plans for your life. Could you imagine being swept away by strangers and taken to a strange place with people you've never met? God chose Esther for that assignment and she went willingly. How amazing is that!

Declaration/Affirmation

My love for You, Father, and desire to do Your will is as strong as the air that I breathe. You are my oxygen the ruwach wind that I inhale to live.

- In You I live, move, and have my being.
- Holy Spirit, you are the true revealer. Open the eyes of my understanding and sharpen my discernment.
- I walk in the spirit because I am Apostolic and a son of God.
- Teach me to do Thy will for Thou art my God, Thy Spirit is good. Lead me into the land of uprightness.
- Nothing can separate me from my Lord; though He slay me, I will forever serve Him.

Prayer

Father, in the name of Jesus I thank you that I am growing stronger daily. You have given me grace with the ability to lay down my life and to die to the things of this world. You've given me a desire to do Your will and I thank You, Father, my strength is in You and not of myself. Amen.

Timing is Everything!

Ecclesiastes 3:1 *To everything there is a season, and time to every purpose under the heaven.*

The time has come that God may use His secret weapon that He had chosen a to sit on the throne as an Apostolic Queen. A decree has been sent out to kill all the Jews and Mordecai tells Queen Esther to go to the king. But there's a small situation; she must be invited by the king or if she comes unannounced he must extend his scepter towards her or she's put to death. Immediately, she calls for the Jews to fast for her and has all her maidens fast with her as well for three days and nights. She prepared herself spiritually to go before King Ahasuerus. Her most famous quote is "If I perish I perish". She needed to see the king. Queen Esther courageously put her life on the line. She was born to do this; God had prepared an Apostolic Queen for such a time as this. This was a kiros moment! Meaning a propitious moment for decision or action and a time when conditions are right for the accomplishment of a crucial action: the opportune and decisive moment. God hid His treasure in an earthen vessel! He knew she would lay her life down to do His will. Can He count on you? Are you willing to lay your dreams and desires down to fulfill the will of God? Are you willing to say, "send me, Father, I will go!" He wants your yes; over and over again!

Declarations/Affirmations

- You have given me favor with You, God and man.
- I am an Apostolic woman of God and great is my faith.
- I walk in authority and holy boldness.
- I'm wise as a serpent and humble as a dove.
- You are my shield and buckler. I fear no evil because You are with me.

Prayer

Father, I thank you for your unfailing love. You will never forsake me nor leave me. You said if I draw nigh unto you that you would draw nigh unto me so I thank you. Your holy angels are encamped about me. One can chase a thousand and two can put ten thousand to flight, so I called on holy intercessors; picking me up in the realm of the spirit to join forces with me against all spirits of darkness. I thank you, Father, because you always hear me! Amen.

CHAPTER 40

LYDIA: THE WOMAN OF PURPLE

By Shevon White-Sampson

She was an affluent businesswoman. She was a worshiper of God.
She was hospitable and a woman with strong discernment. She was
all of that-AND-a sower of great seed!

Like countless other heroic apostolic women on the frontlines, Lydia was one that used her time, talents, and resources to advance God's Kingdom in the European nations, specifically in the ancient Greek city called Thyatira. Her story is told in Acts chapter 16. Lydia was a businesswoman that sold purple. In her era, sellers of purple sold either purple dye or textiles. Whichever type of purple she sold, she conducted her business with integrity. Most of all, she was an example of a businesswoman who made a conscious decision to seek first the Kingdom of God. This was apparent in how she frequently made her adoration toward God by the riverside. She had not accepted Christ, had not yet heard the Gospel until she met Paula and Silas, but she knew God.

God's Spirit led her to worship at a place of prayer near the river outside of Philippi. As Lydia and other women gathered by the river bank to worship God regularly, I believe wholeheartedly that God saw the sincerity of their hearts, how they persisted to be in His presence, so He connected Lydia to His yielded vessel named Paul.

The Bible is clear that God looks at the heart of man.
I, the Lord, search the heart, I test the mind, Even to give every man according to

his ways, According to the fruit of his doings. (Jeremiah 17:10 NKJV)

I am persuaded that the God that knows all and sees all had Lydia in mind when He spoke to Paul through a dream to go over to Macedonia to speak the Gospel. Her story is a true example of how God will go out of His way to make sure that not one of His sheep would be left in the dark regarding the love He had for us and was demonstrated through the price that He allowed His only son, King Jesus, to pay for us.

The Bible declares in John 10:4-6, *"And when he putteth forth his own sheep, he goeth before them, and the sheep follow him: for they know his voice. And a stranger will they not follow, but will flee from him: for they know not the voice of strangers."*

It was the spirit of God that guided Lydia to extending her hospitable nature as well as her home toward Paul and Silas for shelter. God spoke in Lydia's heart to provide shelter for the two of them. By Lydia's obeying the voice of God and extending her home, she earned her place in Biblical history as a businesswoman that was wealthy and still found time to honor God through obedience. Lydia understood that God blesses us to be a steward of His earthly possessions so that we are ready, willing, and able to be a blessing in a time of need.

Through the lens of the life of Lydia we can understand what the Bible is referring to when it says, "For my thoughts are not your thoughts, neither are your ways my ways," declares the Lord. "As the heavens are higher than the earth, so are my ways higher than your ways and my thoughts than your thoughts."

As evident in the writings regarding Lydia, the plans of God were higher than her plans. Lydia may have thought that offering her home was just a small gesture of kindness, but God may have viewed her as being on assignment on Earth to offer shelter to His children as they traveled to deliver the good news of Christ to a whole nation that had not heard the Gospel.

Lydia's life reminds us never to minimize or discount the still small voice of the Holy Spirit and not to ignore the light (or even heavy) tugs on our hearts when God is nudging us to do something, even if it seems small or insignificant in our eyes. That small task could be linked to an entire nation. I encourage you to press into worship no matter how your situation may look. As we can see from Lydia's life, we could be going about our regularly scheduled routine and have a God-ordained encounter in the blink of an eye. Lastly, I encourage you to stay the course and follow the voice of the Holy Spirit who is the comforter and guide.

Lydia Stood Out as a Trailblazer

- Lydia chose to seek first the Kingdom of God
- Lydia had a pure heart that God could open and flow out from
- Lydia was a sower of seed who obeyed the voice of the Lord
- Lydia was diligent in her business affairs and managed with integrity
- Lydia was a child of God who knew how to operate in the world system as a businesswoman, while simultaneously honoring God.

Prayer:

Dear Heavenly Father,

I believe and declare that, like Lydia, my heart is open to You. I seek Your face, Your still small voice, Your light on my path, and Your direction in my life. I ask You to guide me to the right place to receive a blessing and to be a blessing according to Your will and purpose for my life. Proverbs 18:21 tells us that life and death are in the power of our tongues. Therefore, I chose life and declare the following over my life according to Your Word:

- According to John 4:24, I am a worshiper who worships the Lord in spirit and truth.
- According to John 10:4-6, I hear the Lord's voice and do not follow strange voices.
- According to Psalms 32:8, I am being guided with God's eyes in the way that I should go. I will arrive there on time, and I will not miss my God-ordained opportunities.
- According to Hebrews 13:16, You are pleased with me, and You bless me so that I can bless others.

- According to Ephesians 6:10, I am strong in the Lord.
- According to Jeremiah 29:11, I know You have plans to prosper me, to give me a hope and a future.
- According to Philippians 3:14, You encourage me to press toward the mark of the high calling of God in Christ Jesus.
- According to Psalm 23:6, Your goodness and mercy shall follow me all the days of my life. I need not worry, You care for me. I can live a balanced life, be successful, prosperous, and overcome every obstacle because You are with me.

I am anointed, talented, and have grace for this season of my life. Like Lydia, I wear purple, because I have royal blood of the King of Kings flowing through my veins. I wear a robe of righteousness, but not my righteousness. I wear the righteousness of Christ. My DNA is Heavenly, and I wear a crown of favor in all that I do. I am a child of the Most High God and a valuable member of His family, fearfully and wonderfully made. Like Lydia, I sow into the Kingdom and honor God. In the mighty Name of Jesus, Amen.

CHAPTER 41

DEBORAH: AN APOSTOLIC PROTOTYPE

By Noreen Henry

The Book of Judges is about judges leading and ruling Israel. After the death of Joshua, God raised up judges to lead and rule. Deborah is in Judges 4 & 5 and became Israel's judge in the third period. She was the fourth judge, and was the only *female* judge of Israel. In fact, my research says that she is the only female judge mentioned in the Bible.

A Quick Synopsis of Deborah in Judges:

Judges 4 begins with Israel doing evil in the sight of the Lord. Because Israel did evil in the sight of the Lord, they fell into the hand of Jabin, who was the king of Canaan; and the commander of Jabin's army was Sisera.

The children of Israel were oppressed for 20 years by Jabin and cried out to the Lord for help. In that time, Deborah was judging Israel. She sat under a palm tree where she held court and the children of Israel came to her for judgment.

When Israel was being oppressed by Jabin, Deborah sent and called for Barak and said to him, "has not the Lord God of Israel commanded 'Go and deploy *troops* to prepare for battle; take with you ten thousand men; ⁷ and against you I will deploy Sisera, the commander of Jabin's army; and I will deliver him into your hand'" making sure you win the battle. ⁸ And <u>Barak said to her</u>, "If you will go with me, then I will go; but if you will not go with me, I will not go!" [Note: *This shows that men need women, they can't do without us . Another thing to note is that Deborah was the one that sent for Barak.*

216

If she didn't send for him to go to war, they'd have continued to be oppressed. Women are so wise and powerful at leading] ⁹So Deborah said, "I will surely go with you; but understand, there will be no glory for you in the journey you are taking because the Lord will sell Sisera into the hand of a woman."

> *[Note: The level of Deborah's spiritual authority is demonstrated after she summons warrior leader Barak. Deborah tells Barak to fight their enemy, Sisera, because the Lord revealed to her, "I will give him into your hand." And Barak's response is "if you will go with me, then I will go, but if you will not go with me, I will not." He was not willing to go into battle without her. Deborah was the one willing to go to war, and she let Barak know that his decision would mean he would forfeit any credit by saying, "I will surely go with you, nevertheless, the honor shall not be yours on the journey you are about to take, for the Lord will sell Sisera into the hands of a woman* (Judges 4:9)]

To conclude, Israel had the victory and God delivered Israel and subdued Jabin in the presence of the children of Israel. They destroyed King Jabin and Sisera (Jabin's commander of the army), actually escaped, but was destroyed at the hand of another woman named Jael. Note that Barak did not kill Sisera, but Jael did. Deborah had prophesied that this is what would happen (see Judges 4:9b). What Jael did was an act of courage, determination, and fulfillment of God's will. Jael destroyed the enemy. After the battle was won, Deborah wrote a victory song, see Judges 5. And the land was quiet and had rest for 40 years, due to Deborah's ministry.

That's the gist of how the children of Israel were delivered at the hand of a woman, Deborah, and also Jael. *How is God using us to deliver others? Is He even using us?*

Who is Deborah?

Deborah was a heroic woman of history, who possessed many talents. Deborah was a:

- wife
- mother
- prophetess

- judge
- poetess
- singer
- political leader

The name Deborah means: "Bee", as in bumble bee. *[This is an important piece of information to note when studying Bible personality, as a name usually indicates a person's character or their prophetic destiny]*

Deborah, based on her name, is quite an appealing role model because of how bees operate. Bees are intelligent, hardworking, and are busy focusing on their appointed task. Bees are no-nonsense creatures that gets results. The bees' industry is delightfully fruitful. Deborah is like the bee in that she was intelligent, hardworking, and focused on the appointed task and had a great, fruitful harvest.

Why Did God Choose Deborah?

Deborah didn't choose herself. She was called by God, and she didn't neglect or compromise her call from God. One reason God chose Deborah was that she had a remarkable relationship with Him. Another reason is that she was a yielded vessel for Him to use. Apart from having a remarkable relationship with God, Deborah possessed many leadership qualities:

*Special abilities as a mediator, advisor, and counselor;
*Deborah planned, directed, and delegated;
*Deborah was the leader of the nation of Israel and helped to settle disputes;
*Deborah was a prophetess who gave the nation of Israel directions from God;
*She wrote songs;
*She was well-respected by all the people;
*She was active and effective in God's service;
*She confronted wrongs;
*She took action to help others;
*She had wonderful influence; and,

*God used Deborah to bring the erring nation of Israel back to the right way, she led the nation of Israel.

Deborah was a prophet and judge in Israel during the time when Jabin terrorized the Hebrews. In spite of this, year after year, Deborah sat under a palm tree, and people flocked to her for judgments and wisdom.

More of Deborah's Wisdom:

- Deborah knew who fought against Israel [this shows we are to know our enemies].
- Deborah knew who fought for Israel [this is showing to know our friends, know who has our backs]; and,
- Deborah observed who kept away and did not side with Israel [knowing who is not a real enemy but keeping away because of fear or trouble, the love of ease, or not caring, etc. Isn't that what some of us do, choose the easy way out, not caring to confront…?]

My studies show that Deborah's own soul fought against Israel's enemies [meaning, when the soul is employed in holy exercises, and heart-work is made of them, through the grace of God, the strength of our spiritual enemies will be trodden down, and will fall before us].

Deborah's Apostolic Traits:

- Deborah was a godly woman, she had great faith, and was a woman of wisdom
- Deborah possessed a keen sense of discernment
- Deborah believed in the God of Heaven and had courage to follow God's commands, and properly used her tongue
- Deborah demonstrated wonderful influence, and was a source for "peace"

These are all great traits to aspire to. I'm not saying that we don't already have them, but that we have to keep in mind to make sure our traits are affecting others in a positive way.

How do we emulate Deborah's life and character? Is it even possible for us to emulate someone with so many talents?

As Deborah was to the Israelites, so we are to be with others.

Some Things to Do:

- Pray for the salvation of others.
- Live righteously and let our light so shine forth that others will be drawn to Jesus.
- Prophesy to others: uplifting, edifying, and comforting them.
- Confront wrongs and settle disputes positively.

What is fascinating with Deborah is that women were largely subordinate to men, and she didn't allow that to hinder her. Deborah had to have been a remarkable woman to win the respect and admiration of so many, and she must have had a very strong and reassuring presence for Barak to demand her company as he went into battle.

Deborah must have possessed profound wisdom to draw Hebrews from all over Israel for her judgments and wisdom.

- Even her song of victory reflects greatness—my research says that it is considered by many as one of the finest specimens of ancient Hebrew poetry in existence.
- Deborah made herself available to God, and God used her to achieve great things.
- God needs yielded vessels to do His work on Earth, and, there is much work to be done.
- With Deborah's great leadership skills, and her remarkable relationship with God, the insight and confidence God gave this woman, Deborah, placed her in a unique position in the Old Testament. Deborah is among the outstanding wo men of history.
- Deborah's story shows that she was not power-hungry, she was humble. She wanted to serve God, bottom line. Whenever praise came her way, she gave God the credit.

Deborah didn't deny or resist her position in the culture as a woman and wife, but she never allowed herself to be hindered by it either. She didn't allow the fact that she was a woman prevent her from her ministry. Her story also shows that God can accomplish great things through people who are willing to be led by Him. *[Are we?]*

The practical lessons from Deborah's life emphasize the critical role that women have in the world today. God's cause needs women to overcome crisis and to serve.

I encourage the studying of Deborah. Delving deeper into it to get a better understanding and revelation of why women *can* emulate her character.

Affirmations/Declarations:

*I have a great relationship with the Lord and I am full of God's wisdom.
*I am prophetic and I flow in it, and I declare that my discernment increases daily.
*I am a yielded vessel to do the work of the Lord.
*I am intelligent, hard-working, and focused, and I am well-organized, and I plan, direct, and delegate wisely.
*I declare that I am a great mediator, advisor, and counselor.
*I declare that I am a leader that leads after God's own heart.
*I declare that my influence is widely received and heed is taken to it.
*I declare that I am a legacy-changer and a world-changer.

CHAPTER 42

CALL ME ABBY—QUEEN OF ISRAEL

By Jessica R. Jackson

Abigail—not the first individual we visualize when we think of a Biblical or modern-day apostle. Obviously, she's a woman and, in some circles, that disqualifies her in the eyes of many for any office, let alone the apostolic. Apostles serve as ambassadors called to protect citizens, represent the nation, and work for peace. Our Abigail is sent to protect, represent, and keep the peace and do the work of an apostle.

When reading the Biblical accounts of the future Queen of Israel, one can't help but notice the briefness of her story when compared to Hannah, Deborah, and Esther. The heart of Abigail's journey is summarized in one chapter, 1 Samuel 25, and we see a few references to her later in the Scriptures. In terms of major or minor Biblical characters, Abigail is minor—a short story. Thankfully, it's the strength of her character that earned her a page in the greatest story ever told. Her narrative impacted the lives of many, shifting history and earning her a crown. For the sake of this dialogue, let's read between the lines. Abby, as the family may have called her, was beautiful and wise. She was trained in Jewish customs, history, and traditions.

Abby was versed in how to maintain a godly home and to use His character to maintain relationships. Her marriage was arranged to a wealthy man from the line of Caleb named Nabal. Nabal means "foolish" or "senseless," but he was rich and affluent – a rancher and a cattleman. Nabal had the right ingredients and the makings of a perfect husband. As years passed, the marriage lost its savor. Nabal was a drunken wretch of a husband. He was amply named a fool based on his deeds and choices. Poor Abby couldn't even follow her man of God as he followed Christ, but Abby, like many in the household of faith, was content in whatever state she was in until God came to reveal her true hidden purpose.

A sudden call from the Lord required Abby to intervene on behalf of His children. Abigail's story leads to an encounter with greatness in the making, future King David. She averts countless lives being lost in a needless bloodbath because of egos. Abigail becomes an Ambassador, providing governmental legislation for the salvation of a people. Her courage and obedience miraculously delivered her into greatness.

The future king of Israel, David, is on the run from present King Saul seeking to kill him. He and his men are resting in the wilderness of Paran and stumble upon Nabal's shepherds tending to his livestock. They protect the livestock and the men from Nabal's camp, preventing any harm. Later, during the time of a festival, David sends to Nabal for provisions to feed his men and himself. And why not? He should be due some type of blessing. Unfortunately, Nabal, blinded by pride and bad character, refuses to give David and his men anything from his table. He makes a public insult in response to David's request. David's anger is kindled and operating under the influence of offense. David tells his men to put on their swords and purposes to kill Nabal and all the males. A mass genocide of innocent blood was about to take place because of the foolish actions of one man filled with pride.

A servant observed the dialogue between Nabal and David, even David's fury at the disrespect in Nabal's reply to his request. The young man warned Nabal of David's plans for the people. Abby desires to save and spare the people from the curse instigated by the actions of her husband's rashness. I believe the Holy Spirit began to activate the anointing of diplomacy in her life. Abby gathers gifts of wine, grain, prepared meat, and cakes of figs to take to the furious David. Riding her donkey, Abby sees David, leaps off, and falls on her face before him. Abby respectfully and courteously uses diplomacy to intercede on behalf of the people. Next,

Abby prophetically declares in her appeal that there will be a lasting empire for the future king. The moment is reiterated later in Scripture by Nathan and agrees with Abigail's humble words.

Abby recognizes the anointing on this man of God's life, in 1 Samuel 25:28 she declares, "the Lord will certainly make my lord (David) a sure house or an enduring house". Acting as an apostolic ambassador, she rightfully discerns the times and the coming end of King Saul's reign. David is persuaded by her soft answer and it turns his wrath. He blesses God for sending her his way and receives her offerings then sends her home in peace.

Abby returns home after obtaining favor. She finds Nabal incapable of even hearing, let alone understanding what has taken place. He had been feasting like a king and is in a drunken stupor, oblivious to the pending devastation he's set in motion. Alone, Abby decides to rest and sleeps, waiting to discuss the day's adventures when Nabal sobers up. The next morning Nabal listens to his wife's account of all that transpired on the previous day. He's so stunned, Scripture tells us Nabal's heart dies within him; he suffers a stroke. Many believe it was due to the sudden realization of the danger his conduct has put him in. David hears the news of Nabal's death and quickly marries Abigail, remembering all that she brought from her hand.

In Abby's story, God desires to show you how to walk through the situations of life while allowing them to shape you for future Kingdom use. Women and men of God let us look at the lesson Abby taught us on her way to becoming a member of the royal court.

I. Abigail could have easily surmised that if David killed Nabal it would mean the end of her troubles. The end to a marriage possibly filled with days of cruelty and abuse. But, Abigail chose to consider the welfare of Nabal. Saints must always replicate Christ and consider others before themselves.

   o *We declare that you will not think it is robbery to be counted equal with God and lay aside your agendas so that Christ's will might be done.*

II. Abigail demonstrated the proper response to the wounds and bruises one receives in life. She swore to her own hurt and changed not. Her concerns for the needs of others outweighed her safety. The servant and David witnessed Abigail's heart and compassion for others...making her approachable.

- o *We decree that past wounds and bruises will not make you bitter but better allowing you to rise and pull-down strongholds. We declare that out of your bellies will flow rivers of living water to bring life to others.*

III. Abigail humbled herself and allowed godly character guided by wisdom to show her how to appeal to authority. She observed all she was taught and allowed her actions to be guided by the Holy Spirit produce an expected end.

- o *We decree and declare you will walk in wisdom and render honor where honor is due and obey those who have rule over you.*

IV. Abigail continued to mature despite her environment being a place of limitation and obscurity. She observed Nabal's bad behavior enough to recognize it and not repeat it. Faithful and committed to her vows, Abigail went through her processing in preparation for her moment of public reveal.

- o *Lord, we decree that you are workmen that will rightly divide the word of truth and not be ashamed. We declare that your pursuit of Christ's knowledge and wisdom will prepare you to impact the future and change lives.*

V. Abigail's sudden thrust into the governmental role of ambassador placed the lives of her family members in her hands. The threat of annihilation demanded her immediate activation as an apostle to change the course of events.

- o *We decree and declare that you will rise as ambassadors operating with the grace to govern regions and territories. We break every evil sanction, causing a shifting of events, mending of alliances, and overturning of evil decisions so others will be reconciled to God.*

VI.	The Holy Spirit shared Abigail's story to stress that every minute must count. Every man and every woman must be aware of how crucial your act of obedience is to the plan and purpose of Christ. Abby's immediate response in a time of pending war produced a sudden shift, saving a bloodline and catapulting her into destiny. A life of mistreatment, obscurity, and what possibly seemed like lost time, was exchanged for love, blessings, and greatness.

o	*We decree that you will not miss sudden encounters and that what belongs to you will find you as righteous heirs. We declare that as by one man's disobedience many were made sinners, so by the obedience of one shall many be made righteous.*

CHAPTER 43

MARIA WOODWORTH-ETTER: MANIFESTED POWER OF GOD

By Donna Anderson

"Verily, verily, I say unto you, He that believeth on me, the works that I do Shall he do also; and greater works than these shall he do; because I go unto my Father." **John 14:12**

Maria Woodworth-Etter was used mighty by God in the demonstration of miracles, signs, and wonders. Maria caused a cataclysmic shift when she stepped into a region. Maria carried the Apostolic Mantle and sickness, disease dissipated because it was subject unto the authority in the name of Jesus Christ. The weightiness of the Apostolic Mantle caused a transference in people while they were in their homes, businesses, and while they resided on the streets.

A demonstration of the mighty power of God fell within a 25 – 50-mile radius of where Maria ministered. "People climbed in the trees trying to see. The Holy Spirit fell like a cyclone; men and women were tossed as in a windstorm. They fell inside and outside the house. The police standing outside were frightened until they were pale. They said they saw the house shaken, as if in a storm, by the power of God.

Hundreds were saved. People were convicted for miles around." The power of God not only penetrated out of these meetings but it also radiated and caused a transformation to others who were in the circumference of these gatherings. The fire of God descended and caused restoration and transformation while people were receiving a revelation from the word of God. Maria was called, anointed, commissioned by God, fulfilled God's agenda, defended the faith, ministered across cultural barriers, penetrated new territories, and subdued them by the manifestation of the power of God. Her ministry was not geographically or ethnically restricted because it was a move of God which could not be restrained.

Maria was deployed by God into certain regions where transformation would occur with a breakthrough anointing. Maria was referred to as the "Grandmother of the Pentecostal Movement" and she was a powerful evangelist with an apostolic mantle. Every city and state that Maria entered experienced a radical shift, souls were saved, the oppressed were set free, dead were raised, and divine healings occurred. The outpouring of the Holy Spirit upon her ministry led thousands to Jesus Christ. Maria organized churches and established Lakeview Temple. Maria is credited with helping with founding the Assemblies of God in 1914.

Mariah Beulah Underwood was born in Ohio in 1844 to Samuel and Matilda Underwood. Samuel and Matilda Underwood did not practice Christianity until they joined the Disciple Church in 1854. While Maria was attending a meeting at the Disciple Church at the age of 13, she cried upon hearing the word of God. Maria was baptized in water and she wanted the Lord to really save her. "Soon after I was converted, I heard the voice of Jesus calling me to go out in the highways and hedges and gather in the lost sheep. Like Mary, I pondered these things in my heart, for I had no one to hold counsel with. The Disciples did not believe that women had any right to work for Jesus." Maria married Philo Horace Woodworth but could not answer the call because he had no desire for ministry, so she eventually divorced him and married Sam Etter who accompanied her in ministry.

Prior to Maria fulfilling the full mandate from God she experienced the death of her five children and she also had sickness in her own body. Maria felt inadequate because she was not educated. Although she had insecurities, she had a vision from God and she saw grains falling like sheaves and the Lord gave her the understanding that people would fall like that in her meetings.

Mariah was a pioneer who influenced women in ministry. She influenced notable generals such as Aimee Semple McPherson, Kathryn Kuhlman, F.F. Bosworth, and John G. Lake. Maria endured much opposition for the sake of proclaiming the Gospel of Jesus Christ, arrested at age 69, and put on trial for claims of divine healing, with mobs firing pistols and surrounding the tent attempting to kill or tear up her meetings. Maria believed in the manifestations of the Holy Spirit and many people opposed her, especially Apostle John Alexander Dowie who opposed her on "trance evangelism."

In addition to this, Dr. Wellington Adams and Dr. Theodore Driller, campaigned to have her put into an insane asylum because they felt she was using hypnosis on people, but the Lord used Dr. Arthur C. Bell to advocate on her behalf. In spite of the attacks, God protected, shielded, and guarded her against every attack against her and her ministry.

During this time in ministry, Maria endured slander, death threats, and sickness. Maria was humble she persevered, broke barriers and with her faith in God, she walked in Apostolic Authority. People in these meetings put a demand upon the anointing as they were reaching out in faith for a divine manifestation of God.

Maria walked in that Apostolic Mantle as a pioneer, and the power of God consumed her where signs and wonders were established for thousands of people. Many healings occurred in her meetings from leprosy, cancer, paralysis, hemorrhages, crooked limbs straightened out, blind eyes opened, tumors, rheumatism, kidney problems, tuberculosis, spinal meningitis, etc. Through the power of God, Maria spoke the word, laid hands on the sick, and they recovered. Maria traveled to various cities and states where notable miraculous healings occurred. Maria was a resilient trailblazer and catalyst who penetrated territories and caused regional shifts where souls were impacted in church, tent meetings, or in their homes. People gave their hearts to Jesus Christ and experienced visions, trances, and many were baptized in the spirit while attending these meetings. The power of God was known to rest in Maria's meetings especially when a woman died; Maria prayed over her and rebuked the demon of death, and commanded her to live and this woman was brought back to life again.

Maria tore down demonic forces and strongholds through faith, prayer, intercession, walking in the power and authority of God, and obedience to the word of God. God sealed her with the spirit, anointed her, and sent her forth. She laid Biblical foundations as she was a pioneer who seized new territories for the glory of God.

It is possible to walk in this mantle that Maria Woodworth-Etter was carrying by walking in faith, obedience to His word, praying, following His commands in addition to lining yourself up with the word of God. If God has called you to walk in this Apostolic and Prophetic mantle, it is obtainable. Stand on His word and decree and declare the promises of God over your life, bind up the spirit of fear, heaviness and infirmity, loose joy, peace, and healing over your life. As Maria healed the sick and set the captives free via laying on of hands, speaking to them, and commanding the demonic spirits to come out or praying over handkerchiefs and seeing massive deliverances, you can do this also if you have the right posture towards God.

Maria's Apostolic Traits:

- Trailblazer
- Forerunner
- Penetrated Territories
- Resilience
- Pioneer
- Power Gifts

Prayer

Everyone who is willing and ready to receive this mantle of the supernatural, I pray their hearts be open and tender to receive the word of God to penetrate in their innermost being, eyes to be opened now in Jesus' name to see beyond the core of your being that they will be able to supernaturally discern between angels and the demonic hosts. Father, I pray for the anointing to be so prevalent in their lives that when they walk by people, deliverance will be manifested by the power of God as they remain in covenant with You. Lord, let their hands drip with oil that when they lay hands or speak to individuals in authority, that deliverance will immediately come. Signs, wonders, and miracles be bestowed upon every righteous believer in covenant connection with you. I speak to their ear gate and their eye gate that they will see and hear correctly and obey Your voice only, God. I bind fear, mind-binding spirits, and the demonic host that will come against your destiny and I loose the Holy Spirit and the power of God. Lord, I am asking for a manifestation of Your presence to rest upon every individual who desires to walk in this mantle. I pray that they will be strengthened as they ward off every attack. Power of God, fall upon them now in Jesus' name. Shift them in the spirit now; give them a divine visitation of Your glory. Lord, carry them up in another realm in Your spirit. Let them feel the weight of Your glory.

References:

1. Maria Woodworth –Etter Collected Works. Whitaker House 2013
2. Maria Woodworth- Etter Collected Works. Whitaker House 2013
3. Liardon, R. (1996). God's Generals. New Kensington, PA: Whitaker House
4. King James Bible

CHAPTER 44

MARY'S APOSTOLIC ASSIGNMENT

By Cheryl Weems

"And Mary said, behold the handmaid of the Lord; be it unto me according to thy word. And the angel departed from her." Luke 1:38

The Apostolic embarkment of a young woman named Mary into the second most significant work the world has ever seen is rarely viewed through an apostolic lens. However, Mary's journey sets in motion a movement of obedience which builds a system to guard the greatest work to ever hit the Earth. This work results in fishermen, tax collectors, doctors, and tradesmen joining a movement that later brings the description, "these are they that come to turn the world upside down" (Acts 17:6). Apostles do things that have never been done, which results in the invasion of Heaven on Earth. This movement began the moment Mary's world turned upside down, a place commonly occupied by those known as the sent ones. Mary's life displays many traits that believers today can model to release a move of God in their individual spheres.

Apostolic Ascension (Mary Received a Word that Brought Upgrade to the Region)

Luke 1:26 And in the sixth month the angel Gabriel was sent from God unto a city of Galilee, named Nazareth, vs.27 to a virgin espoused to a man whose name was Joseph, of the house of David, and the virgin's name was Mary.

To ascend is to go up or climb, to rise to a higher place or altitude. Mary lived in Nazareth, a town in the low valley, surrounded by high mountains.

The area was known as impoverished, which would relate to a present-day ghetto. So much so that the Scripture presents the question, can any good thing come out of Nazareth? While Mary is going about her day-to-day rituals, she receives an encounter that changes the trajectory of her life. This word brings ascension to her life and the city of Nazareth.

As a believer, God will place a move of God in you that will first bring upgrade to your life, then cause upgrade to the area you've been assigned. The move of God for your life is meant to impact your world and the world around you. Apostolic ascension is the grace to birth a move in a city, sphere, or territory and raise it beyond its current state to meet the standard of Heaven.

Apostolic Agitation (What Mary Carried Caused Agitation to Existing Systems)

Matthew 2:16 Then Herod, when he saw that he was mocked of the wise men, was exceeding wroth, and sent forth, and slew all the children that were in Bethlehem, and all in the coasts thereof, from two years old and under, according to the time which he had diligently inquired of the wise men.

Agitation is to trouble the mind or feelings. Herod received news from the wise men about Mary giving birth and, based on the announcement, of the one that is born king of the Jews. He became troubled and gave instructions to kill any children within the region that were of a specific age. The announcement of a move of God always triggers the rise of demonic warfare to come against what is being birthed in the Earth. Mary received a strategy and that strategy stood until the warfare ended with the death of Herod.

As a believer, there will always be a counter-strategy to safeguard what you are releasing against the agitation of systems and demonic pursuit. The exciting point to remember is that we glory in our ability to overcome!

Apostolic Activation (Mary's Influence Caused Jesus to Respond)

John 2:1-11

Vs 4 And Jesus said to her, "Woman, what does this have to do with me? My hour has not yet come." Vs 5 His mother said to the servants, "Do whatever he tells you." V6 Now there were six stone water jars there for the Jewish rites of purification each holding twenty or thirty gallons. V7 Jesus said to the servants, "Fill the jars with water." And they filled them up to the brim. V8 And he said to them, "Now draw some out and take it to the master of the feast." So they took it.

Activation is to set up or formally institute or make reactive. The wedding at Cana was a significant point in Mary's assignment. She was called and commissioned to a work that bore such a significance that the world has never returned to its previous state. In the delicate balance of maternal and matriarch emotions, she pushed on her assignment until there was a Divine release. Jesus was in a place where he had his disciples with him at the wedding, but was hesitant to release miracles due to timing. We see Mary's natural and spiritual authority in Jesus' decision to respond to the need of the event outside of his appointed time. We learn that the apostolic authority that Mary housed caused an advanced release. Jesus later said that he does nothing apart from his Father. This tells me that Mary had influence.

We can extract that God uses the system of activation to accelerate purpose and cause believers to walk into their moment!

Apostolic Apex

John 19:25

Now there stood by the cross of Jesus his mother, and his mother's sister, Mary the wife of Cleophas, and Mary Magdelene.

Apex is the top or highest point of something. We find Mary at the foot of the cross at no doubt the most significant season of her assignment, both personally and spiritually. She's there watching fulfillment of the original word the angel Gabriel released to her over 30 years ago. At this pinnacle is the epitome of pain and pride as Jesus is saving his people from their sins. Mary's apostolic journey carried her from birthing the move of God, nurturing the move of God, to now releasing the move.

We will do well by gleaning from the finishing principle displayed through this portion of Mary's story. There is an anointing to finish seeing a mandate to its completion that is released and required to secure apostolic assignment! You too can finish strong.

Apostolic Traits We Can Take Away:

- God determines what we carry, when we birth, and our job is to submit to his call.
- You can release upgrade to people, systems, and regions.
- There will always be a Divine strategy to make the warfare against you and your assignment null and void.
- There is a system of activation that produces acceleration of purpose and causes you to maximize moments for the miraculous.
- What you are birthing will take you to the Apex of both your person and your assignment.
- There is an anointing to finish. Finish strong!

Apostolic Prayer:

God, we thank you for the apostolic call on our lives! We thank You for the grace to take the journey of obedience that changes territories, systems, and standard service. We accept every assignment, knowing that there is a great release of purpose; the kind that changes everything! We ask that You continue to keep us sharp as arrows in Your quiver as we take this moment to say yes to Your Heavenly target. Nations will never be the same, cities will never be the same, our region will never be the same. Thank You for choosing us as women on the frontlines, on the cutting edge, birthing that which has been prophesied and is now set to be released. Use us as You did Mary, according to Your word! In Jesus' name we pray, Amen!

Sources:

"Mary the Blessed Virgin"-
Http://www.catholic.org/saints/saint.php?saint_id=4967

"Who was the real Virgin Mary?; She is the icon of womanhood-with 2000 years of myths-making attached", The Guardian (1959-2003_; December 19th, 2002. ProQuest historical newspapers: The Guardian and The Observer pg. A8)

CHAPTER 45

MARY MAGDALENE— APOSTLE OF JESUS CHRIST

By Sadra Davis

Romans 5:17 (AMP) *"For if by the trespass of the one (Adam/Eve), death reigned through the one (Adam/Eve), much more surely will those who receive the abundance of grace and the free gift of righteousness reign in [eternal] life through the One, Jesus Christ [and his bride: those who carry His gospel].*

In this great hour of awakening and anticipation for the greatest harvest of all time, God is calling us higher in the knowledge of His will, plans, and purposes. I know that over the years, some, like Paul, have felt restrained from teaching on many things due to the carnality and the infantile state of the church at large (Heb. 5:11-14; 1Cor. 3:1-5). However, now is the time for all the scales to be removed from the eyes of the church (ekklesia) so that we might forge ahead in power, possessing the whole Earth for the glory of God.

In Genesis 1:26 "God said, Let us make man in our image, after our likeness: and let *THEM* [male and female] have dominion [reign] over … all the earth [but not one another]." As with everything that was made on Earth, women also came forth from the heart of God, and were filled with purpose *and* leadership. In verse 28 of Genesis 1 we see this as they were both "commissioned" with the assignment to "be fruitful, and multiply, and replenish the earth, and subdue it: *and have dominion.*" In this chapter, I intend to enlighten you on the apostolic commission given specifically to

Mary Magdalene, and the key role she played in the restoration of women's equal place in being ambassadors of the Kingdom of Heaven.

In the framework of Jesus' ministry, we see in almost every encounter that he had with women he capitalized it to remove the stigma and misogynistic ideologies around women being treated and regarded as less than men, sinful, sexualized, and as property. We see these women being uniquely empowered as fully equal and worthy to carry out their initial godly commission. His ministry to and with Mary Magdalene was not different, but it, unlike the others, set a tremendous precedence for women called to apostolic ministry. Let's examine the Scriptures for specific clarification of this. Luke 8:1-3 is where we see the reference to Mary's encounter and note hers along with several other women's active roles in Jesus' ministry. Mary experienced deliverance of seven devils and the infirmities that they were causing in her life. The usage of the number seven infers that she was in complete bondage, yet the deliverance of seven represents full purification and consecration (Easton, M.G.). Her faithful commitment and *followship* of Jesus would be attributed to this great liberation. Going forward, Mary Magdalene showed herself to be one the most faithful disciples and later apostles of the Lord Jesus Christ. She never left his side even when her life could have been in jeopardy, and was obedient as a true son/ambassador, unlike Peter, who denied the Lord thrice when feeling threatened, or Judas who was drawn away by lust.

The resurrected Christ represents the "door" for all humanity to re-enter their pre-sin state of Gen. 1:26; being "born-again" (Jn. 10:9 & Jn. 3:3). What has been overlooked is the *full significance* of the risen Christ's *first encounter* being with Mary Magdalene. Understand that the resurrected Christ also represents the "New Testament" the "revised or restored order" (Heb 10:9; Rom. 5:18; 2Cor. 5:17). This encounter was the climax of all the previous encounters he had concerning women, and here he affirms it by appearing in resurrected form before Mary Magdalene, commissioning and affirming her, and then sealing the eyes of the twelve that there would be no doubt of God's choice to use women in leadership.

In John 20:17-18 "Jesus saith unto her, Touch me not; for I am not yet ascended to my Father: *but go* **to my brethren**, *and say* **unto them, I ascend unto my Father, and your Father; and to my God, and your God.** Mary Magdalene came and told the disciples that she had seen the Lord, and that he had spoken these things unto her." However, based on the continued opposition and rejection of women in leadership, we know that this spiritual transaction, of Mary and the risen Christ, has certainly been disregarded. This was her first act as an apostle and denotes an emphatic restoration of equality first and specifically to the very twelve men that he also chose to be his apostles. Christ rebukes them for NOT believing; both what the apostle [apostolos /sent one/Mary Magdalene] had said, and what had been prophesied (concerning his death and resurrection, that God's spirit would equally be upon ALL flesh, both sons and daughters as in Genesis, etc.). Let's look at the Scripture in Luke 24 with the Holy Spirit's breath upon them for new revelation:

Luke 24:15-16, 25, 30-31

(KJV) "¹⁵ And it came to pass, that, while they communed together and reasoned, Jesus himself drew near, and went with them. ¹⁶ But **their eyes were holden [restrained/seized by the Lord] that they should not know him…** ²⁵ **Then he said unto them, O fools, and slow of heart to believe all that the prophets have spoken:**… ³⁰ And it came to pass, as he sat at meat with them, he took bread, and blessed it, and brake, and gave to them. ³¹ And **their eyes were opened, and they knew him**; and he vanished out of their sight.

(AMP) "¹⁵ While they were talking and discussing it, Jesus Himself came up and *began* walking with them. ¹⁶ **But their (eyes were [miraculously] prevented from recognizing Him… 25 Then Jesus said to them, "O *foolish men*, and slow of heart to trust *and* believe in everything that the prophets have spoken!**… ³⁰ And it came to pass, as he sat at meat with them, he took bread, and blessed it, and brake, and gave to them. ³¹ **And their eyes were opened, and they knew him**; and he vanished out of their sight.

This act of the resurrected Christ "breaking bread" or a fresh covenant with the men to cleanse their hearts, minds, and egos from the stains of sin and their misogynistic ideas and behaviors is what the Lord wants to do with all of us. We have allowed the "traditions of men" and societal norms to supersede Kingdom standards. Men were never to have dominion over women, nor women to have it over men. However, in the fear of the Lord, both men and women are to execute any and all orders and commissions given by the Lord to be carried out on Earth. These Scriptures remove any doubts about whether women have been apostles and/or apostolic.

Let's recap this revelation in simple terms:

1. Women, including specifically Mary Magdalene, were in fact disciples; and apostolic believers of Jesus Christ.
2. Mary Magdalene served as a "proxy" for women to be fully restored in their place of dominion, free from the inhibition of men, and we see her preceding several other women apostles in the New Testament (i.e. Junia and Priscilla).
3. The resurrected Christ is the sure and only "door" for our entrance into a restored life of power, dominion, and apostolic (ambassadorial) living.
4. Diligence in discipleship is the foundation of sonship/apostolic living. Every believer can and should mature and reach this level; being apostolic.
5. To be apostolic is to be aligned with the doctrine of the apostles (Christ being chief) and to be carriers of the Kingdom (liberating others from sin, sickness, spiritual death, poverty, and the bonds of Satan) (Mark 16:17-18).
6. To be an apostle is to have a direct commission from the Lord, coupled with Heavenly wisdom, knowledge, power, an aggregate authority level, and often a direct physical visitation or encounter with the risen Lord.

The great Sojourner Truth's favorite quote targets the foolish thought processes that would keep women restrained from leading, it states that "if the first woman God ever made was strong [influential] enough to turn the world upside down all alone, these women [of faith] together ought to be able to turn it back, and get it right side up again! And now they [are positioned] to do it, the men [need to gracefully] let them" (Wallace 2015).

Prayer

Father, in the name of Jesus we renounce and pull down every stronghold that would prevent us from viewing women in leadership through Your eyes and plans. We embrace Your will and release ourselves to move into actions that partner with this revelation and understanding concerning apostolic women being on the frontlines executing Your will on Earth with full Heavenly clearance (2Cor. 10:4-6; Rom. 12:2).

References:

Mary Magdalene, Apostle of Jesus Christ

Easton, Matthew George. "Number 7 in the Bible - What Does It Mean and What Is the Significance?" *Easton's Illustrated Bible Dictionary*, Third ed., Thomas Nelson, 1897, www.biblestudytools.com/dictionary/seven/.

Wallace, Gail. "5 Black Women in History Every Egalitarian Should Know." *The Junia Project*, The Junia Project, 21 Feb. 2015, juniaproject.com/5-black-women-every-egalitarian-know/.

All Bible quotations are taken from the Comparative Study Bible, Revised Edition (KJV, AMP, NIV), copyright 1999 by Zondervan; The Holy Bible, New International Version, copyright 1973, 1978, 1984 by International Bible Society; and The Amplified Bible, copyright 1954, 1958, 1962, 1964, 1965, 1987 by Lockman Foundation.

CHAPTER 46

THE WOMAN WHO BELIEVED IN MIRACLES: AN ENCOUNTER WITH KATHRYN KUHLMAN

By LeeChunHwa Stovall

Finally, be strong in the Lord and in the strength of his might.
Ephesians 6:10 ESV

The Moment I Met Kathryn Kuhlman

"I believe in miracles!!!" rang from the television as I sat on Mother Jeffrey's couch this particular Sunday afternoon. The sound of this woman's voice was so different; I don't think I had ever heard anything like it before, it immediately grasped my attention. As I looked at the television, trying to see in between the lines and interference, I hear the sound of an organ and the voice once again saying, "I believe in miracles, because I believe in God!" That statement penetrated deep into my core; as I sat on the couch drinking my glass of water, the statement kept replaying in my head over and over. I was a new believer, and a fresh convert from Catholicism, so the talk of miracles intensely peaked my curiosity. The power that resonated from her voice seemed to pull me deeper into the television, although I was new to Christ, I could sense this woman had a very strong relationship with the Lord. Mother Jeffrey began to introduce me to the woman on the screen, "Kathryn Kuhlman is her name!" she said, "She's long been gone with the Lord, but her ministry is still with us". I instantly knew that I wanted to know more about this woman who believed in miracles.

Every week, I would sit on that couch and watch a different video of Kathryn Kuhlman, and just as Mother Jeffrey said, you never grew tired of watching her minister. One of the last moments I spent with Mother Jeffrey before she went home to be with the Lord, we were watching a video, she began to share that the Lord was going to raise up many more women, like Kathryn Kuhlman and the great pioneering women that came before and after her. Her very last words were, "GET READY"!

Who was Kathryn Kuhlman?

Kathryn Kuhlman came unto salvation at the age of 14 during a revival at a Methodist church. At the age of 16, she graduated from high school and began traveling with her sister, who was married to a traveling evangelist. Kathryn remained with them, as a part of their ministerial team in Idaho, until her sister decided to go on to South Dakota with her husband. A local pastor offered Kathryn the opportunity to preach at an old pool hall that was converted into a mission, and this is where the ministry of Kathryn Kuhlman began. She traveled to several cities before establishing the Denver Revival Center in Denver, Colorado.

During the height of her ministry, she secretly married a gentleman, this brought much scrutiny to her ministry and everything that she diligently built began to dissolve. Eventually, she and her husband divorced. She had been ministering in Pennsylvania, she began to see her ministry reshape and become reestablished. From that point forward, she never allowed anything to distract her from fulfilling the assignment and call of God on her life.

Along with her itinerant ministry and holding meetings at the Tabernacle, she developed her radio ministry, sharing unprecedented truths that shook the core of Christianity. A woman of great humility, she never wanted to be known as a "faith healer," but as an "ordinary person" or a "handmaiden of the Holy Spirit"; she despised some of what she witnessed from some of the "faith healers" of her time. Kathryn began to learn more in-depth about the often ignored third person of the Holy Trinity, the Holy Spirit. She learned the principle that healing was provided at the moment of salvation. This revelation began to transform her ministry and the lives of those who attended her meetings and supported her. In one of her crusades, a woman miraculously received a healing without anyone touching her, followed by another miracle, and another miracle. Word began to travel about the miracles, her meetings grew in size, and her worldwide ministry was birthed; television broadcasts were incorporated, and she became a household name. She headquartered her ministry in Pennsylvania, and it remained there beyond her death, until 2016.

More than a Conqueror

When you think about the ministry of Kathryn Kuhlman, you cannot help but think of the strength and tenacity she carried within her; fueled by the power of God, she was able to withstand many storms and resiliently bounce back with greater stature and influence. Throughout her life and ministry, she faced many obstacles and setbacks, but she never allowed them to defeat her. Those who remember her ministry have often stated that she was a force to be reckoned with, and she accepted nothing less than that which was pleasing to God the Father; that is a tremendous way for your life and ministry to be remembered.

What made her the force that she was? It was the strength of the Lord that sustained and carried her. It was her intimacy with the Father, and her sensitivity to His presence. Although during that time, women were more frequently looked upon as mothers, missionaries, and evangelists in the church, Kathryn Kuhlman carried many apostolic traits that you and I, along with so many other women carry. We have been given these traits to deposit and birth the next generation of warrior women, who will take the Kingdom by force. It has been the deep hunger and desire for something more and greater to take place in the Kingdom that has caused great movements to come forth; and it is because of the spirit of strength and might that rests in the loins of trailblazers that we, as women, can begin to take our rightful place in the Kingdom.

- *INTIMATE WORSHIPPER* – Kathryn was known as a woman of great intimacy with the Father. It will take women who are sensitive to the ebb and flow of God to orchestrate the next great moves that are coming forth. The next coming revivals will be a result of women who have taken the lead of Mary and rest at the feet of Jesus.

- *INFLUENCE* - She was a woman of great influence. Kathryn Kuhlman's ministry far surpassed denominational barriers, and she even played a major role of influence in the mountains of religion, government, media, and entertainment. The next dimension of influence will be orchestrated by women who have confidently assumed their positions within the seven mountains of influence and the Kingdom of God.

- *RESILIENCE* – Kathryn Kuhlman was able to withstand the pain, disappointment, ridicule, and failure of her actions and decisions that caused trauma to her ministry. She had the strength and stamina to not only be restored, but to exceed the limitations of what could have caused her to be stagnant. The Junias, Deborahs, Annas, Esthers, and so many more that are coming forth will stand in the confidence of the Lord, gaining ground for the next move, not being held back by their past, the opinions of man or society; they will go forth in great expectation and in great faith that the Lord is on their side.

- *FLEXIBLE/ ADAPTABLE* – Kathryn understood that in order to have a fruitful and productive ministry, one must be able to be flexible and not broken. She had the ability to adapt to the change of current within her ministry. The women who are rising into position will be sensitive to the current of the river; they will know how to establish, move, and execute simultaneously, while understanding that their ability to withstand the winds, waves, and storms is by them being anchored in Christ and the leading of the Holy Spirit.

- *VISION* – Kathyrn was a woman of great vision; she had the ability to see far beyond what was present. The daughters of the Kingdom who are coming forth will have the ability to see beyond dimensions and dispensations, but they will see with the eagle eye vision of the Lord. They will not be limited by opinions and man-made borders; they will have conquered with great might.

PRAYER

Father, anoint your precious daughter to be a trailblazer. Give her strength and courage to pioneer with great power, tenacity, and freshness. Let her heartbeat be aligned with Your heartbeat, as she embarks on the path that You have predestined; order her steps to her expected end and grace her to surpass the limitations of man, but to walk in Your authority, empowered to build and establish. Allow her vision to remain focused, never to be distracted, or run off course. May she forever be steadfast and relentless in her pursuit of You and Your will for her life, and the Kingdom. May she always remember to look to the hills where she will receive her help and her passions be ignited by Your fire. Allow Your fruit to be increasingly demonstrated in her life. AMEN!

CHAPTER 47

HULDA—PROPHETESS AND SCHOLAR

By Shelley M. Fisher, PH.D

"The Lord announces the word and the women who proclaim it are a mighty throng:" **Psalm 68:11 (NIV)**

God uses whoever He pleases, whenever and wherever He desires. Information about Huldah, the prophetess, is unobtrusively tucked into 2 Kings 22:14-20 and 2 Chronicles 34:22-34. She spoke, the king listened, and a nation was saved. Huldah was the wife of Shallum, who was keeper of the king's wardrobe. She lived during the reign of Josiah in Jerusalem (3285-3316) and resided in the part of Jerusalem called the Mishnah, or the college. The Hebrew word for college is *Mishnah*, and it means a place of repetition. Since the core of education then was oral, teaching was repetition. Popular belief is that Huldah was a teacher, a scholar, and she wrote Hebrew Scriptures (Mariottini, 2013). She had a school for Jewish women and taught them about God, and things pertaining to mothers and daughters, asserts Mindel (2003).

For a woman to have been used so powerfully and to have her name mean "weasel" seems a paradox at first glance. However, an interesting fact about the weasel is it does a war dance and its prey has been known to die from fright just by watching the weasel dance (Horowitz, 2015). Huldah was a warrior who walked in dominion and authority. She unabashedly said to Hilkiah, "Tell the person who sent you here that the people have sinned, and God will destroy them. He will not destroy you because when those lost scrolls were found you rent your shirt and cried out to him" (2 Kings:18-20).

Most writers agree she was kinswoman to Jeremiah. In this time of history, Zephaniah and Jeremiah were the Major Prophets, but God gave His word to save a nation to a woman to deliver. He is no respecter of persons. The fact that she was consulted rather than Jeremiah speaks volumes of her character and respect (Zondervan, 1988).

Some opine that God used Huldah because Jeremiah was out of town (Kohn, 2017; Mindel, 2017). While others seem to view the situation of Huldah through the lens of the man as the head. The Scriptures remind us that the carnal mind is no match for God (Romans 8:7). Still, others challenged audiences with the question: would you want to receive a prophecy from a man rather than a woman (Legge, 2007)? This question has a myriad of implications.

"Tell the person who sent you…" is a source of offense for some writers who thought Huldah was disrespectful because she didn't say "the king" (Legge, 2007; Kohn, 2017). This kind of thinking limits God to man's capacity. God's authority supersedes the landscape of masculine superiority and self-centeredness. Regrettably, a woman prophesying to a king or any male is a conundrum to some. To deliver this message unabashedly and to say to the delegation, "Tell the person who sent you…" Huldah was God's chosen vessel who operated in her God-given authority with holy boldness. She knew God's voice. It's credible to say she was a woman of prayer and power who had a love relationship with God.

Gender bias and religiosity are blinders to spiritual maturity. Our God, the giver of every good and perfect gift, is magnified through Huldah. Not only does He endow the gift, but He makes room for it. How fruitless it is of man to "kick against the pricks" in lieu of accepting the import of God's word.

Huldah did not fit the stereotype of women of her day. She not only had a relationship with King Josiah, who reigned for thirty-one years, but she also had a relationship with the King of Kings. To support the tenant of her relationship with the King of Judah, during the repairing and cleaning of the temple, a lost scroll was found with God's law written on it. Hilkiah, the High Priest, gave the scroll to Shaphan (the king's secretary) who read it;

then gave it to the king. The scrolls indicated neither the people nor their ancestors had obeyed God's commands. After reading the scroll, the king in anguish tore his clothes in terror. (2 Kings 22:1-13). He commanded Hilkiah, Shaphan, Asiah, Ahikam, and Achbor to petition the Lord to see what they should do.

Hilkiah, the priest, led the charge for all of them to go to Huldah, the prophetess. What would be the premise for their going to see Huldah? She obviously was well-respected, a woman of great faith, knowledgeable of the Scriptures, and of moral character (Kohn, 2017). These are qualifiers for hearing from God. The men didn't go to Jeremiah, or Zephaniah, but they went to Huldah. God knew who He wanted to give His message.

Even more important than Huldah's relationship with King Josiah, was her relationship with the King of Kings. Huldah gave the delegation the word of the Lord, telling them of the destruction the Lord was sending on them because of their worshipping of other Gods. This would not take place until after King Josiah's death because of his contrition, crying out to God and tearing his clothes. The message was taken to the king (14-26).

King Josiah expunged the idols from the temples and restored the city to its former place of worship. Huldah, the Female Prophet of God who saved a nation, authenticated the scrolls found as Scripture. She interpreted and applied it by giving the Word of the Lord about the situation. She exercised authority over men within the confines of her God-given authority (Valentine, 2007). This passage not only shows us that God gives the gift of prophecy to women, but he also honors humility. The implications for today are that we lace our callings and gifts with humility, and the body of Christ needs to align its actions with the word of God.

After Kings 2 and 2 Chronicles 34, the pages of the Bible no longer give way to Huldah's voice. But after the temple was restored, gates were named after her to commemorate her work. Her story is encouraging to the apostolic women of today. Know that God has chosen you, and He has given you the tongue of the learned to speak a word in season to those who are weary (John 15:16; Isaiah 50:4). No man can stop who God anoints and appoints. Stir up your God-given gifts. Huldah already paved the way for you, apostolic women. Don't be intimidated by those who have a form of godliness denying the power thereof by viewing women as lesser vessels, or who relegate women to their rigid thinking. It is God who gives favor to man. It is God who positions and promotes; this comes through prayer, fasting, and moving in the things of God.

There is much work to be done. Statistics tell us that 68% of the people who attend church do not believe in a moral absolute (Boice, 1996). The conditions in our families, churches, communities, businesses, and government need a "sent one." The Gospel needs to be taken into all the world. Whom shall I send and who will go for us?

Apostolic women, God needs you. Just as the sons of Issachar knew the times and seasons, know that now is your time and your season. It is a time of acceleration. God wants to work miracles through you. Yield to His leading. Consecrate yourself and thirst after Him as the deer pants for the water brook. God has used you, is using you, but there is more He wants to do through you. You must die to self, going beyond the Vio Dolorosa – the place of preparation for death and burial—to the cross the place of death, burial, and resurrection.

Power, dominion, and authority belong to you. He's giving you new wine for the challenges that lie ahead. He's new and fresh every morning, and a new day is dawning. God is calling His daughters out of obscurity. Come forth! He will give you no rest until you embark on His quest to bring salvation to those He loves.

Summary:
- Women who are obscure in the Bible have been used mightily by God.
- God used Huldah to save a nation.
- God is the giver of every good and perfect gift.
- God chooses, anoints, and appoints those to do His bidding on Earth.
- The body of Christ needs to align words and actions with the word of God.
- God has equipped women to bring the Gospel to a dying world.

Declarations:

- I am bold in the Lord and in the power of His might.
- I can do all things through Christ who strengthens me.
- Lord, here am I. Send me.
- Lord, think through my mind, move through my hands, and order my steps.
- I am a spiritual entrepreneur. I do the bidding of My Father.
- I die to self, so God can be glorified in me.

Prayer

Father, thank you for Your presence in my life. You chose me; what a humbling thought. I purpose to walk worthy of you bearing fruit in every good work and growing in the knowledge of You, my God. Your word says that if I am willing and obedient, I will eat the good of the land. I am willing and obedient. Ignite the fire of the Holy Ghost in me to do Your will. In Jesus' name. Amen.

References:

Boice, J.M. (1996). *God's City Christians in a Crumbing Culture*. Illinois: InterVarsity Press.

Hirsch, E.G. and Selihsohn, M. (2002). Executive committee of the Editorial Board. The Jewish

Encyclopedia. The Story of Huldah the Prophetess. Retrieved December 15, 2017 from http://www.womwninthebible.net/women-bible-old-new-testaments/huldah

Horowitz, K. (2015). 7 Fierce Facts About Weasels. Retrieved December 11, 2017, from mentalfloss.com/article/641937-fierce-facts-about-weasels-weasel war dance.

Legge, D. (2007). Little Women Part 5: *Huldah the Prophetess.* Preach the Word. Retrieved from www.preachtheword.com /sermon/women05.shtml

Kohn, Leah. (2017). Women in Judaism. The Prophetess Huldah: Her Message of Hope Part I

Series: Women in Judaism Level Beginner.

Legge, D. (2007). Little Women: Part 5. Huldah the Prophetess. Preach the Word. Retrieved

December 18, 2017 from
httpd://preachtheword.com/sermon/women04.shtml

Mariottini, C. (2013). Huldah the Prophetess. Retrieved December 16, 2017, from https://claudemariottini.com/2013/09/02/huldah-the-prophetess.

Mindel, N. (2003). Huldah the Prophetess. Retrieved December 22, 2017, from http://www.chabad.org/library/article_cdo/aid/112503/jewish/Huldah-The-Prophetess.htm

Valentine, B. (2006). Huldah Who? The Forgotten Ministry of a Lady Prophet. Retrieved

January 6, 2018, from http://stonedcampbelldisciple.com/2006/06/27/huldah-who-the-forgotten-ministry-of-a-lady-prophet/

Zondervan (1988). The Woman Who Unveiled the Future of Nation. Retrieved December 21, 2017, from https://www.biblegateway.com/resources/all-women-bible/Huldah

CHAPTER 48

PRISCILLA: AN ESTEEMED LEADER IN THE EARLY CHURCH

By Valarie L. Randleman

For we are His workmanship, created in Christ Jesus for good works,
which God prepared beforehand that we should walk in them.
Eph 2:10 NKJV

Preface: There are silent heroines that grace the annals of human and Church history. When we discover their story afresh, our lives are enriched because we took the time to READ their story. And in reading their story, this points directly to His story. Thus is the account of Priscilla of New Testament times, in ministry alongside her husband, Aquila. Their story is referenced in six passages (Acts 18:1-3,18; Rom16: 3-4; 1 Cor 6:19: 2 Tim 4:19), in which three places Priscilla's name is referenced first, and other passages name Aquila first. This may have occurred to reflect the equality in their relationship and the beauty of team ministry, displayed through their marriage, as well as the collegial partnership with the apostle Paul.

"Leave Now!" The edict was released and its intended audience clear-all Jews residing in Rome were ordered to depart [cf Acts 18:1-2]. What do you do when you must exit in haste and go to the next place? Renner makes this compelling observation: "So although the devil thought he was shutting down forever the powerful ministry of Aquila and Priscilla by expelling them from Rome, he was actually positioning them to move up to a higher level of ministry than they had ever experienced" (Renner, p 121). The sudden expulsion from Rome placed this humble couple with the great apostle of the New Testament (Acts 18:2). This kairos timed event provided years of collegial friendship in addition to a shared occupation that the Roman edit could not have anticipated or envisioned. Doesn't this sound like God turning the tables for a Divine setup?

Now banished from Rome, Priscilla and Aquila forged ahead and took up residence in Corinth. It was here in Corinth that Paul sought them out (Acts 18:2). Paul lived and worked with them while establishing the church in Corinth. What a priceless opportunity for this faithful couple! Doing life and business together brought forth a new sharpening and grounding in the word, especially for Priscilla. She would grasp Scriptures at a deeper level and her skill as a teacher was tremendously enhanced. Undoubtedly, she and Aquila had been servant leaders while in Rome, opening their home as a gathering place for fellowship and instruction. Now in Corinth, the ministry opportunities increased and team ministry now included the apostle Paul.

Her involvement in spreading the Gospel was exponential and from Corinth came Ephesus, where they stayed to labor with the early church. Priscilla and Aquila with the apostle Paul became a new apostolic team that would advance the early Church. This camaraderie and support from this couple would refresh and provide a safe haven for this pioneering apostle, who worked untiringly in spreading the Gospel.

As Paul mentored and taught both Priscilla and Aquila, the next account demonstrates the effectiveness in what was imparted to them to then "explain the way of God more accurately" (Acts 18:26),

Apollos was a Jew hailing from Alexandria and is described as "an eloquent man, mighty in the Scriptures, fervent in spirit" (Acts 18:24,25). Priscilla and Aquila had an opportunity to hear him teach the things of God, but only up to John's baptism. This dynamic duo filled in the gaps of information that Apollos was presenting as truth.

He was now armed with a more complete picture of Jesus' birth, ministry, crucifixion, and ascension. It is to Priscilla's credit that Apollos, now equipped with powerful revelatory truths, could more vigorously refute before the Jews that Jesus was the Christ (Acts 18:28). She taught him with humility, tact, and courage, giving him the necessary edge to be an early defender of the faith.

Finally, enough cannot be said of Priscilla's consistency to persevere in tough times, to travel with Paul alongside Aquila, and her love for Christ. She helped to establish churches in Corinth, Ephesus, and Rome. Paul, in approaching the final days of his life, sent this greeting to his close friends: "Greet Prisca and Aquila, and the household of Onesiphorus" (2 Tim 4:19). He remembered the time they literally put their necks on the line for him, without giving the context, yet the churches established at that time were aware of their courageous stance for a dear friend (Rom 16:3-4).

Let's salute Priscilla as a respected apostolic leader with a zeal to see the Kingdom advance and God to be exalted. You as a reader of this anthology are invited to the table and His scepter is extended to you and you have access. Access granted is His heart's desire for you!

Summary:

- In the midst of social upheaval and turbulence, keep your focus [cf Heb 12:2]
- What can appear at first glance to be evil or unexpected, remain open to the leading of the Holy Spirit to work it out for your good [Gen 50:20]
- Be willing to be stretched in your understanding, as you may have an opportunity to do so for another now or in the future
- Be willing to reproduce the greatness poured into you by seasoned, mature saints that you can make a mark in your generation
- There was a progression of responsibility that happened to Priscilla and Aquila; at each juncture they had to move in obedience and move forward by faith
- Priscilla was held in high esteem by the Apostle Paul and exemplifies collegial respect that can occur between sons and daughters
- Godly friendships can refresh, encourage, and bolster the faith of those on the frontlines as Priscilla and Aquila provided for Apostle Paul

Prayer

Lord, empower the company of apostolic women to arise and roar as the Lion of Judah. Let them rule in the midst of Your enemies as You send each one and place each one according to their designated purpose and destiny. The breaker anointing will expose, dismantle, and annihilate demonic snares intended to derail these daughters from fulfilling their purpose. Contend with those that contend with them as Jehovah Gibbor. When You arise, Your enemies are scattered. We choose, as a company of apostolic daughters, to walk fearless, complete all assignments placed in our hands, and declare great exploits to come forth through us! In Jesus' name. Amen

Decrees & Declarations

- I decree and declare Your daughters are skillful in the wielding of the sword of the Lord and ruling in apostolic authority
- I decree and declare that we are covenant daughters of the Lord that pattern our lives and speech in humility, integrity, exemplifying the character of our God
- I decree and declare we will take the first step, to move in a proton anointing that causes us to go first to break through new territories and blaze a trail for others to follow
- I decree and declare that just as Priscilla was a sent one and went forth, bless those that are aligning to Your eternal purposes and moving in their designated metrons by Your power & authority
- I decree and declare that the Holy Spirit infuses each daughter with tensile strength, a face like flint to weather adversity, the tongue of diplomacy as a skilled ambassador, and hinds' feet to make leaps of faith all the days of her life, in Jesus' name.

References

Judy L. Brown, *Women Ministers According to Scripture* (Kearney, NE: Morris Publishing, 1996).

Loren Cunningham and David Joel Hamilton, *Why Not Women?* (Seattle, WA; Youth With A Mission Publishing, 2000).

New Spirit Filled Life Bible, New King James Version,

Prude, Joseph L, *Female Apostles* (Cleveland, OH; BattMorr Publishing, 2007).

Rick Renner, *Dressed to Kill* (Tulsa, OK: Teach All Nations, 2007).

Michelle McClain-Walters, *The Deborah Anointing* (Lake Mary, FL; Charisma House, 2015).

CHAPTER 49

THE PHEBE ANOINTING FOR KINGDOM BUSINESS

By Sandra Hill

From time and memorial, God has used women to fulfill His plans and purposes for mankind. Women from all walks of life, small and great, women of world-renowned or nameless, God has used as His valued vessels of honor. In every arena of life, God has purposed to utilize women as His hidden treasures. In business, in the home, in every arena of life, be it social, civil or moral, by design woman is one of God's choicest vessels.

Many women time after time have said, like Jesus, "I must be about my Father's business." Phebe was one of God's chosen women, who was about her Father's business.

> *I commend unto you Phebe our sister, which is a servant of the church which is at Cenchrea: ² That ye receive her in the Lord, as becometh saints, and that ye assist her in whatsoever business she hath need of you: for she hath been a succourer of many, and of myself also.* (Romans 16:1, 2)

Phebe was a servant of the assembly of the people of God at Cenchrea. Cenchrea was a port city and a city of commerce and trade. This church name represented a "millet," which is a small cereal grass which produces in abundance. I believe that the small seeds she planted within the Church at Cenchrea produced Godly fruit in abundance. As a servant, she planted love in everything she put her hand to. Love was the apostolic anchor that allowed Phebe to produce great fruit. Within this passage of Scripture, you can feel the love and care received by the Apostle Paul from this great woman of God.

The harvest of the millet is favored due to its productivity and short-growing season under dry, high-temperature conditions. No matter the seed Phebe planted, it was favored even under the toughest conditions. Her life as a servant produced such great fruit, founded in love, that Paul called her to cultivate that same fruit in the assembly of saints at Rome. Phebe was being sent to Rome on an apostolic mission.

Woman of God, be encouraged with every seed you plant. Just as the millet seed is productive and reliable in poor, droughty, and infertile soils, so is every seed God gives you to plant. Decree and declare into every work of Kingdom business you are called to accomplish, that it shall flourish. Also imagine that every God-assigned seed you plant will also flourish in fertile, and good ground, additionally producing an abundant harvest.

1 Corinthians 3:6 I planted, Apollos watered, but God [all the while] was making it grow and [He] gave the increase. (AMPC)

The Request to be Received

God is sending a preceding word for His women to be received, just as Phebe was received. Paul's admonition was for her to be received with the highest degree of respect. He challenged the saints to have a higher standard of dignity and wisdom for all servants that came to serve them, but specifically for this woman of God. You and I are to be received wherever God sends us. What God has given women to plant is to be respected, accepted, embraced intimately, and to flourish as the millet seed. You will be received in a Godly manner, according to the weight of glory that is upon your life. This reception is with respect, love, favor, and tender care that is over the top and according to God's standards!

Within Phebe's mission as a servant of God, she was assisting people and bringing order to Kingdom business, this too is our mission. God has assigned you to be accomplished whether in your home territory or on an apostolic assignment. God calls women to fulfill His business and secure what is needed within every Kingdom mission with abundance.

Just as Phebe was, you also are a succourer. A succourer was a woman set over others as one who protects, who supports, who encourages apostolic, prophetic, and kingdom causes. A succourer includes the ability to provide protective supervision. Phebe was well able to aid others with the natural and spiritual resources God provided for her. Her testimony through the Apostle Paul was she blessed many and was a personal blessing to him. Because of the anointing on her life, no one was too big or too small in their position or status to receive from her life.

Pray in the Assistance Needed

Woman of God, as you are sent on your God-given assignments, ask God to send the resources and anointings needed. This includes human resources, economic resources, intellectual resources, mentorship resources, natural resources, and spiritual resources. Paul requested support for whatever type of business Phebe needed to conduct. Whatever God-given Kingdom assignment you are walking out, the abundant anointing is available for the asking.

Apostolic strengths exemplified by the life of Phebe:

- She exhibited love and servanthood
- She was about the Father's business
- She thrived in a place represented by small seeds flourishing under favorable and unfavorable conditions
- The way she conducted God's business allowed her to be sent on an apostolic assignment
- The fruit of her business for God allowed the saints to be challenged to a higher standard
- As a succourer, she was set over God's business to protect, support, and encourage
- She was given the resources to complete her Kingdom assignment

Prayer:

- Father, I thank You that I am a servant of the assembly of the people of God wherever You would have them gathered and that love is the anchor of my servanthood.

- Father, I thank You that just as Phebe was in the church at Cenchrea –I will be about Your business and bear fruit in abundance.
- Father, I thank You that where You send me apostolically, the small seeds I plant, the crop is favored due to its productivity and short growing season under dry, high-temperature conditions. Father, I thank You that this seed is cultivated globally.
- Father, I thank You that I am encouraged with every seed I plant, just as the millet seed is productive and reliable in poor, droughty, and infertile soils, so is every seed You give me to plant – I decree and declare it shall flourish. Thank You, Father, that every seed I plant will also flourish in fertile and good ground, also producing an abundant harvest.
- Father, I thank You that ,just as Phebe was received, I am received and what You have given me to plant is accepted and embraced intimately. Thank You that I am received in a Godly manner according to the weight of glory that is upon my life with proper respect, love, joy, favor, and tender care.
- Father, I thank You that Your people assist me by presenting every resource needed for any Kingdom business You have assigned to be accomplished. Father, I thank You that the need for every Kingdom assignment is met, with abundance.
- Father, just as Phebe was, I am also a succourer: a woman set over others as one who protects, who supports, who encourages apostolic, prophetic, and Kingdom causes, and one who provides protective supervision.
- Father, I thank You that I am able to aid others with the resources You provide me. Thank You for the many things You have blessed me with as a succourer, and the many to come.
- Thank You that, as Phebe served the Apostle Paul, I will be blessed to serve other apostles and five-fold ministry giftings as well.
- Father, I thank You and receive this anointing for Kingdom business and will walk in the complete fulfillment of it with every assignment You give me.

In Jesus' name, Amen and Amen.

CHAPTER 50

HULDAH: A DAUGHTER OF ROYAL EXCELLENCE

By Michelle White

Huldah is known and ranked among many men and women prophets recorded in history possessing the gift of prophecy. Her name means, "weasel." She was married to Shallum (nephew of the prophet Jeremiah), the keeper of the royal wardrobe. Huldah was a teacher of the Word of God (the law or Torah) to many women and children throughout the city. Josiah was reared early under the godly influenced teaching of Huldah, who nurtured him early in life to become "a God-fearing man."

So it was, when the "Book of the Law" which was discovered in the House of the Lord by Hilkiah and the words contained was read to the king, he tore his clothes. It prompted him to search for the revelation-knowledge of the discovered truth. Without question, by Divine direction, Huldah was quickly approached.

As an apostolic leader, she laid the foundation (1 Corinthians 3:10 KJV) early as a prophetess (Acts 2:42KJV), teacher, and prominent member of the royal wardrobe, trained and developed women and children (Ephesians 4:12). Huldah sent confirmation via the Word (Revelation), which caused an impartation for the King of Judah to initiate reformation, which lead to Kingdom Order (first by way of repentance) that impacted the entire region (Acts 13:4 KJV).

"Submitted and committed women are nurturers by nature. Submission brings strength and a submitted vessel gains power to resist. WHEN the enemy meets real resistance, he will flee. Within a woman, the Holy Spirit establishes a nurturing spirit that will not allow her to push away her young but nurse them and care for them. The wise women learn his devices. Once you learn what he is "trying to do" use your strength for positive purposes (T.D Jakes). Huldah's nurturing of Josiah early in his life was impactful as recorded in the prophecy, "….because your heart was tender and you humbled yourself before the Lord…2 King's 22:19." Humility is the catalyst for radical change to birth reformation. Reformation, according to Webster's means, "the action of process of reforming an institution or practice." God used Huldah to deliver a prophetic message that altered the course of an entire nation. King Josiah grabbed hold of the prophecy, and he and other people took a stand and made a covenant before the Lord.

Reformation institutes "re-alignment" which brings about God's intended order. Though the process may first be painful, it is by far purposeful for our good and God's Glory and Honor due Him. "The Spirit of reformation is the Spirit of change. It blesses and strengthens the church and keeps the church moving toward the fulfillment of the Great Commission"(Apostle John Eckhardt). Each of us has all been in a wilderness season or seasons of uncomfortable change. However, God has commissioned us to rise ABOVE the depression, despair, divorce, derailment, and destruction and see through the lens of God, DESTINY as we walk in full deliverance, being the agents of change the world is desperately waiting to come forth.

In "God's Apostle Revived" by Dr. Paula A. Price, she says, "The Apostle's mantle includes warfare, strategy and rulership. The Apostle surfaces as an "arch warrior, a chief strategist and competent captain and an able guard over his jurisdiction." God has positioned each of us with Kingdom authority (Apostolic Grace) to initiate a movement of God in the places (territories) we are granted access to influence the Kingdom. The same Spirit in Christ Jesus is alive, active in us, and GREATER works shall we do.

Huldah was used to inform Josiah how to essentially reinstitute order first with reverential fear of the Lord. It did not take place the first day Hilkiah went to Huldah. It was first instilled in Josiah when he was a young child.

"So shall they fear the name of the Lord from the West and His Glory from the rising of the sun. When the enemy comes in like a flood, The Spirit of the Lord will lift up a standard against him" (Isaiah 59:19). Faithfulness, the requirement of a successful steward, is a character trait of the fruit of the Spirit which serves as a guiding culture principle for living as Kingdom citizens. Pistis, as defined in Strong's Concordance, in Greek means "faith, belief, trust." To possess the quality of being found trustworthy is found in the root of the receptive believer who has allowed God's Divine access to be used by Him. For those called to serve as Apostolic Leaders of God's people, faithfulness should be highly ranked in ministry rather than success, recognition, or popularity. Obedience was found at the basis of the heart of Josiah early in his life as well as I am confident it was with Huldah which serves as the foundation of this story. It further reveals how one act of obedience can fearlessly change the course of an entire nation. The Spirit of Grace is allowing for the Great Outpouring on all the flesh to bring about the Greatest Reformation Revival. The Promise of the Spirit is to boldly and confidently declare, "I AM Strong!"

- Commit to remain accountable to God
- Commit to carefully and faithfully do what is written in the Word of God
- Commit to the Gospel
- Commit to the call to be the courageous example
- Commit with an attitude of gratitude and boldness

Prophetic Prayer: In the Name of Jesus, may Your Grace become our love source to drive us to reach uncommon heights and deeper depths to do exceedingly, abundantly above ALL we ask or imagine according to Your power that is at work within us. May we become the FIRE (Fresh, Innovative, Radical, and Explosive) starters for reformation change; walking free and standing firm KNOWING whom You have made and called us to be in Your Kingdom. God Almighty, YOU declare the word of the Gospel with power and we (the warring women of Zion) deliver its message. May we ARISE and Your Glory, God, OVERFLOW as we become the next group of *Unexpected Global Game Changers*!

Declaration: We will move into EVERY Divinely-ordained and orchestrated opportunity God has made readily available to us. We will embrace the present and forsake the poison of the past as we press through toward our PROMISE! We are Mighty Women of Valor. We will go in the strength God has given us because He has said it is ours to possess. We shall defeat EVERY ENEMY that attempts to overtake us and we shall be used in a GREAT way even if we feel as if an army is rising against us. You, God, are looking for those who will take heed of Your Word and see ourselves as You have created us to be. God, You are calling forth Your Warriors. We will not be fearful or fainthearted. We will walk in faith and will not be moved by circumstances.

We will operate in "frontline faith" regardless of what is seen or heard in the natural and will take You at Your Word to rescue and deliver the captives. Our mind SHALL remain sharp, our thinking intuitive and innovative as we continue to advance into all You have called us to do. We will not fear the unknown, knowing You have provided everything needed to accomplish Your purpose and plan set out for our lives. We will seek Your counsel continuously to receive clear understanding and keen discernment for the tasks ahead, as well as wisdom and direction.

Prayer and intimacy shall be our portion as we store Your word in our heart. We realize the greatest blessing lies in the past of what we are willing to leave behind. I ask You Father, in Jesus' Name, to make every crooked path straight, for we KNOW You have already encamped Your legion of angels to surround us and the Blood of Jesus to cover us. You have created and called us for such a time as this to stand strong in the face of adversity and not to be confused. You have called us to conquer difficult situations. We submit our lives in total surrender to You, Father, knowing You will give Divine wisdom, discernment, and understanding for the days ahead. We shall RISE UP mightily, in Your strength to carry out the assignment you have personally given to each of us clothed in EVERY piece of armor praying ALWAYS in the power of the Holy Spirit, staying alert and persistent in our prayers at all times…In Jesus' Mighty and Matchless Name, Amen!"

CHAPTER 51

SHEERAH RISES!

By Dr. Betty Mitchell

Colossians 2:17 "All those things are mere shadows cast before what was to come; the substance is Christ." **MSG**

Hebrews 10:1 "The old plan was only a hint of the good things in the new plan." **MSG**

Ephesians 4: 11a "He handed out the gifts of apostle…" **MSG**

Tucked obscurely (as if to insinuate insignificance), we find in the Book of First Chronicles, a thread in the full story; a type and shadow of things to come pointing to the full manifestation of the Plan of God; recordings of names, genealogies, family trees, acts, stories large and small. The Holy Spirit included them in the Grand story of Salvation. Boring… but when REVEALED, pearls of great price can be mined, bringing edification, comfort, and exhortation.

It's A Girl!

"Now his daughter was SHEERAH, who built Lower and Upper Beth Horon and Uzzen SHEERAH." (1 Chronicles 7:24 MSG)

For a brief backdrop, Ephraim, her father, was the second of two sons born to Joseph, the dreamer and Asenath, an Egyptian woman which the pharaoh gave to Joseph as wife and founder of one of the twelve tribes of Israel. His name, Ephraim means "double fruitfulness" signifying that Joseph, his father, had been made fruitful by God in the land of his affliction, suffering. Note: Biblical names had spiritual significance attached as a means of record keeping, chronicling. First Chronicles 7: 20-27 gives us a glimpse into some family happenings. Eight sons are listed, including two, Ezer and Elead, who were killed by men of Gath after stealing their cattle. As the story continues, the father, Ephraim, mourned many days. During this time, another son, Beriah was born AND A DAUGHTER, SHEERAH (in a good majority of research materials and commentaries her name is either not mentioned or explained away).

Down But Not Out

"Now may the God of hope fill you with all joy and peace in believing, that you may abound in hope by the power of the Holy Spirit." (Romans 15:13)

Misfortune strikes, dad is elderly, two brothers killed...where do we go from here? In this dismal picture, Father Ephraim could have very well adopted a pessimistic view of "all is lost." Or perhaps in the spin of grief, sorrow, the trauma of it all, he forgot his name's meaning, "double fruitfulness." But God...God remembers the covenant with his ancestors, Abraham, Isaac, and Jacob and He (God) RISES—a **Kairos** moment!

I Rise

"But for you, sunrise! The sun of righteousness will dawn on those who honor my name, healing radiating from its wings..." (Malachi 4:2 MSG)

Thus SHEERAH RISES! Fathered by the same father, raised in the same home, instructed in the same Torah, observant of her famed father's conversation (manner of life) and business dealings; the dots began to connect for SHEERAH.

First Corinthians 1:26-29 NIV ...think of what you were when you were called... But God chose the foolish, the weak, the lowly so that no one may boast before Him.

SHEERAH pondered, "Why sit we here and die? Not my fault that I have a different Earth suit." "Little girls with dreams become women with vision" (Unknown). She exhales the frustration, futility, and anxiety of it all, then bows and inhales the vision of God and roars, "I RISE, I TAKE MY PLACE, I RECEIVE MY PORTION, I RECEIVE MY INHERITANCE.

Sheerah the Builder

"Come, let us ARISE and build, I am mantled (covered by my Father)."

Isaiah 61:1a, 4 MSG – *"The Spirit of God, the Master, is upon me because God anointed me… They'll rebuild the old ruins, raise a new city out of the wreckage. They'll start over on the ruined cities, take the rubble left behind and make it new."*

Isaiah 58:12, MSG – *"You'll use the old rubble of past lives to build anew, rebuild the foundations from out of your past. You'll be known as those who can fix anything, restore old ruins, rebuild and renovate, make the community livable again."*

SHEERAH began to build…and SHEERAH built. Three cities: Lower and Upper Beth Horon, the site of numerous wars… one instance in particular, where Joshua , a relative of SHEERAH, defeated five kings as God threw them into total confusion… God himself hurling hailstones upon Israel's enemies; more died from the hailstones than from the sword in response to Joshua's prophetic decree (see Joshua 10: 12-14) and Uzzen Sheerah. As Winston Churchill once said, "Give us the tools and we will finish the job". That she did!

Clearly, the apostolic grace was upon this daughter of the Lord! Through the power of God, she was unstoppable. She quelled the voices of apathy, doubt, unbelief, criticism, and fear, including fear of failure. She defied age-old instructions, "color safely, stay within the lines", "don't shatter the stained glass ceiling." At this Kairos moment and time in her life, she ceased to be a well-behaved woman. "Well behaved women seldom make history" (Laurel Thatcher Ulrich). This quote is not a tease to misbehave in order to be remembered, it is simply a sad but truthful reminder that many women who made quite the impact upon history are poorly and sorely often overlooked—Not SHEERAH!

Apostles are graced to pioneer, trailblaze, go where others haven't gone before, envision the impossible, build the unlikely… it is a gift, an office bestowed by the Chief Apostle, the Lord Jesus Christ. It is repeatedly included in the salutations of the New Testament letters to the churches- GRACE, mercy, and peace be multiplied to you. SHEERAH BUILT THREE CITIES—MUCH GRACE!

Summation:

- Apostles are sent to re-present the heart of the Father and build the Kingdom.
- Apostles are graced to finish the work.
- Apostles endure great opposition because they bring order into confusion.
- Apostles receive keys; direct revelation, strategies, patterns, and vision from the Father through intimacy with Him.
- The apostolic grace is not limited to the pulpit; it operates in the marketplace as well.

Apostolic Prayer:

Father, in the name of Jesus, I pray and declare that those with apostolic grace upon their lives will awake to the plan and call of God upon their lives and ARISE to build in their sphere of influence. I break off limitation, inferiority, low self-esteem, lies of the enemy, fear in all forms, and I **now**, by the Power of the Holy Ghost, create space for them to hear the voice of God with clarity and distinction. Be free to obey God and be the blessing you were designed to be in Jesus' Name!

Declarations of Faith:

1. Father, I receive multiplied grace through the apostolic anointing YOU have bestowed upon my life!
2. Looking unto Jesus as the author and finisher of my faith, I arise and courageously build the Kingdom.
3. I have the keys of revelation, vision, provision, supernatural strength, wisdom, understanding, and ALL that I need to fulfill my assignment.
4. By faith, I fully receive and possess my inheritance. Give me this mountain!

5. I am in no way terrified of my enemies.
6. I run with vision from God, speaking, declaring, decreeing it until it can speak for itself.
7. My obedience to the call paves the way for others to experience great victory in their lives.
8. I can do and will do ALL things through Christ who empowers me!
9. I leave a rich legacy to my heirs.
10. I win!

CHAPTER 52

HARRIET TUBMAN: THE APOSTOLIC FREEDOM FIGHTER

By Yolanda Mosby

Harriet Tubman was born into slavery in Maryland and later escaped to her freedom in the north in 1849; she became one of the most well-known conductors in operation of the Underground Railroad. However, not without complications, Harriet had to fight to stay alive after being hit in the head by a heavy iron weight. After refusing to help aide the punishment of another slave, the overseer picked up the iron weight to throw it at the slave but instead it hit Harriet in the head, nearly crushing her skull. The traumatic head injury left Tubman unconscious for days and caused pain and seizures throughout her entire life.

In 1844, Harriet married a free man named John Tubman, which caused her last name, Ross, to become Tubman. She also took on her mothers' first name, Harriet. In 1849, Harriet became worried that she and many other slaves were going to be sold, so she decided to run away. Her husband refused to join her; therefore, she and her brothers followed the North Star that would later guide them north to freedom. After her brothers became terrified, they turned back, but Harriet continued until she reached Philadelphia. She later found work as one who would serve others in-home and saved her money to return to help others escape the hands of slavery.

Over the course of a 10-year span, Harriet took the chances of running the painstaking personal risk to free and lead hundreds of family members and other slaves through the plantation system to their freedom on the secret network of safe houses. Tubman had also become the "Moses of her People." Many slaves dreaming of freedom sang the spiritual "Go Down Moses." So many slaves hoped the Lord would deliver each of them just as he empowered Moses to deliver the Israelites out of Egypt.

Tubman helped 300 people to freedom by making 19 trips to Maryland. During these dangerous journeys, she also rescued members of her family, which also included both her parents, who were 70 years of age. At some point, rewards for her capture totaled $40,000. Nevertheless, she was not caught nor did she ever fail to follow-through to deliver her passengers to safety during each of her missions. Tubman had her way of saying, "On my Underground Railroad I (never) run my train off (the) track (and) I never (lost) a passenger."

After becoming a leading abolitionist before the American Civil War, Tubman also helped the Union Army during the war; she also managed to work as a spy and a nurse for the federal forces in South Carolina amongst so many other challenging roles. Tubman dedicated her life after the Civil War ended to helping impoverished former slaves and elderly people.

During the course of Harriet Tubman's apostolic mission, her story speaks for her life as an anointed and devoted vessel of God. She took her apostolic mission to heart without hesitation. When she asked her husband to escape with her he refused, nevertheless, Tubman did not allow her husband's decision to keep her from escaping slavery for herself, nor for the future of others who would soon need her help.

Harriet Tubman was called the "Moses of Her People." Likewise, God is calling **you** to complete the apostolic mission He has assigned to you. God has called you to rise up with the power that He has bestowed upon you, to engage in Great Exploits that will set the captives free—for this is the Great Commission that God has given each of us as born-again believers. God has given you the power and authority to rise up as a *change agent* in your generation!

Apostolic Empowerment Scriptures:

Jeremiah 1:10 (KJV) "See, I have this day set thee over the nations and over the kingdoms, to root out, and to pull down, and to destroy, and to throw down, to build, and to plant."

Matthew 18:18 (KJV) "Verily I say unto you, Whatsoever ye shall bind on earth shall be bound in heaven: and whatsoever ye shall loose on earth shall be loosed in heaven."

Luke 10:19 (KJV) "Behold, I give unto you power to tread on serpents and scorpions, and over all power of the enemy: and nothing shall by any means hurt you."

Ephesians 4:11-12 (KJV) "And he gave some, apostles; and some, prophets; and some evangelists; and some, pastors and teachers; For the perfecting of the saints, for the work of the ministry, for edifying of the body of Christ."

Titus 3:5 (KJV) "Not by works of righteousness which we have done, but according to mercy he saved us, by the washing of regeneration, and renewing of the Holy Ghost;"

Declarations:

1. I will rise up to fulfill my God-given assignment to set the captives free by any means necessary—people are waiting for my arrival.
2. I will rise up to fulfill my God-given mission. I will monitor my post and region, to assess the damages in order to execute the appropriate strategy that will bring restoration and revival.
3. I will rise up to operate in my God-given authority to divide and conquer, uphold and put down, bind and loose, declare and decree, denounce and proclaim, to pray and fast. I will sound the trumpet, cry aloud, and spare not concerning that which God has assigned me to.

CHAPTER 53:

THE EXTRAORDINARY
LIFE OF GLADYS AYLWARD

By Terry Ricklefs

Gladys Aylward is little known, but her life was extraordinary. I did not hear of her until a friend of mine loaned me a book on her life over 15 years ago. Since I then had a ministry call and a call to the nations, I was very eager to hear her story.

Aylward was born in 1902 in London, England to a working-class family. Since her teens, she worked as a domestic housecleaner. Her heart began to burn to go to China as a missionary, and on every occasion she had, she would study the Chinese culture. However, she was denied by a Chinese missionary society, as they felt she was not qualified to go. She had many naysayers who felt she was just a housecleaner and not much else.

Through the rejection, she remained firm and unwavering about her call, and insisted she was going to China. She was able to find another job as a housecleaner, and began to save every penny she made for her train ticket across Europe, through Russia- to China. She was also determined to get experience in preaching, and stood on a soapbox at Hyde Park in London to train herself. Finally, she obtained her train ticket, and was given a contact named Jeannie Lawson, who she was supposed to meet upon her arrival. The journey by train to China was very perilous, but the Lord and His angels protected her and saw her to her destination.

Gladys met Jeannie and helped her for a time with the inn she owned- a place of refuge for mule train drivers. Gladys had to learn the Chinese language, ways, and culture, and despite the hardships, she fell in love with the people and wanted to spend the rest of her life there.

Jeannie Lawson died a short time after Gladys arrived in China. Gladys was thrown into a tailspin, but the Lord was faithful to open another door for her. The mandarin of the village learned of her and asked Gladys to become his official foot un-binder. She agreed, and began to liberate many Chinese women in this way. Foot binding had been an ancient custom in China, where the feet of young girls were rolled under.

This is an excerpt from an article that describes foot binding, from the South China Morning Post:

"Like opium dens, sedan chairs and bat-winged junks, women with bound feet were once stereotypical to China…Deliberately crippled to conform to male ideals of beauty, these strange, pathetic creatures to Western eyes embodied the mysterious ways of the East…Early travel accounts describe the "alluring" manner in which Chinese women with bound feet walked, as they gently swayed and tottered, usually with an amah on each arm for support. Physiological reasons for this "attractive" faltering gait were never seriously questioned by casual observers."

Gladys did a good job at loosing the feet of the women and children of the district, and the Lord gave her favor with the mandarin, who eventually converted to Christianity.

Gladys was born with black hair, which was unheard of by those of British descent. The Lord had fashioned her from birth! This must have helped the Chinese to be able to relate to her.

It says in Psalm 139, "My frame was not hidden from You, When I was made in secret, And skillfully wrought in the depths of the earth; have seen my unformed substance And in Your book were all written the days that were ordained for me, when as yet there were none of them! How precious also are Your thoughts to me, O God! How vast is the sum of them!"

After Gladys had been in this country for a while, news that Japan was going to attack China soon, caused much fear and panic among the people. A group of orphans was brought to Gladys, and she was given a letter saying if she could get the orphans to a certain place, she and the orphans would be safe from the Japanese, and all would be given food and shelter. Gladys embarked on yet another journey through mountain terrain, and she and the orphans made it safely to where they needed to go. The Lord protected them in specific ways, such as security across the Yellow River crossing, as the Japanese did not patrol that area the week Gladys and the orphans were passing through.

Gladys was a woman who walked in fellowship with the Holy Spirit and received His direction. This is possible for any servant of God. We can know the mind of Christ for our lives on a daily basis. We can know by the Spirit if we are walking on the path He has for us, or if we have strayed from it.

Gladys carried a burden of the Lord for China that she could not shake. The Old Testament has a few references to the English word "burden." One of these is the Hebrew word, *Massa*. The Lord saw the wars in China that were about to happen and the Heavenly Councils were asking, as well as the Lord Himself, "Who will go for Us?" They found Gladys was willing and available. Gladys claims, however, that she was not the Lord's first choice for this mission.

God is a *sending* God, notes Isaiah chapter 6 when Isaiah saw the holiness of God:

> *"Then one of the seraphim flew to me with a live coal in his hand, which he had taken with tongs from the altar. With it he touched my mouth and said, "See, this has touched your lips; your guilt is taken away and your sin atoned for."*
> *Then I heard the voice of the Lord saying, "Whom shall I send? And who will go for us?"*
> *And I (Isaiah) said, "Here am I. Send me!"*

Isaiah then began to receive the message, the burden, as the Lord said, "Go and tell this people, etc.," He then obeyed the vision.

This further describes the *Massa burden of the Lord*—from thequickenedword.com.

Zech 12:1 AMP

The burden or oracle (the thing to be lifted up) of the word of the Lord concerning Israel: "Thus says the Lord, Who stretches out the heavens and lays the foundation of the earth and forms the spirit of man within him."

A Bible concordance reads, Massa' (mas-saw'); from OT: 5375; a burden; specifically, tribute, or (abstractly) an utterance, chiefly a doom, especially singing; mental, desire, burden, carry away, prophecy, song, tribute.

The *Massa burden of the Lord* is a by-product of intimacy with God. Out of your times together, He reveals the burdens of His heart, like a spiritual seed planted in the womb. Not many may understand what you carry, and you will be brought into the fellowship of the sufferings of Christ. Nonetheless, the Lord is looking for those willing to carry these burdens.

A Prophetic Prayer: "Lord help me to step forth in the courage and boldness of Gladys Alyward. She inspires my life, and I decree that if she can overcome so many obstacles, there is nothing I cannot accomplish for You, if I move out in faith and obedience to Your call, You will protect me in Your hand in all things, according to Psalm 91. When I get discouraged, help me find strength by Your Spirit and in the testimonies of the lives that have passed on before me.

What qualities did Gladys possess that we can claim for ourselves?

1. Endurance- Gladys had to endure hard physical, psychological, and emotional challenges. When she finally arrived to her destination with the orphans, she collapsed from exhaustion.
   Declaration: "I can do all things through Christ, who strengthens me!

2. Courage- She had to face many situations with extreme courage, such as going into a prison to try to stop a riot. She succeeded and brought Divine order to the facility.

   Declaration: "There is nothing I will face apart from the grace of God!"

3. Compassion- The love and compassion of God flowed through her, she reached out to people of all ages, especially children. The mandarin of the village came to trust her in time.

Declaration: "I have been crucified with Christ, and it is no longer I who live, but Christ who lives in me!

4. Empathy- Gladys tried to emphasize with those around her. She lived among them, and felt their pain. She did not arrive, stay for a few weeks or months, then return to a more comfortable life.

   Declaration: "I am able to love with the love of Christ!"

5. Adaptability- Gladys had to adapt to a culture that was completely foreign to hers, yet she overcame this through her faith and trust in God.

   Declaration: "I am adaptable, and an overcomer!"

ABOUT THE ANTHOLOGIST

I.R. Womack is the CEO and founder of Alpha Book Publishing. He's a best-selling author, teacher, preacher, and missionary. I.R. Womack is also the founder of the Kingdom Ministry Institute. He travels internationally, conducting miracle crusades and training the body of Christ and organizations in various areas, including fivefold ministry, healing ministry, deliverance ministry, prophetic ministry, entrepreneurship, and financial empowerment. He's married to Shavonne, and they have four wonderful children.

MEET THE CO-AUTHORS

Dr. Yolanda Powell

Dr. Yolanda Powell is a 2nd generation Apostle with a prolific call to Marketplace Ministry. She serves as a founding Board Member & Tier-1 Leader of the EPIC Global Network (Extraordinary People Influencing Culture) with Apostle Axel Sippach and has a unique mantle to scale the 7-Mountains and train others to do the same. This cutting edge trainer and master communicator is also an international speaker, author and mentor who serves as President & CEO of her own communications company, Yolanda Powell Transcontinental, LLC. Her premiere training and coaching programs are designed for Kingdom leaders, Marketplace ministers, Global gatekeepers and Corporate executives - across seven continents - on how to develop their Life Message & Signature Talk as a living trust to creatively showcase Christ in the public square and advance His Kingdom around the globe. Dr. Powell has been in ministry for nearly four decades and is also the visionary & senior leader of Dominion International Ministries, "an embassy of training and development for Kings & Priests," located just outside Washington, DC. To learn more, visit her website at www.yolandapowell.com.

Deborah Sheppard

Deborah Sheppard is the co-founder of Unveiling Word Ministries Newnan, Ga., with her husband, Apostle Wayne Sheppard. She is a loving mother of three wonderful boys, Immanuel Griggs, Darrell Griggs, and Elijah Griggs. She is the author of

"The Essence of Spiritual Discipline: Principles of Successful Discipleship" which was released in April, 2018 (available at www.amazon.com).

Apostle Deborah Sheppard Graduated from Newnan High School in 1986, she received her Master's in Cosmetology in 1993, her second Degree in Business Administration in 2005 at the American InterContinental University, and went on to receive her third Degree in Accounting/Banking in 2012 from the Rasmussen University in Ocala, FL. She is also a graduate of Leadership Coweta 2013's Coweta County Chamber of Commerce.

Nicole Davis

Nicole Davis has a passion for family, women, and leadership development which has evolved and strengthened over many decades. As a wife of over 25 years and the mother of two adult sons, family enrichment has been her number one priority. Her passion for the topic of *leadership* started during her years in the United States Navy. From there, she has provided education and training to leaders in several arenas and on various levels including collegiate, non-profits, corporate, government, and church. She is also a certified mediator, facilitator, conflict coach, and marriage trainer. As a Christian leader, Nicole has served in multiple capacities within churches to strengthen and develop ministries and programs. She has gained affection by both couples and women for her teaching and leadership style for being loving, firm, but fair.

Along with her husband, Tony, she has co-authored multiple books which include: the 3-book DONE RIGHT SERIES: (1) *Parenting Done Right is Hard Work But It's Worth It*, (2) *Marriage Done Right is Hard Work But It's Work It*, and, (3) *Leadership Done Right is Hard Work But It's Worth It*, to bring voice to what God is speaking regarding FAMILY dynamics and the conduct of the individuals within them. She is also a co-author in two anthologies: SPEAK TO THE MOUNTAINS! and JUNIA ARISE: APOSTOLIC WOMEN ON THE FRONTLINES.

Having grown in wisdom regarding maintaining a loving marriage and rearing children who are god-fearing and successfully fulfilling purpose within their respective professions and gifts, God has released Tony and Nicole to now share what it takes to grow and maintain strong marriages and "train up a child in the way he should go." They have co-founded an organization, *Empower to Engage*, focusing on enhancing marriages, families, and equipping men and women to exemplify godly leadership in their sphere of societal influence. Visit their website www.empowertoengage.com.

Michelle Brown-McKoy

Michelle Brown-McKoy is an ordained Apostolic-Deliverance Prophet who is well known for her strong zeal, genuine love and desire to see people healed, delivered and empowered to living a life of freedom and fulfilled prophetic destiny. She serves a dual role as a Marketplace Minister influencing the nations having worked as a Christ Ambassador at the United Nations and for former NY Senator, and U.S. Presidential candidate Hillary Rodham Clinton. As God's Prophet, she has been charged with ensuring that justice prevails, saints are empowered, set free from bondage and God's design for creation manifests to cause global transformation throughout the nations. Prophetess Brown-McKoy is a Kingdom strategist, advocate for justice, social reformer, entrepreneur and empowerment coach. With her strong love for Christ and dedication to Kingdom advancement, she thrives on training, equipping and mentoring believers so they can advance in their prophetic destinies. Her mandate is to impact individuals, the Mountain of Government and the other mountains of influence so that they can come into divine alignment with God's original plan and purpose for the Earth. Prophetess Brown-McKoy is the visionary and founder of O WOW! Women's Empowerment Group and Prophetic Charge Ministries in Bronx, NY. She is a well sought after author, speaker and co-author of Speak to the Mountains. Michelle is an Independent Certified Coach, Trainer and Speaker with The John Maxwell Team. She is also a member of EPIC Network under the leadership of Apostle Axel Sippach.

For booking inquiries, please contact:
Phone: (914) 330-0695
michlsmckoy@gmail.com or
owowempowerment@gmail.com

Thapelo Kgabage

 Thapelo Donald Kgabage was born in a town called Taung, Leshobo Village (Mokgareng) located in the North West province, South Africa and currently residing at Potchefstroom (North West Province, South Africa). Thapelo is a certified accountant by profession and works as an auditor for the South African Supreme Audit Institution. He is also a business man running a consultation company that has helped many companies with its administrations and major projects. Thapelo is a young ordained minister of the Gospel of Jesus Christ who began preaching the Gospel of the Lord Jesus Christ at a very young age of 10 years. He is a conference speaker, motivational speaker, mentor, the author of the book entitled "The Benjamin Generation" and he has been involved in lot of ministries including outreaches as well as crusades across South Africa. Thapelo has impacted many lives around the communities he is based, and he is much known for the sound prophetic and apostolic teachings, he also worked and helped establish many ministries with the teachings and the administration ability. Thapelo is mandated and graced by the Lord Jesus Christ to impact his Generation, he is called to discover and voice the revelations and the mysteries of the kingdom of God as kept in the Holy Scriptures, minister love, align the church to the correct prophetic times, he is called to sound a trumpet and declare the kingdom to the nations, he is called to reveal the mind of God in these latter days in his generation across the nations of the world.

Cherie Banks

Cherie Banks is the mastermind behind the moniker, CEO Influencer™. Her visionary leadership contributed to generating the 1st billion dollars for an international Fortune 500 company with consecutive results. She is a success leader, business investor, and serial entrepreneur with a multi-million dollar brand. Cherie is a highly-sought after industry expert for her business mastery, strategic planning, market penetration, growth expansion, global alliance, leadership development, ethical integrity, PR/media relations, crisis management, conflict resolution, and human capital commitment. She also serves as a chief strategic advisor, fiduciary board member, and social good advocate for non-profit organizations. Cherie is an honored recipient of prestigious awards in business, law, education, and community. Notably, Cherie is an apostolic visionary and prophetic voice in marketplace ministry with a profound anointing in business, wealth, and legacy. She serves as a pastoral confidant and spiritual advisor to CEOs, corporations, church leaders, and faith-based ministries. Cherie has an M.A. in Pastoral Studies from Loyola University and an Honorary Doctorate in Divinity. She also has a J.D. from Loyola University School of Law and a B.A. from DePaul University. Cherie was a founding board member and vice magistrate of Phi Delta Phi Honorary Legal Fraternity. She studied European law at Oxford University in the United Kingdom. Additionally, Cherie was distinguished as a United States honorary guest at the European Parliament, Council of Europe, European Courts of Justice and Human Rights, European Union, and NATO. Cherie earned highest honors distinction for academic excellence and moral character with notoriety on the President's Scholar Guild, Golden Key International Honor Society, and National Dean's List.

Anita McCoy

Anita McCoy, with over 30 years of ministerial leadership, is a dynamic woman that God has raised up to advance His Kingdom. In 2009 Anita started "The Healing Clinic", a transformation center with an emphasis on apostolic teaching, strategic prayer, prophecy and the ministry of healing. In addition to this, as Founding Pastor and Director of Field of Dreams Harvest Ministries (2013), Anita has a mandate to raise leaders through apostolic and prophetic training, and discipleship. She has ministered in various parts of the United States, as well as East Africa and India. Anita also serves the Northwestern region of Pennsylvania as Vice President of Leadership Development of Aglow International, an international Christian organization of women and men comprised of over 200, 000 members ministering in 171 nations worldwide. Anita, a graduate of Bloomsburg University of PA, received her Bachelors of Science in Education with a minor in Speech and Audiology and credits her love of education and revealing truth as key components that fuel her passion to reproduce reproducers who are equipped and empowered to fulfill their God-ordained destiny and influence all cultures of society through the dynamics of Heaven's Kingdom Culture.

Shelby Frederick

Shelby Frederick, who is affectionately known by her social media followers as "Lady Jewels", is a rising apostolic prophetic leader whose unique communication style bridges generational gaps, using "Life Keys" to convey kingdom principles for successful living. She is the founder of God's Precious Jewels, a women's ministry which has birthed several extensions including Jewels Speak Radio Show, War Room Warriors Prayer Ministry and Sisterhood Fellowship. With over a decade of experience as a Licensed Massage Therapist, her knowledge and training allows her to holistically educate the public on the benefits of alternative therapies, including the incorporation of essential oils in daily living. Her vision as a Wellness Specialist is to equip women with holistic strategies, inspiring them to take personal responsibility for their emotional wellness as they make positive impacts in their spheres of influence.

Michelle Thomas

Michelle D. Engram Thomas
schmichleythcth@hotmail.com
(312) 479-0265

Michelle Engram Thomas is a newly-published author who has been writing most of her life. She was born in Chicago, Illinois to a WWII veteran and his bride, both preacher's kids. Michelle attended a Baptist church with her parents, later following her mother to a UCC-affiliated church. Michelle attended several schools and even helped to integrate one in Chicago, then proceeded to graduate from NIU with her B.S. in Biology,. She became an ASCP-Certified Cytotechnologist and worked for a few Chicago-area hospitals. She lived in Chicago until she decided to give the USAF a try. The military did not disappoint. She lived in Texas for a few years and was introduced to Pentecostalism at Livingway Christian Church under the leadership of Steve and Becky Fender. This introduction propelled her into the lifestyle of more than just attending church on Sunday. Seeking to satisfy this hunger for more knowledge of God, Michelle relocated to Tulsa, Ok. to attend ORU. Her spiritual eyes became enlightened and the rest is history. Michelle has been divorced for many years, is a mother, and currently resides in Lafayette, LA awaiting further instruction from the Lord concerning her life's purposes in God.

Ladonna Jackson

Prefacing her salvation at the age of 20, LaDonna Jackson had a generational "birthright" to a call in ministry. Her family moved from Kansas City, Kansas to Houston, Texas when she was very young. Soon after, LaDonna became adamant about her marketplace pursuits. She obtained three college degrees: BA (Sociology/ Human Development and Family Studies); BM (Music Education); and MM (Voice Performance). In the near future, she plans to pursue an MA and PhD in speech language and pathology to become a fully licensed singing voice specialist. Her desire is to study voice disorders and become a voice coach for many, including those in Hollywood. Other than marks in education, LaDonna has had an opera singing career onstage with appearances in Carnegie Hall, Uganda, and the Amalfi Coast. Her next step is to turn these opportunities into global missions.

LaDonna currently serves at Free Indeed Church International in Houston, Texas, under the leadership of Apostle Johnny and Prophetess Jenice Gentry. She is actively involved in the prison ministry aspect of Community Works CDC, a non profit geared towards missions, and the re-entry of ex-offenders into society. She is also involved in Free Squad, the ministry's evangelism team.

Jackie Betty

Jacqueline Wade Betty wore the mantle of justice long before she realized it. As a young girl growing up in Jamaica, she was very vocal in her views of unfair treatment of others and often defended them. It mattered little to her that she sometimes suffered. What mattered is that her intervention got positive results. Her heart for justice is real, and she demonstrates this in her work. The judicial link between her call to champion the cause for justice and her love for accounting merged in an unusual way. A successful Charted Accountant of England and Wales who practiced in a Third World country soon learned that moving to the First World was extremely challenging. Though she quickly gained the equivalent Certified Public Accountant (CPA) license and could practice accounting, the opportunity never materialized. Thank God, she quickly learned that she could choose to take these disenfranchising punches as blows or as challenges. These punches activated another part of her purpose- writing. Her 9 years' tutoring experience in an English and Literature environment at a state college drove her to explore historical works of inequality and justice in systems. As a CPA, she is skilled to administer financial accounting laws. Now, her skills are channeled to matters that weigh heavily on equality and justice. Among other work of poetry and music is her webpage, www.kingdomjusticealliance.com. She writes to bring awareness to her readers and invites them to purposefully unite and balance the scale of justice.

Cassandra McKissack

Cassandra McKissack has added sparkle to any setting as she instills in audiences the ability to own their power and discover their possibilities. She has been seen on TBN, The Word Network, STL 10, TV 4, 'Here & Now,' show and other TV stations across America. She has also interviewed people from all genres, including Bishop William Murphy; Dr. Bobby Jones; Dr. David Knight, Bernita Ewing (actress in TD Jakes movie), and many more. Ms. McKissack loves people and positivity. Cassandra has earned multiple degrees, and her ministry is called McKissack Ministries. Her ministry gifts are evangelism and prophecy.

Carla Louis-Wallace

Carla Wallace is the business owner of M.O.Y.A. Productions, LLC and Centurion Health and Wellness Solutions, LLC. She is a Registered Nurse, who is currently employed by a national health care company in the Market Place as a Regional Nurse Consultant for the Texas region. She is an author, a mentor and a sponsor to many Kingdom Business Owners and start- up companies. She is a visionary who carries the Joseph anointing, who loves equipping, empowering and launching people into the things that will help advance the Kingdom of God. She is an Ambassador with a Kingdom Business with marketplace influence.

Connie Strickland

Connie Strickland is a commissioned Apostle that has a global mandate to preach the message of the kingdom as she travels to nations around the world. Her anointing is evident as God uses her to carry His Glory into regions eradicating the power of darkness and empowering, activating, and releasing believers into their God-given purpose. Apostle Strickland is the overseer of C.G.K.C. (Chosen Generation Kingdom Center) AHOP (Apostolic House of Prayer) and CSMI (Connie Strickland Ministries International) headquarters in Houston, Texas. She is an apostolic trailblazer that God has preserved for this generation and future generations to birth out MOVES of God that will manifest transformation and reformation in the regions assigned to her. Apostle Strickland is a market place leader, author and ghostwriter and serves in the UAAFI Network as Apostle of Foreign Missions, under the leadership of Apostle David Pittman.

Deborah L. Anderson

The Ambassador and Speaker of the House! Deborah is a frontline warrior in the army of the Lord whose ministry carries an apostolic and prophetic anointing as a Trumpet of God, called to relentless to serve the Lord as a builder of ministries nationwide. She is the Founder of Fully Persuaded Ministries International that has successfully edified, strengthened and built up the Kingdom ministries whose footprint is on the foundation of several church plants for over 25 years. A Graduate of Washington H.S. with an Associate Business degree from Michiana College of Commerce, a B.S. Degree in Theology from Calvary Temple Theological Seminary & Bible College, a Paralegal Certification from Southwestern Professional Institute, and holds a Bachelor Degree in Business Administration (Summa Cum Laude) from LeTourneau University. Having a governmental anointing, she serves as the Precinct Chair for Senate District 17, Precinct 804 for the Texas Democratic Party, a member of the Christian Legal Society, a national organization of lawyers, judges and legal professionals and has served as a Board Member of several non-profit organizations utilizing her legal background and ministry experience for organizational development and as a Judge for the InterFaith Freedom Initiative (IFI) in cooperation with the Texas Department of Criminal Justice for successful transition from prison and re-entry to the community. A published author of *"Apostolic Women Birthing Nations – A 21st Century Guide to 21st Ministry"*

Kenna O'Flannigan

As an office gift to the Body of Christ, Kenna O'Flannigan operates as a watchman prophet inspired by Holy Spirit. Kenna is the founder of Tsaphah Ministries whose mission is to restore order and integrity to the Body of Christ through prophetic insight and biblical wisdom. With an eye toward Order and Protocol, the Lord uses Kenna to identify areas in ministry and personal character that are left open for the enemy to attack and to provide insight for realignment, strategy, and ultimate victory. Kenna is the author of <u>Watchman Prophet</u>, a blog and developing online community for Kingdom servants under prophetic orders to give divinely inspired warnings from the Lord. (https://tsaphahwatchman.com). The opportunity to contribute to Apostle Sippach's "Junia Arise" project serves as Kenna's sophomore contribution to the community of prophetic scribes, with "Speak to the Mountains" being her first contribution. Kenna's legal background as both a court reporter and paralegal provide a foundation for awareness of protocol, permissions, accountability, and access, which uniquely qualify her intelligent expression and studied insights. Readers will find the genuine wisdom trustworthy for life application. Elder Kenna is both a minister and a mother. She is the resilient mother of four adult children, and an Elder-Elect at New Nation Church. Her leaders are Pastors Chris and Felicia Dexter. Stable and rooted in the faith, Elder Kenna renders loyal, honest, and caring service to the Body of Christ at her local church and in her spheres of influence. Junia Arise carries a profound significance at this stage in Kenna's life, as she is an emerging leader and voice in the Kingdom. Kenna's life verse is Ezekiel 3:17, which says, "Son of man, I have made thee a watchman unto the house of Israel: therefore hear the word at my mouth, and give them warning from me.".

Kierra Douglas

Kierra Douglas is a native of the District of Columbia, Maryland, and Virginia(DMV) area. She is a graduate of Suitland High School and Prince George's Community College, with an Associate's degree in General Study. While working in the corporate job field, Kierra was a Professional Writer and Editor at the world's largest credit union. She also successfully held a position as a Professional Trainer/Facilitator while working towards obtaining her degree to become a School Teacher. Kierra attends Beyond the Veil Worship Center church, under Apostle Wanda Sisco in Washington, DC. Kierra served on the Outreach Ministry, Liturgical Dance Ministry, and as a Soldiers of Joy Bible Study Teacher for the teenagers, before taking a leave of absence due to illness. Kierra has proven to be an over comer, as she has survived having brain surgery in 2007. As a result of a rare autoimmune illness, Kierra had to learn how to walk again, lost and regained her vision several times, and still suffers with debilitating muscle spasms and nerve pain. Through all of these challenges, Kierra was able to start her own business – 3KD Enrichment. Within this business, Kierra has created an Anti-Bullying App that allows children to anonymously report bullying in their schools. She is also working on self-publishing her first children's book on stopping bullying in school. God has great and mighty exploits to do through Kierra, and she is not allowing anything to stop her or slow her down!

Cecilia Davis-Jackson

Dr. Cecilia Jarmon Davis-Jackson is a retired English and philosophy teacher. She has a Master's Degree in Education and in Clinical Counseling, a Doctorate in Divinity, has over 30 years of experience in ministry and education and holds various licenses and certifications. Cecilia is an author of 30 professional publications, inspirational speaker, Biblical educational consultant, curriculum developer, intercontinental leader of Kingdom International Nations for Christ, and Co-Founder of "I AM" Fellowship's Non-Conventional School of ministry (with her husband for 37 years, Dr. Michael Jackson). Additionally, Cecilia is currently an adjunct professor at a college, founder of Reaching Women and Children for the Nations and Christian Community Outreach, Inc., functions as an experienced leader in the Kingdom of God, and has a passion for apostolically imparting doctrine with practical application. Apostle Jackson's God-given anointing charismatically influences and shifts the atmosphere in audiences of cultural, ethnic, and socio-economic diversity as her lectures impact cross-generational gatherings. Contact: drcjackson3712@gmail.com, www.authordrcjackson.com, www.iamfellowshipministries.com, 513-278-7170, or PO Box 355, West Union, Ohio, USA.

Jeannette Connell

Jeannette Connell is married to her husband George Connell of 31 years. They have six children and currently reside in Troy, Mo. She is an apostolic leader who has served for the past 25 years in building the Kingdom of God in multiple churches. She has been active in prophetic intercession; children and youth ministries; counseling; deliverance, writing and church planting. Jeannette is currently functioning as an apostolic leader and founder of Troy Freedom Outpost in Troy Missouri. TFO also serves as a ministry base for Spiritual Cleansing ministry in which she birthed several years prior. It is a team ministry of inner healing, freedom, teaching, training and equipping the body of Christ in spiritual warfare. She is an author of her first book, _Spiritual Cleansing getting to the root_ and has currently published her third called _Spiritual Cleansing of the bloodline_ and also a Handbook. She is ordained through Cornerstone Ministries Inc. in New Mexico. She and her team do mission work in the First Nations tribes. She also is a part of the ISDM - International Society of Deliverance Ministries.

Josiah Lane

Josiah Lane is a man after God's own heart, first and foremost. He has attended Lee University where he received his Bachelors degree in theological studies, and is headed to Seminary to earn his Master of Divinity. Women becoming leaders is a passion of his, and he has a great desire to see it carried out today. Josiah currently resides in the city of Cleveland, TN where he voluntarily helps lead youth for Dwelling Place Church International.

Michelle J. Miller

Michelle "The Barrier Breaker" Miller is a corporate lawyer, speaker, managing real estate broker and global visionary. She has learned to identify adversities and tragedies of life as catalysts of success. Today, Michelle shows others how to use these catalysts of character building as pathways to becoming champions of change. She shares her story as a means of encouraging other to pursue their dreams.

Michelle received her Bachelors of Arts from the University of Illinois at Urbana-Champaign and she holds a Certificate of Chinese Law from the Beijing University of Political Science & Law. She began law school as a single mother and obtained her Jurist Doctor from the DePaul University - College of Law while caring for her daughter and working various jobs. Michelle received scholarships from the Cook County Bar Association, the Black Women Lawyers' Association, the DePaul Chapter - Black Law Student Association and the DePaul University College of Law while attending law school. Michelle is an Illinois Managing Real Estate Broker. She also participated in a Spring Law Comparative Constitutional Law Program in South Africa. She holds certificates in Conflict Analysis, Negotiation & Conflict Management, and Interfaith Conflict Resolution from the U.S. Institute of Peace. Michelle also holds a Doctorate in Ministry in Theology from Word Bible College. She most recently received her Masters in Laws in International Business & Trade Law at the John Marshall Law School. Michelle currently works as Corporate Counsel for CNA. She is also the owner of Michelle J. Miller International, LLC. She is the Founder of Micaiah School of the Prophets and in 201 she will be launching her exclusive Italian leather and suede shoe line, Exousia Shoes and the Michelle J. lifestyle brand.

Loria M. Morrison

In 1994, Loria received a visitation from the Lord Jesus Christ who told her, "There is still hope", when those words were imparted to her, she immediately received Jesus Christ as her personal Lord and Savior. She was instantly set free and delivered; she describes the experience as weights and chains falling off of her! The very same hour he gave her three instructions in which she quickly obeyed, he said, "Put on your white suit, go find your sister and tell her what I did for you, and go to the church you visited two weeks prior. That day it was evident of the apostolic commission to GO and be a mighty witness! That evening, she arrived at the church she was instructed to go to, the pastor of the church asked her if she had something to say, she declared, "Yes, I got saved today and I'm never turning back"! She operates in a strong apostolic and prophetic anointing which is evident with many receiving salvation, healings and deliverance. She founded More Power Radio/Revival Crusades, Co-hosted Oneness in Christ Television Ministry. Loria is an Apostle and Senior Pastor of Christ Has Risen International Ministries. Her ministry is known internationally as well as throughout the east coast.

Adrienne Sumler

A New Orleans native, an Apostolic Admiral and a worshipper after God's own heart that's Apostle Adrienne J. Sumler. She has over 25 years of ministry and 18 years as the founder & Senior Leader of Kingdom Ambassadorial Worship Center International; an apostolic hub center. When she is not ministering to the flock she can be found in intercession or bringing God's people through deliverance. As an apostle to the nation's, a spiritual mother to many, a natural mother to four and a wife to Claude Sumler Sr. She is blessed to call Apostle Axel Sippach her spiritual Father and is a member of the EPIC Family. If this is your first time hearing of Apostle Sumler for the first time, it certainly won't be your last!

Jacqueline R. Simmons

Jacqueline R. Simmons, is an Epic Global Network leader. She has been married to George Simmons for 12 years with two sons. She has been in ministry for 20 years preaching and teaching, along with intercessory prayer. Jacqueline is emerging apostolic voice speaking into the lives of those who are lost and perishing to turn their hearts back to the Father. She's director caring for Alzheimer & Dementia patients at an assisted living facility. Jacqueline is also an independent sales director for Mary Kay to build and empower women leaders across Southeast Texas.

Uloma Chinwe Obi

Uloma Chinwe Obi is a Pastor, Published Author and Transformational Leader. Uloma holds a Bachelor of science degree in Political Science and a Masters in Industrial and Labor Relations. She is the Vision Coordinator of House of Rehoboth International, a church based ministry and Dominion Africa aimed at providing platforms and opportunities to showcase Africa to the world. Uloma makes her home in Spring Texas with her husband with whom she spends time 'cooking up a storm '.

Karen S. Williams

Min. Karen S. Williams, a prophetic voice, award-winning author, and scholar, lives in Metro Detroit. She is an ordained minister and a staff pastor with Southfield, Michigan's Good News Christian Center Ministries. An author and public health manager, researcher and program developer with 25+ years experience, her heart is to minister healing, inner healing and deliverance ministry via teaching, speaking, writing and social media help to equip men and women who have suffered trauma, toxic stress, and adverse life experiences to "pay their personal relationship with Christ, healing, freedom, wisdom, life stories as well as their spiritual and natural gift forward" as they win other women to Christ. Min. Williams has a regular podcast titled "Miriam's Cup Messages with Min. Karen Williams" on Spreaker network and has written for "Global Prophetic Voice", "Spirit Fuel", and other publications. Follow her or contact her on Facebook at "Miriam's Cup Messages with Min. Karen Williams", at miriamscupmessages@gmail.com it in the web at www.Karenswilliams.org.

Crystal Billingsley

Crystal Billingsley is the founder of a trailblazing restoration ministry, called Place of Shiloh. She has the honor of helping people overcome trauma by utilizing Heaven-sent healing activations that reveal how to rebuild life after deliverance. She has written a book, "Wounded Feet Be Healed", that ministers to people suffering from torn mantles and in desperate need of restoration. Crystal Billingsley has the grace to coach people out of hiding by sharing influential insights that carries the power to help individuals regain confidence in their tailor-made callings from God and become reactivated in the arena called life. She currently lives in Indiana with her husband, Bryan, and their five children.

Robinette D. Cross

Robinette D. Cross is a native of Richmond, Virginia. She attended Spelman College in Atlanta, Georgia where she earned a Bachelors of Art in History with a concentration in Africa. Robinette is a dedicated servant of God and is committed to living a Kingdom lifestyle. Using the Apostle Paul as a blueprint, Robinette believes that an effective citizen of the Kingdom has a fully developed arsenal equipped with language skills, knowledge of multiple cultures, and boldness for God. She understands that showing believers how to develop their arsenal will make them stronger warriors who are able to "go forth and make disciples of all nations". A dedicated member of Alpha Kappa Alpha, Robinette is committed to the instruction, education, and the upliftment of humankind and, as global citizens, ensuring that all who wish to have access possess the fundamentals needed to be successful in academics and cross-cultural understanding.

Bessie Foster

Chief Apostle Bessie Foster, a native of Phoenix, AZ, and a mother of two children. She accepted Christ and the Holy Ghost in 1975 while attending First Pentecostal Church under the leadership of now deceased, Bishop A.C. Eddings. Apostle Bessie Foster accepted the call from God in 1998, was licensed as a Evangelist in 2000, and placed under study by Suffocate Bishop David Eddings. In October 2000, she was ordained Elder through Christian Fellowship Ministries, Inc. of Arizona by Prophet Ronald Dubrul and a graduate of Christian Fellowship Bible College. In 2001, she served under the Full Gospel Baptist Church Fellowship of Arizona by Bishop Henry L. Barnwell. She served as the Director of Protocol in the Full Gospel Baptist Church Fellowship under the direction of Overseer Love. In November 2002, she was ordained as Pastor and Bishop and in June 2008, she was ordained as Prophetess through Overcomers In Christ located in Phoenix, Arizona by Chief Apostle Robert James Anselmo and Apostle Edith Anselmo. Commission November 2014 as an Apostle under Apostle Kluane Spake at Sword Ministries in Atlanta , GA. She travels back and forth overseas planting churches and equipping the saints for the work of the ministry, counsels the five- fold ministers, leaders, and others as well as having crusades throughout Africa and wherever the Lord sends her. She has been entrusted by the Lord with spiritual sons and daughters who she covers in Africa and the USA which consist of 30 churches, 7 School of Ministery, 3 ministry, and 6 orphanages. Assistant Pastor in the Phoenix, Arizona about 11 years. She is the Director and Founder of Train Em Up Ministries for 20 years and where she deals with healing and deliverance since 1997. From 1996, until 1999 she attended Disciple Training Institute, under the direction of Rev. Paula Hunter at Pilgrim Rest Baptist Church. She holds a Bachelor Degree in Religious Education from Anchorage Theological Seminary and Bible Institute in Texarkana, AR, a Master Degree in Religious Education and Doctorate of Divinity from Modesto, CA and Pastoral Degree from Azusa World Ministry Training Institute in Phoenix, AZ.

Alandis Porter

Apostle Alandis is a seasoned Apostolic voice and prophetic teacher with a down to earth style. Apostle Alandis carries a heavy healing and deliverance mantle. She is an Apostle of love, intercession and wealth. Committed to building and educating others to exemplify the heart of God. Apostle Alandis is currently the visionary of Kingdom Advancement Global Ministries, the Dean and an instructor in the T.E.A.R.S Training Academy, the Apostolic covering and overseer of Kingdom Advancers Global Network, Radio Personality and published author.

Cynthia Bolden Gardner

Apostle Cynthia King Bolden Gardner is the founder of Greater Love/ New Mercy Seat Ministries, Inc., Indian and African Alliance. She is the spouse of Pastor Bennie Seales Gardner, Sr. residing in outer JACKSON, Ms. Apostle is an Amazon/Kindle Bestseller in Religion, Counseling & Social Issues and the sole author of 17 books including law and poetry. She has a Doctorate of Divinity from the ABC (Annie B. Campbell) School of Ministry; BSFS Humanities in International Affairs 1978 and Juris Doctorate 1981 from Georgetown University. Apostle has worked corporate and government including Jones, Day, Brown & Bain, US Dept of Justice and San Diego County where she received Attorney of the Year in 1999. Her passion is helping disadvantaged youth, disenfranchised Minority males, the Mentally Challenged and homeless. She is an accident advocate and activist.

Joyce Stevens

Joyce J. Stevens was born in Johnson City, Tennessee; to the late William and Eloise Malone. She was the youngest of ten children. Her parents reared her in a strict religious home and church environment, which became the foundation for her ministry. God has been gracious and allowed His favor to shine upon her as she now functions as the senior pastor of New Life Worship Center, a progressive, non-denominational church, in Tucson, Arizona. She is the visionary for several ministries that are extensions of the church. Her passion for "Building God's People to Advance the Kingdom" has led to the development of an annual conference, *Latter Rain*, purposed to bring believers from all denominations and races together for corporate worship. The *Naomi and Ruth* ministry is a program designed to allow seasoned women to mentor younger women. *Reaching in Love Ministries* provides Apostle Stevens the opportunity to share her wisdom and experiences with men and women called into ministry. Finally, with the help of community agencies, she has recently formed *New Life Directions*, a program for teenage girls and young adult women confronting the issues of abstinence and pregnancy. Apostle Stevens has a master's degree in Human Services from Lincoln University in Kennett Square, Pennsylvania. It was there she met and married her true love Clarence Stevens. To this union was born three wonderful children, Mark, Cassandra and Clarence III, all of which are active in ministry.

Apostle Paula R. Hines, D.D.

Dr. Paula Hines is the Director and Founder of RPH Ministries (a 501C3 organization) and Founder of "The Embassy" headquartered in Phoenix, AZ. Apostle Hines has been in ministry for over 30 years. She is a Kingdom Strategist who defies the traditions of men while leading with a no-nonsense mentality bringing order and clear vision to the Body of Christ. Through her God-given apostolic and prophetic teaching and preaching ministry; strongholds are pulled down in the lives of men. Dr. Hines is a gracious, gifted and giving Woman of God.

Bonnie Scott

Apostle Bonnie Scott was raised in Fort Lauderdale, Florida and currently lives in Ridgeland, Mississippi. She became Quicken and born of the spirit of God 1987 and almost immediately Bonnie encounter a visitation from the Lord only a few months of her salvation giving her detailed instructions. Immediately drawn into intercessory prayer not knowing or understanding what was happening to her she simply yielded to the unction, urge's and burdens to pray in the Spirit. She would have lots of visions and dreams finding herself prophesying, laying hands, flowing in Revelation knowledge, healing and deliverance. She's also a playwright, author and lastly but not the least she loves the Lord with all of her heart.

Shevon White-Sampson

Shevon L. Sampson is an author, entrepreneur and businesswoman who believes that serving the community and finding success in business go hand-in-hand. Her life-long passion for serving others led her to write her first book, "The Heart of a Sower". She has also developed a companion game board that teach money management from a biblical perspective. In addition to this fun for all board game and self-help workbook she has created a devotional. She hopes to help and inspire others with this collection, designed to get people thinking about not only their finances, but how the decisions they make about what they keep and what they give can impact their future and the futures of others. Sampson is chief executive officer of Sowers Reap International. Sowers Reap International is the distributor of her works, including "The God Bank", "2 SOW OR NOT 2 SOW" Board Game, "The Heart of a Sower" workbook, and "Kingdom Keys for Seed Sowers" devotional. Sampson received her Bachelor of Science in Business Management at Grand Canyon University in Phoenix, Arizona. After many years as a successful business leader, she returned to school and will be completing her Master Degree in Business Management Fall 2018.

Noreen Henry

Noreen N. Henry is a native of London, England and migrated to the United States in her late teens. Noreen is the Founder and CEO of Victorious Living Culture LLC, is an author, and her book "Victorious Living: Guide to a Happier Life" is a multiple #1 International Bestseller and #1 on the Hot New Releases list. She has obtained an AAS degree, an Administrative Assistant certificate, a diploma and six certificates from Rhema Correspondence Bible School; certificates of Taking Care of People God's Way, Christian Counseling 2.0, and Eating Disorders from Lighthouse University, has attended The Healing School; and has various other certificates. Noreen is currently pursuing a Bachelor's degree in ministry. She is an ordained minister through Joan Hunter Ministries, and is a life-long learner, that continues to study the Word of God daily. Noreen is an avid reader, and spiritual mum to many. Noreen is a member of AACC, 4CA, KBA, and is certified member of the John Maxwell Team. She is passionate about the things of God due to her life experiences and cares a great deal about people and society. Noreen has gone through a lot of major challenges in her life that has made her into the person that she is today, and she plans to make the world a better place, being a legacy changer as well as a world changer; The song "People Help the People" was dedicated to Noreen by one of her nieces. Noreen resides in New York City and has three children and two grandchildren, at the moment.

Jessica R. Jackson

Apostle Jessica Jackson is the founder of Order in the Courts ministries. Apostle Jackson is committed to sharing biblical truths and unlocking the mysteries of heaven so none will stumble. God has blessed her to faithfully serve in ministry for over 30 years from the dishwasher to the administrator. Professionally, she has successfully worked within the financial industry for 20 years as a System Engineer. In 2013, her childhood pastor, Bishop Oscar Turner, Th.D., officially ordained her in the office of Apostle the place God called her to walk within. Apostle Jackson is a saved and successful single focused on expanding the Kingdom of God.

Cheryl Weems

Cheryl Weems is a native of Towson, Maryland where she attended Mt. Calvary AME Church under the leadership of Rev. William A. Gray III and Rev. Dr. Ann F. Lightner-Fuller there she received the call to preach at the age of 14. Cheryl preached her initial sermon at age 18 while serving at Harvest Christian Worship Center in Baltimore, MD under the leadership of Pastor Melvin G. Boulware, Sr. Over the years, she has served in various ministries within the church to include the Steward Board, Music Ministry, Christian Education and Finance Team. Cheryl is able to serve multiple capacities in ministry as a result of her God given gifts. One of Cheryl's areas of focus is ministry team development. This passion was sharpened during her time at Kingdom Worship Center, under the leadership of Bishop Ralph L. Dennis and Bishop Gregory A. Dennis. She preached her initial sermon in the AME Church in February, 2012 under the leadership of Rev. Tracey Victor-Butler who has served as a mentor to her through Daughters of Destiny over 20 years. Following her initial sermon she was admitted into the Baltimore Annual Conference April, 2014.In July 2015, Cheryl connected with Leviticus International Fellowship a team of church planters and ministry development team. In January 2016 she received the invitation from Apostle Joseph T. Hackett and Pastor Marlon R.. Anderson to pastor the Leviticus Church in Richmond, Virginia. Cheryl accepted the invitation and began Pastoring in March and ordained an Elder with the fellowship in May, 2016. Cheryl is the very proud mother of two children, Darian and Aaron.

Sadira Davis

A true loyalist of the Sovereign Lord, Sadira's intimacy with him and the spirit realm spans back to her early childhood. Dedicated to the advancement of the Kingdom of God, restoring purity and honor to the prophets office, and building leaders in ethics, spiritual protocols, and soundness in their soul: heart, mind, emotions is her passion. Being conscientious is second nature yet her tenderheartedness, tact, and genuine love for all humanity has afforded her the opportunity to touch and transform many lives throughout her life from prostitutes and pimps to politicians and preachers. Her nurturing, protective, "motherly" love, is often felt in her warm demeanor. Respectively she is known for her explicit candor and advocacy for truth and justice.

LeeChunHwa Stovall

Apostle Dr. LeeChunHwa Stovall is an apostolic leader who has been commissioned to bring healing, revival, deliverance and direction through prophetic insight, impartations, revelatory teaching and breakthroughs in a rare ministering style where the divine wisdom of God flows. She and her husband, Pastor Leonard Stovall are the founders of Global Fire International Alliance and the Senior Leaders of Fresh Encounter Church in Atlanta, Georgia. They also are the founders of the Lamad Leadership Institute, a ministerial educational and training center, Gethsemane House, an organization dedicated to the wellness of pastors and ministry professionals and Daughters of Devorah, a discipleship organization for women operating or emerging in church or marketplace leadership. LeeChunHwa travels throughout the United States working with several regional bodies, establishing, training and equipping individuals and teams in apostolic foundations, prophetic ministry, prayer, worship, spiritual warfare, deliverance, and healing ministry. She also works very closely with senior leaders training them how to identify and establish church government, leadership development and training within their local bodies. LeeChunHwa has a double Doctorate in Christian Theology and Divinity, and holds several degrees, awards, acknowledgements and certificates in various areas of ministerial training.

Shelley M. Fisher, PH.D

Dr. Shelley Fisher is a native of Gary, Indiana. Her foundation was shaken in 1986 when she began to hear God's voice: "Whom shall I send and who will go for us?" "Receive your sight...the God of our fathers has chosen you, that you should know His will, and see that Just One, and should hear the voice of His mouth. For you shall be His witness unto all men." Dr. Fisher is continuously emptying herself of doctrine and tradition to embrace the spiritual nature of God. She is a Certified Mentor – one who can lead you through life's experiences using the Bible as the focal point. Dr. Fisher is the former Northwest Indiana Coordinator of Prophetic Intercessors, past president of Gary Educators for Christ and Women's Aglow International. She is a former principal, teacher, consultant, author, and Adjunct Professor of Organizational Behavior. Dr. Fisher serves as an associate minister at her church, First Baptist, Gary, IN, and is a volunteer chaplain at Methodist Southlake Campus. She is married to Alfred Fisher and they are the parents of two children and a grandson. Her passion is to see people complete in Christ Jesus.

Valarie L. Randleman

Valarie is the Founder of SEEC, Soaring Eagles Equipping Center, an apostolic and prophetic equipping center whose mandate is to equip believers and to mature them to attain their full stature in Christ. Her early beginnings of being mentored in the prophetic by her mentor, Apostle Adrienne Hawthorne, was a springboard to her ultimate call as an apostle. Her call to apostleship in 2005 was recognized in her being commissioned and set apart in 2013. In 2012 and 2013 ministry trips to Cuba shifted her focus to the Latino community, expanding her ministry to include bilingual training & equipping. Also, in 2014 a new mobile team ministry was launched called Marketplace Gatherings (MPG), meeting in a friend's hair salon to equip believers through books and challenging them to become proton believers-to accelerate, mature, and to be relevant in the world we live. Of recent times, Valarie recently transitioned out of higher education as a sign language interpreter in 2017 to focus on expanding the Kingdom through co-laboring with Glory House International, located in Rochester, New York, under Pastor Melvin & Ashley Cross,Jr. She enjoys time with her friends, traveling, reading, and collecting books. Valarie has an 13 year old godson, Xavier, who is being prepared to fulfill his prophetic purpose to go to the nations.

Sandra Hill

Sandra Hill is in passionate pursuit of advancing the kingdom of God as an enthusiastic, on-target and practical teacher of the word of God. She shares her gifts with the world as a mentor, minister, speaker and author. She is founder of the Academy of the Scribe, with a mandate to ignite, instruct, accelerate and activate present day scribes in their God given assignments through workshops and mentorship. As a serial entrepreneur she owns a bookkeeping business, a community development corporation and a publishing company. She is an ordained minister of the Gospel of Jesus Christ. Sandra has been married to the love of her life Ronan Hill for over 30 years.

Michelle White

Michelle M. White is a native of Louisiana. She later moved to Texas where her career took flight for 22 years until recently returning back home. Michelle's educational background consists of Nursing, Liberal Arts and Criminal Justice. Michelle's greatest business achievement thus far has been the launch of her catering business named after her children "Cambri's Catering." The Business has opened many doors of opportunities to cook and cater for great men and women of God as well as prominent business owners between Texas and Louisiana. Michelle is a prophetic intercessor who is extremely passionate about speaking in the lives of people especially women who have been bruised, broken and rejected. Michelle's reminder to them is Through Him, With Him and In Him is the ability to laugh, live and love again!

Dr. Betty Mitchell

Apostle Betty Mitchell presently serves as the senior pastor of Thee House Uv Beth-El, Minneapolis, Minnesota. She is the founder of Reaping the Harvest Ministries (501c status). The mission is to RE-PRESENT the KINGDOM through education and humanitarian efforts, establishing an apostolic network; ANNA, providing training through Eagles Landing 5 fold/ Officers School and a monthly regional prayer initiative Women on the Wall.

Yolanda Mosby

Yolanda R. Mosby is an author, prayer intercessor, speaker and entrepreneur who stands firm on the word of God. As a minister of education, she is very passionate about teaching others about God's word. She has received an Associates Degree in Christian Theology in 2015. Yolanda resides in the Florida with 5 wonderful children.

Terry Ricklefs

Theresa (Terry) Ricklefs received her BA in Communication Studies at SUNY Cortland, in Cortland, NY in 2011, and is also a photographer, graphic designer, author, and screenwriter. In 2002, she began playing the harp prophetically. Terry is also a prophetic leader on Facebook and has written many prophetic teaching articles with custom graphics such as *the Seer Anointing, the Demonic Roundtable, Power Objects* and *the Psychic and the Prophetic.* These were based upon her life experiences. She has one daughter and resides in Rochester, New York.

Donna Anderson

45305159R00177

Made in the USA
Middletown, DE
16 May 2019